The Handbook of

PROFESSIONAL SERVICE MANAGEMENT

JOHN H. WELLEMIN

The Handbook of

PROFESSIONAL SERVICE MANAGEMENT

CARING FOR THE CUSTOMER BEFORE, DURING AND AFTER THE SALE

Studentlitteratur | **Bratt Institut für Neues Lernen** | **Chartwell-Bratt Ltd**

Cip-Kurztitelaufnahme der Deutschen Bibliothek:

Wellemin, John H.:
Handbook of Professional Service Management
/Caring for the customer before, during and after
the sale/ John H. Wellemin –
Lund: Studentlitteratur
Goch: Bratt-Institut für Neues Lernen Gmbh
Bromley: Chartwell Bratt Ltd
ISBN 91-44-99581-4 (Studentlitteratur)
ISBN 3-88598-044-4 (Bratt-Institut)
ISBN 0-86238-050-2 (Chartwell-Bratt Ltd)

Second Printing
Printed in Sweden
Studentlitteratur
Lund 1984

ISBN 91-44-99581-4 (Sweden)
ISBN 0-86238-050-2 (England)
ISBN 3-88598-044-4 (Germany)

Hardcover edition:
ISBN 91-44-95221-X (Sweden)
ISBN 0-86238-069-3 (England)
ISBN 3-88598-045-2 (Germany)

Contents

Preface

This book has been compiled for the use of active Service Managers and other executives in commercial or industrial organisations responsible for the after-sales support of customer equipment.

It recognises the need of experienced managers to keep abreast of general trends and latest techniques in the service business, and for potential management to learn the basics of service management.

Each chapter deals with one or more clearly defined issues but as these are often interrelated with other subjects in the book, they are cross-referenced to enable the reader to refer to other aspects covering the same subject matter.

As the book is intended for "beginners", i.e. potential Service Managers, as well as for experienced executives, each subject covered addresses every point from the basic to the more sophisticated approach. There is no single path to resolving issues, each case has to be considered on its own merits, bearing in mind the size, type and aims of the business in which the reader operates or intends to operate.

It is important to remember that even though a particular approach or method has been successful for a company in the past, it will be necessary to review the validity of maintaining this course for the future at regular intervals; everything changes, markets – customers expectations, competition, our own company's maturity, as well as society and technology – it would be unreasonable to expect our customer service management approach of yesteryear to be valid unaltered for a long period.

In consequence, it may well be that some, or even many, of the methods described in this book are known to the reader, but there are likely to be others which may be new and which sow a seed in the mind of the reader. He may not use the idea immediately or exactly as described, but it is hoped that some of the concepts may initiate a train of thought which will adapt the idea to the specific requirements of the individual.

To those of you who find that they are already using *all* the latest concepts and most sophisticated ideas mentioned in this book, let me say: "Congratulations, you can now sleep more soundly, knowing that you utilise the latest techniques in service management".

To the rest of you, and I suspect it to be the great majority of my readers, let me wish you a lot of fun in considering and modifying some of the ideas put forward in this book and I sincerely hope, and expect (!), that it will help you to operate a more efficient, cost-effective, customer orientated, profitable and *happy* service operation.

Introduction

The Changing Role of Service

Since the earliest days of mankind, when "things" went wrong, they had to be repaired. This could be done either by the user himself or by some other person who may have been more dexterous, or more knowledgeable, or have the requisite tools to effect the repair.

The need in the past, therefore, was entirely "technically" orientated, i.e. requiring manual dexterity, special knowledge and experience or necessary equipment. A typical example may be a blacksmith who was able to shoe a horse or repair the simple agricultural tools used at the time.

As more and more products and machines were put on the market, all requiring repair and maintenance to a greater or lesser extent, so Service Departments were created in the manufacturing companies or in their dealers and distributors. Independent service companies, whose sole purpose was the repair and maintenance of equipment made by someone else, were also set up.

Technology progressed further and the equipment tended to get more complex and with more of it around, an ever-increasing need for servicing was created. Just look around your factory, office or even your home or street and you will find yourself surrounded by equipment requiring service. Add to it the repair of "Public Utilities" we take for granted (power stations, gas works, water and drainage pumps, telephone switchboards etc.) and you will see what I mean.

In general, the servicing of products has been carried out quite efficiently and many courses teaching the technical skills are being conducted both publicly (by schools, colleges and other institutions) as well as by manufacturers for their own staff or that of their dealers, distributors and, in some cases, even for their customers.

It is not, in fact, the technical aspect of servicing which has tended to be neglected, but the professional approach to service management. It is not surprising that this has happened because the pressures on top management have been from different directions, so they were willing to allow the best Technicians or Service Engineers to be promoted to service management, without giving them management training or helping them in developing their management skills.

The major energy of top management was devoted to designing products with more features (additional bells and whistles), mechanising the manufacturing process, devising more imaginative marketing programmes, financing the business, developing new sales incentive schemes and, more recently, trying to pull together the information from separate and divergent departments into a manageable information and accounting system.

Over the past two decades or so, top management in some companies have begun to realise that their dependence on their After Sales Service support to the customer was changing drastically. This is due to a number of reasons which we should analyse in a little more detail:

1. Customers are becoming more and more dependent on the efficient operation of their equipment. Whereas in the past the breakdown of a lathe in a factory or a typewriter in an office was inconvenient, it was not a "show stopper". Today's equipment in factories and offices is often interconnected with other operations and the breakdown in one unit may hold up the work of a large part of the operation. In consequence customers are becoming more sensitive and knowledgeable about the up-time of their various pieces of equipment which has an effect not only on the reliability demands a customer makes on the supplier of the product but also on the response time and repair time. This may mean a need to be able to provide a variable and flexible service to individual customers, and for the service department to be able to plan, control, cost, and measure the provision of that type of service.

2. There has been constant economic pressure on the manufacturer or supplier of the service. Service is labour intensive and the cost of labour has been rising more rapidly than most other costs, particularly when taking into account the gradually shortening work hours per year (longer holidays, shorter working week) and the increasing social security costs (health-insurance, pensions etc.). Competition has also become more severe and it has not always been possible to increase charges in line with rising costs. Yet, the manufacturers and suppliers rightly require an increasing profit contribution from their service departments.

3. Competitive products intended for the same market segment are becoming more similar in the eyes of many customers. The quality of service and the

reputation for service of the manufacturer or supplier are becoming increasingly an area of differentiation between competitors in the eyes of customers.

4. At a time of recession or small economic growth, customers are increasingly selective in seeking value for money (not necessarily the "cheapest") when they purchase their service. Service contracts in the eighties are no longer bought – they have to be sold.

5. As general management had concentrated its modernisation expenditure on mechanising factories, automating the office and computerising their accounting procedures, the modernisation of service management tools and techniques has been neglected. The time for applying more sophisticated management techniques within service has been postponed.

6. Social changes, which affect our society in general, are being felt even more strongly in a service department because service is (as mentioned earlier) very labour intensive and the service force in many industries is working out in the field under less supervision or contact with colleagues than operatives in a factory. These social changes must be recognised and suitable management actions taken.

All these changes are altering the knowledge and skill requirements of service management. There is a growing need to broaden its outlook and up-date its knowledge at regular intervals, to appreciate what is being done in other companies and to adapt some of these practices to their own specific situation. In short, service management is required to be highly professional. It must be familiar with general management concepts and know-how to adapt these to the *specific* needs of service management. The professional Service Manager is an integral part of a company's management team who has to understand the needs of the business and how any company decision will affect "service" and how any service action may affect the company as a whole.

In this book I will try to review *some* of the different approaches that have been taken by various companies. It will be appreciated that I cannot encompass all the new techniques and that none of them can be adopted universally. There are many influences which will affect the best approach at any time and even if a method is good for a company today, it may not be right a few years later, when the market may have changed, the company grown, its philosophy and strategy altered and its management style modified. The professional Service Manager is sensitive to changes in climate and will adjust his management approach accordingly.

SECTION I

Objectives of a Service Department

In a generic way we could simple state that in almost every industry the objective of Service could be summarised as:

"To create and increase customer satisfaction

and

to generate reasonable profits to the company.

This can only be achieved through a highly motivated and willing service force."

Figure 1. *Balancing Service Objectives*

This type of generic goal is an acceptable philosophy but fairly meaningless for service management in establishing quantitative and qualitative goals against which to measure achievements. It is only these quantitative and qualitative measurements which will enable meaningful cross-functional decisions to be made.

Let us therefore look at some of the ways of establishing the parameters which will enter into the balancing of customer satisfaction, direct profits from the service operation and some of the indirect profit contributions the service force can and should be encouraged to make.

Customer Satisfaction

Before we can satisfy customers we must establish what his genuine needs are, whether service can fill these needs, the cost of doing so, and the willingness of the customer to pay the price.

It is important to establish these needs before the equipment is sold to a customer and for reasonable service plans to be made.

You will question whether all customers have the same needs and the obvious answer is in the negative. Nevertheless it is important to establish a certain pattern of customer requirements, build up a Mr. Average Customer profile, segment this average as much as required (e.g. by geography, by industry, by size, by application etc.), and then be flexible enough to establish individual customer criteria if required.

So let us look how these customer needs can be identified:

(i) If we are establishing these needs for a product or equipment similar to one our company already supplies, the easiest way is to establish the customer satisfaction level to individual parameters of the service we are supplying and, if possible, compare it to that of our competitors. We also need to prioritise the various parameters according to the importance customers attribute to them. A well designed questionnaire in the hands of a skilled interrogator often is a useful aid. Don't be afraid to ask customers, they will be glad to give you this type of information. Care must be taken on who in the company provides the information as the priorities may differ. For instance, the customer's management may be more interested in the quality and quantity produced by our equipment whereas an operator may be more concerned about ease of approach to service, cleanliness of the workplace after servicing, and friendliness of support.

(ii) If our service is to be carried out on a product or equipment in a market segment new to our company, the approach is somewhat more difficult but basically similar; potential customers must be questioned about their needs. As our own company is likely to have little experience in the new market segment, more help may be needed from external research facilities.

(iii) It is useful to get a small panel of customers' opinion leaders into a workshop session at which the relative importance of the parameters to be included in the survey are identified.

(iv) Subsequent audits of the actual level and comparative (with competition) level of satisfaction should be carried out by visits to a small number of important customers and by a more general solicitation of comments of a larger group of customers with a questionnaire.

(v) The trend in the number of complaints from customers can also be an indication of customer satisfaction. It will certainly be appreciated by everyone that each complaint must be investigated thoroughly and the customer concerned notified of any remedial action taken.

The difficulty with all these approaches is that it builds on current experience and expectations but these expectations can often change quite rapidly. We therefore must anticipate the likely needs of customers and, if feasible, even influence his expectations to give us a competitive advantage.

An example of how customer perception and with it his expectations can be influenced, is the well known manufacturer, let us call him the AB Corporation, who had a very high reputation in one segment of the market. He came out with a product for another segment where his initial product did not come up to reliability expectations existing in the new segment. AB Corporation had a very large service force trained for their traditional products but due to the higher than expected call rate, was unable to train sufficient engineers for the new ones to be able to give the very fast response times the new segment was accustomed to. AB Corporation decided to send their existing service force, who had only minimal training on the new product, to customers, thus satisfying the demand for fast response time, even though it meant that in most cases a second call by a fully trained engineer had to be made to make the equipment operable. AB Corporation obviously felt that once the customer knew that his machine was being dealt with (due to the arrival of the first engineer) the "steam" was taken out of the situation.

Once we have established the parameters and priorities influencing customer satisfaction we need to establish how we can measure and control each factor. We need to be as specific as possible to enable us to plan our service operation and to deliver the type of service that will give customer satisfaction.

Management select wide list of potential parameters affecting customer satisfaction.

Selected group of potential customers in workshop session identifies important service parameters and weights (prioritises) them.

Develop questionnaire. Care must be taken that wording is clear so that questions imply the same meaning to all respondents and to evaluators.

Carefully select potential respondents. Conditions will dictate whether survey should be done by telephone, personally, or by written response.

Evaluation of response
*Statistical:*Well proven techniques for evaluation exist.
Comments: This must be done by experts with an open mind. It is too easy to say that a comment was made only once and is therefore invalid. It may be a good idea worth pursuing.

Develop and cost alternative service strategies.

Select strategy which will form basis for tactical alternatives to be made available.

Figure 2. *Prioritising customer satisfaction parameters*

Let us examine what customers are likely to need:

(a) Customers will want the maximum availability of their equipment. This means a number of things, some of which are fully or partially within the control of service, whilst others are largely outside their control but they may nevertheless be partially influenced by service. The customer does not, and should not have to, distinguish which department within the company is responsible to satisfy his needs.

   (i) Reliability is primarily designed and built into a product but service has an important role both in influencing the customer's perception of product reliability by good servicing, availability of parts, fast response time and skilled customer relations, and in feeding back information to Engineering and Manufacturing to influence product modifications (ECO-Engineering Change Orders) and future product design. Specific factors for measuring reliability will be discussed in the Forecasting, Planning and Budgeting Section and these factors can be quantified.

   (ii) On the (hopefully few) occasions when the machine does break down and requires service, the customer will need easy access to the Service Department (see Service Control under Management Tools of Service Management), a reasonably rapid appearance of the Technician or Service Engineer on his premises – this is known as Response Time – and then a quick and efficient repair. The measurement here is obviously hours and minutes.

   (iii) Once the repair has been effected the customer is unlikely to want return visits by the engineer. He wants the problem to be resolved. That means the engineer must be knowledgeable to find the fault, well trained, logical and must have the necessary spare parts and tools available to effect the repair and the appropriate test equipment to check that everything is operating satisfactorily. This is measured by the number or repeat calls or re-calls.

(b) The customer will expect reasonable costs for the parts and the service provided. It is often advantageous for both the manufacturer and the customer to enter into a maintenance contract (see Service Revenue in Service Management Section) which will speed up the procedure and clearly identify the customer's commitment. This is, of course, measurable in monetary units.

(c) The quality of the output of the machine or product must remain within the specified limits. Where these can be quantified easily there is not much of a problem (e.g. measurement of size, surface finish, temperature, weight, brightness, noise level etc.) but for some products this may not be so easy. In most instances, however, some measure can be established.

(d) The customer naturally prefers a pleasant relationship with the manufacturer (see Customer Relations) and his staff. This may often justify certain shortfalls in other areas. This is likely to be the area most difficult to quantify. Some indication of this may be found in specific comments during customer audits, in questionnaires and in letters of complaint or commendation. The rate of repeat orders is, of course, the most telling evidence of customer satisfaction.

Service Profit Contribution

We must separate the cost stream and the revenue stream to enable management to influence the profit contribution of the Service Department. We are talking here in tangible monetary units – the intangibles such as helping to build a Company Image or providing Market Intelligence will be covered separately.

Cost Effective Operation

Whatever the treatment of service revenues may be in different companies, it is almost universal for a Service Department to have an analysis of its cost. Although Accounts Departments sometimes believe that service costs are an absolute value, they are so only in relationship with a fixed level of service to the customer. If we change the level of service, we automatically change the parameters affecting costs.

The way the costs are broken down will differ from company to company but the Service Manager must ensure that the way costs are broken down help him to manage the service force. In consequence he must establish which cost factors are meaningful to him and then agree with the Accounts Department to provide the data to him in this way.

Typically he would separate manpower oriented costs from spare parts, from fixed costs and from information processing costs. He would also try to separate direct labour costs (cost for people actually working on the equipment) from indirect costs (management and other support costs). Travel costs would also be broken out. A happy medium must be found so as not to break down his costs into so many "buckets" that it is expensive to obtain and administratively impossible to utilise effectively, or having such large divisions that the movement of one factor counterbalances that of another, thus making it impossible to identify areas of strengths and weaknesses. The table in Figure 3 shows a typical breakdown of costs. The crux is that he must be able to identify areas where action is necessary or, at least identify the need for further investigation from his cost statements. A product line statement is often very useful for making service management decisions and is necessary for establishing whether customer pricing (see Service Revenue in Service Management Section) is profitable. The difficulty often is in the area of indirect costs, i.e. how to attribute cost which cannot be clearly identified to an individual product.

Let us look at a specific example. Let us assume that the Service Department services three major product lines (A, B and C). Let us further assume that product A is a low cost product costing say $1000, B is the mid-range product at $10,000 and product C at the top end at $100,000. For simplicity's sake let us assume that Service Revenue is 10% per year of product cost, response time requirement is the same on all products and the mean time to travel is ½ hour, the same on each product family. Let us assume that product A has a mean time to repair (MTTR) of 1 hour and requires 4 calls per year, product B's MTTR is 1½ hours and 12 calls per year, and product C's MTTR is 2 hours and needs 48 calls per year. If we look at the table in Figure 4, we can see that direct time (Total Work plus Travel Time) is equal on the three product lines. But how do we allocate other costs? (Management, Work Control, Travel etc.). If we allocate these costs by direct time, each product line would be charged with a third of the costs. That appears fair as far as management is concerned, as management tends to be directly proportional to the number of engineers. But is it a fair way of allocating costs of travel, administration and telephone/work control?

1. Total Headcount

2. Salaries and Wages
3. Social Benefits
4. Other Benefits
5. Contract Staff

6. Total Employment Costs

7. Cost of Spare Parts
8. (Spare Parts Returned for Rework)
9. Net Cost of Spare Parts
10. Cost of Consumable Items
11. Other Material Costs
12. Company Vehicles
13. Travel Costs
14. Communication Costs
15. Material and Parts Movement Costs
16. Rental Costs
17. Depreciation
18. Outside Purchased Services

19. Total Operating Costs

20. Rent and Rates
21. Public Services
22. Maintenance of Premises
23. Other Occupancy Costs

24. Total Occupancy Costs

25. Internal Recharges In
26. Internal Recharges Out
27. Internal Recharges Net

28. Provisions

29. Total Net Overheads

Items 1 to 6 inclusively are often broken down into so-called 'Direct' and 'Indirect' costs.

Figure 3. *Example of Cost Breakdown of a Service Department*

Product Line	A	B	C
Cost each $	1,000	10,000	100,000
Service Revenue each $	100	1,000	10,000
Number serviced	20,000	5,000	1,000
Total Service Revenue	2,000,000	5,000,000	10,000,000
Number of calls per year	4	12	48
Total Calls per year	80,000	60,000	48,000
MTTR hours	1	$1\frac{1}{2}$	2
Total Work Time hours	80,000	90,000	96,000
MTTT hours	$\frac{1}{2}$	$\frac{1}{2}$	$\frac{1}{2}$
Total Travel time hours	40,000	30,000	24,000
Total Work Plus Travel Time hours	120,000	120,000	120,000
Of Direct Time %	$33\frac{1}{3}$	$33\frac{1}{3}$	$33\frac{1}{3}$
Of Number of Call approx. %	43	32	25
Of Revenue approx. %	12	29	59
Of Number of M/cs approx.	77	19	4

Figure 4. *Product Line Statement*

Travel and telephone/work control expenses are dependent on the number of calls (43:32:25); invoicing, assuming all servicing is done on a maintenance contract basis, depends on the number of machines (77:19:4). Another way often used because of its simplicity is by revenue (12:29:59). Obviously each of these methods of allocation will give widely differing results.

It is recommended to choose the most appropriate division of cost on *each* of the major cost parameters rather than use a flat allocation procedure across all costs. Some may argue that it is an unnecessary refinement to split the cost of individual items by different methods but it is necessary to clearly understand what creates the cost and to allocate it to the product involved. This will enable correct management decisions to be made for running a cost efficient operation and recovering the appropriate amounts from customers. Cost objectives are almost always set to a service department; frequently these cost objectives are not linked to the level of service to be given, although this is necessary to become a meaningful target.

Service Revenue

Whether service is actually credited with the revenues it generates or not is a separate issue. The fact remains that service does generate revenue even if we only consider rented equipment, where no separation of revenue by function is made by some companies.

Basically we can look at service revenue in two streams:

- where the cost to the customer is charged as part of a whole and
- where the customer is specifically charged for the service provided.

Let us first examine the costs included in an overall price to the customer.

□ Warranties – the length of warranty varies according to product, industry and it is sometimes used as a tactical sales tool e.g. some car or television manufacturers have recently extended their warranty periods to obtain a tactical advantage over competition and to demonstrate their confidence in their products.

Although customers are not charged for warranties, they naturally pay for it in the purchase price. Service Departments must therefore be able to identify the amount of effort spent on installing products and servicing them under warranty to be able to plan and manage this area. In many companies these costs are recharged by the Service Department to Sales or Manufacturing, as appropriate.

□ Rental Equipment – here again the service costs have been included in the rental charged to customers and Service needs to be able to identify these costs and, if appropriate, recharge Sales.

□ Free Trials, Exhibitions, Demonstration Equipment – All service costs associated with these events fall into the same category as rented equipment. It is a promotional cost and should be recharged to the department responsible for incurring the expense. It is sound management practice to show cost in the area responsible for incurring it as it makes the relevant manager more aware of what is the total cost of his decision. This makes it easier for him to decide whether the whole approach is viable or whether another programme would be more cost effective.

I have seen managers who assumed that the service force is a fixed cost which can be excluded in calculations evaluating the costs of campaigns, little realising that the costs were planned into the Service Deparment's budget based on previous experience.

The other major area of service revenue is charges for service made to customers. The whole area of Maintenance Contracts, their pricing and selling will be discussed in greater detail in the 'Service Revenue' part of the Service Management section.

In addition to Maintenance Contracts other areas of revenue from customers are from:

☐ Extra requirements on and above a Maintenance Contract. This may involve the resiting of a machine, the training of additional customer staff, repair of machines damaged by customer negligence or subject to an insurance claim, service outside agreed periods (e.g. during weekends or on second shifts) and other unplanned activities.

☐ Service to machines not on a Maintenance Contract. – In some industries this type of ad hoc service is very usual. This is carried out on a Time and Material (T+M) basis, where the supplier of the service has a fixed charge per hour and a price list for spare parts and consumable items, and charges accordingly. Garages are a typical example. Many companies combine work on contracts with T+M activities and we will discuss the advantages and disadvantages from both the customer's and the supplier's point of view in the Service Revenue section.

☐ Revenue from other sources. – Some companies also service equipment not supplied by them, either on an ad hoc basis (e.g. garages) or on a special agreement with a competitive or a non-competitive manufacturer. This is particularly widely used in the more outlying areas where it may be uneconomical for every manufacturer to have his own servicing facilities.

More and more, so called Third Party Service Organisations are springing up who service equipment in competition to the manufacturer. This type of company has been operating in the USA for many years and some have sprung up in Europe and elsewhere during the past decade. They are a challenge to the Service Organisations of established manufacturers and they ensure that these organisations keep on their toes and provide a cost effective service to the customers.

Service Revenue is becoming an increasing proportion of the total revenue in many companies in most industries, and there is more competition for this lucrative market. Service nowadays has to be actively sold by the manufacturer – he can no longer sit back and wait for the customer to simply buy it. (See Marketing Service).

Service should be set clear objectives of the level and type of revenue it is expected to achieve. These targets are usually expressed both in monetary units (e.g. £ or $) as well as market share, expressed both as a percentage of existing business and contracts from new placements.

Now that we have identified service revenues and service costs we can draw up a simple Profit Statement. Figure 5 illustrates one way of depicting such a statement.

Revenue

1. Revenue from Maintenance Contracts
2. Revenue from Time and Material
3. Other Service Revenue from Outside Sources
4. Sub-total – Total Revenue from Outside Sources
5. Imputed Revenue from Warranty
6. Imputed Revenue from Rentals
7. Imputed Revenue from Other Sources
8. Sub-total – Total Imputed Revenues
9. Total Revenues

Expenses – Direct costs

10. Variable Labour Costs
11. Semi-Variable Labour Costs
12. Spare Parts Cost
13. (Returned Parts Credit)
14. Net Parts Cost
15. Consumable Costs
16. Total Direct Costs
17. *Service Contribution*

Expenses – Allocated Costs

18. Selling Costs
19. Service Support Costs
20. Customer Administration
21. General Administration
22. Distribution Costs
23. Other Costs
24. Total Allocated Costs
25. Provisions
26. Total Expenses
27. Profit Before Tax

Figure 5. *Example of a Service Profit Statment*

Building the Company's Image

It has been realised for some time that Service is too expensive an asset for a company to be used solely for the installation, repair and maintenance of equipment. It is not only the machine that needs servicing but the customer as well. This goes beyond maintaining good customer relations and involves projecting the desired Company Image to the public and for Service to be an integral part of a company's marketing mix.

Why has this change occurred? In the first half of this century most companies were satisfied if Service performed its traditional role of product maintenance. Technological innovation has, however, also brought with it the difficulty for customers to differentiate between competitive products intended for the same market segment – the product features the customer wants to utilise are almost identical, prices tend to be in the same range and so customers are turning to the quality of, and reputation for, after sales service of the manufacturer or supplier to differentiate between competitors.
You will note that I have carefully separated "the quality of service" from "the reputation". The quality is something "real" which is attained by achieving the customer satisfaction objectives mentioned earlier in this section. It is something more often recognised if it is absent than appreciated when it is there – in fact it is taken for granted.

Reputation, on the other hand, is partially based on quality and partially on the image created. This image can be influenced in a number of ways and usually it is cheaper to influence the image of service than to improve the level of service. Some of the ways a desired image can be created include suitable advertising and public relations activities (recently there has been a substantial increase of these), selective prioritisation of key customers, enhanced preventive maintenance programmes, and improved customer education.

Often a number of these activities can be combined to increase the effectiveness. For instance, one multi-national company wanted to project an image of an important national entity in the country in which it is operating. Customer training was typically undertaken in branch offices where video monitors were used for other purposes. During the customer training programme the national Managing Director of the company appeared on the screen of the monitors and after a short introduction during which he talked about the growth of the national entity, he led the group (on video tape) through the national headquarter building, the local workshop or factory and he showed what happens in the branch to incoming requests for service from the customer. All this created the desired image of an important national entity which, by the way, is part of a large world-wide organisation, and which has good facilities for handling customer calls. Furthermore, it made the customers understand more fully what is involved in responding to their requests.

In this way customer training was combined with a public relations exercise to create the desired image.

Selective prioritisation of customers must be used sparingly lest the prioritisation becomes a standard which may be expensive to maintain. On the other hand, if we have had a lot of difficulties with a particular installation, there is no reason why we should not temporarily modify its priority. Equally, if we happen to know that a competitive piece of equipment is on trial at a particular customer, it may well be desirable to ensure that this customer is especially well supported by us at this stage.

Care must be taken to think through the full consequences of certain image-building campaigns. They may back-fire. I remember a Spanish company who advertised its good service by showing four Service Engineers playing cards with a caption explaining that they were there waiting for customer calls. When a customer then had to wait for a couple of hours or more for the engineer to arrive to repair his machine, the customer welcomed him with a sarcastic "Sorry to have interrupted your card game – did you at least win as you made me wait so long?" Or, another company in Australia, who wanted to show how simple their equipment was to operate, who showed a TV advertisement of a monkey working their machine. Operators had their leg pulled and requested a transfer away from that company's machine. Both advertisements created the intended image but also introduced undesired "side effects".

Image is created not only by the company itself but often by the customer's own staff. Their attitude to the supplier and his product at every level of the hierarchy is often crucial for purchasing decisions. If a decision maker asks for some work to be done and the operator of a machine that is having its PM procedure performed says "I cannot do it, that so and so machine is not working again", sounds different from the same operator saying "I will do the work shortly – at the moment the machine is having its preventive maintenance performed". The lesson must be that everyone in a company needs to have the right attitude to the company and the right image of it. Whereas objectives can be made specific, effectiveness is difficult to measure.

Market Intelligence

The service force is probably more often in touch with the customer and on a more intimate basis (albeit at a lower level in the customer's hierarchy) than any other function. They are out there in the field, often spending many hours with the customer's own staff. They are bound to get information which can be of immense importance to our company. They know

- □ When customers may be dissatisfied with our equipment or company.
- □ When additional equipment or an upgrading is needed.
- □ When competitive products are being considered.
- □ How competitive equipment is performing.
- □ Likely future requirements of individual customers.
- □ When customers may consider moving premises or taking on additional tasks.

All this information is there, in the heads of our Service Engineers. Service Management has to ensure that this valuable information is shared with areas of the company where this type of information can be utilised, i.e. Sales, Marketing, and Engineering.

This information will only be "unlocked" when Service Management positively encourage this flow of information, give suitable recognition to the engineer involved and provide feedback on what action has been taken with this information.

The first two of these Service Management actions are entirely internal to the department, the last action needs to be agreed with other functions, and formal procedures must be laid down.

This type of activity can also be clearly identified as an "Objective" for a Service Department.

Technical Feedback

This is, in a way, an extension of market intelligence to cover the performance of your own product. Details of Service Reporting (which includes technical feedback) will be covered in detail in Section V, Management Tools for Service Management. The reason for mentioning it here, is that it is a clear objective for any service organisation to provide technical feedback to its Engineering, Manufacturing and Quality Assurance departments. The need for this feedback must be made clear to every Service Engineer so that he accepts it as part of his job, just as much as maintaining customer machines or any other task. This technical feedback can be made in many different ways, depending on the nature of the product, its position in the product life cycle, the numbers involved and a number of other factors. Typically, companies require a full and in depth feedback at the early part of the life cycle, often performed as a pre-launch trial or a full launch reporting procedure. Later it may be sufficient to have a more superficial technical feedback, or only a sampling procedure, or a feedback of exceptional failures. Whichever it is, it is not sufficient to have a procedure unless it is consequentially enforced. Included in this procedure should be an indication to the service force on how the information is used. This is particularly important where the feedback is coupled with a Suggestion Scheme, where Service Engineers are encouraged to propose improvements to obviate the failure. In these cases, each individual suggestion should be logged and each proposer should be informed whether his suggestion has been accepted and if not, why it has been turned down. This information should reach the proposer within a reasonable time. It is highly demotivating for engineers to spend time and effort in making proposals and then not hearing anything for a long time.

In many companies awards are made to the proposers of suggestions which are either worthwhile but rejected for practical reasons (e.g. the product is on the declining part of the product curve, or the modification would be uneconomical), or for suggestions actually accepted and implemented. Most of these companies use a formalised method of establishing the level of the award which is usually linked to the profit impact of the suggestion. Even in companies who do not have a formalised Suggestion Scheme, it is recommended that they publicise the names of proposers of worthwhile suggestions as this type of recognition is highly motivational, and is likely to encourage other good ideas to be put forward.

Whereas technical suggestions are an objective in companies all over the world, the only country where I have actually seen that the quantity of these proposals targeted (by small groups) is in some Japanese Service Organisations. This enables them to some extent to control the number of proposals being put forward.

Marketing Support

Whereas it may be obvious to top management that one of the objectives of a Service Department is the support of Marketing, it is nowhere near as obvious that this also entails involving Service management in the preparation of marketing plans to enable them to have the right resources available at the right spot at the right time.

It also means specifying this support requirement as part of the objectives of the Service Department.

It involves not only the physical support implied above but also the clear identification of each Service Engineer with the objectives of the company. The engineer can only identify with an objective if he knows what it is – the full and detailed statement of company objectives is therefore essential. All too often the objectives of the Sales Department are not compatible with those of the Service Department – the customer is caught in the middle and may decide to change his allegiance.

The physical support of Marketing sometimes required of Service include:

- ☐ Unplanned Sales Drives, which need to be supported by a larger number of exhibitions, demonstrations and installations than originally envisaged.
- ☐ Unusual Applications, which may need the re-adjustment or alteration of equipment, which may in turn lead to a higher call rate for Service.
- ☐ Opening up of Unplanned Geographical Areas, which may increase travel time and expense and reduce the service coverage in planned areas.
- ☐ Promises Beyond the Agreed Level of Service, which may take the form of faster response times, out of normal working hours coverage or earlier installation.
- ☐ Extensions to Warranties or "Free Trials", which may again reduce the service coverage of other customers.

A balance must be found by management to allow sufficient flexibility of the whole organisation to satisfy customers' legitimate requirements and allowing each Salesman to give away too much of the company.

All these activities can be more easily catered for if Service is involved in the planning cycle, which enables the objectives to be prioritised jointly.

Satisfied Service Force

All the objectives so far mentioned depend heavily on the full co-operation of the whole service force – as the saying goes: "you can lead a horse to water but you can't make it drink". The best prepared schemes and carefully quantified plans will only become effective with the whole-hearted support of the staff who have to implement these schemes and plans.

We will discuss the motivational practices applicable specifically to the service force under the heading "Managing the Service Force" in Section IV, "Service Management". Here I want to cover the setting of objectives for measuring the level of satisfaction of a service force. As we all know, that is not as simple as using a thermometer and reading whether the temperature is "normal".

Yet, even when we measure the temperature of the human body, we need to establish first of all what constitutes "normal". And even if the temperature is normal, the body may still be "ill", i.e. abnormal, and other indicators are used by the physician and compared to a standard or norm, e.g. pulse rate and rhythm, chest sounds etc.

In the same way it is not possible to pick on one measure to determine the level of satisfaction of a service force. Furthermore, it is probably more important to establish a *trend* for the various parameters than an absolute level which is likely to depend as much on the definitions and yardsticks used by individual companies.

Let me illustrate what I mean by taking one of the widely used measures for the determination of employee satisfaction: the rate of attrition, i.e. the percentage of leavers to the total staff employed in a particular department or area. This measure is so popular because it is so simple to obtain, it is one which can easily be compared to the attrition rates in the industry in general or to specific competitors in particular, and between individual departments in the company. All this would indicate that an absolute measure is reasonable. But let us look at it in a little more detail. Are we comparing like with like? When we compare the attrition rate with that of other companies, is the definition of attrition the same? Do we all include all leavers, or do some of us exclude, for instance, those retiring at their normal retirement age, or those whom the company has asked to leave? Are all companies treating promotions or transfers to other functions the same way when comparing attrition of Service Engineers? If we look at comparisons within the same Company on an inter-departmental basis we can ensure that all the above factors are treated the same way across all departments. We then have to consider whether the mobility of certain types of staff is greater throughout the industry than that of others. For instance, in many countries the mobility of Salesmen tends to be higher than that of Service Engineers but this may not be true everywhere – in some of the African countries where there is a desperate shortage of skilled technicians their movement is higher than that of salesmen. International comparisons are equally dangerous because of cultural differences, e.g. the attrition rate in Japan is likely to be lower than in the USA.

Enough said – it is trends in attrition we are going to utilise. Even here we will obviously need to take external influences into account. It is likely, for instance, that during a time of high and rising unemployment the average rate of voluntary attrition is going to reduce – I am using the term "average rate" advisedly, as it may well hide a qualitative problem, i.e. that the best engineers are leaving but the remainder are staying.

Attrition is only one of the measures of satisfaction and not necessarily the most meaningful one. A low level of attrition can be induced by excessively high rates of pay in comparison to other companies but that does not make for a happy or satisfied service force. As we will see when we examine motivation factors, below standard pay for the job will cause dissatisfaction, but above standard pay for the job will not cause satisfaction.

In consequence, a company needs to establish the attitude of its employees to their jobs, to their colleagues, superiors and to the company itself. This is not easy to determine as many of us will find it difficult to identify individual factors which affect our attitude to our environment. Often we need to establish the cause factor rather than the way it manifests itself before we find an area which can be actioned.

Let me again give you an example from a real situation. Efficiently conducted attitude surveys in a large service organisation established a great deal of dissatisfaction with the reporting system. This was surprising, as in the company concerned the reporting system had been effectively streamlined and the amount of reporting had been reduced over time and the need for written reports by the engineers almost eliminated. It took some sensitive questioning to establish that it was not the reporting system as such that the Engineers objected to (although that was what the attitude survey indicated) but rather the way results from it were used. In fact what had happened in a relatively inexperienced group of first line managers (i.e. direct managers of Service Engineers, let us call them Field Service Managers from now on) was that in the twice annual reviews the Field Service Managers based their evaluations entirely on the numerical results of the reporting system. That led to engineers "massaging" their reporting inputs which had an adverse effect on many decisions taken from these reports and that in turn disillusioned the Engineers and also made them feel that the wrong Engineers received good reviews. Once this was understood by the company, remedial action was taken by breaking the direct link between reporting and reviews, additional training for the Field Service Managers in leadership qualities was given and it was explained to them that the reporting system was only one of many tools available to them in evaluating Engineers and they were encouraged to spend more time out in the field with their Engineers. The results were quite striking; the reporting became "honest", the quality of the Field Service Manager's support to his Engineers improved and the dissatisfaction with the reporting system disappeared as a factor in the attitude surveys.

The reason I went into some detail in this particular case was to demonstrate the need for management to understand the real cause of any dissatisfaction and to show that some action should be taken by management from the results of the surveys – if no action is taken, surveys are useless.

The wording of questionnaires must be devised by experts to ensure that there is no ambiguity or bias. The wording should not be changed frequently to establich genuine trends which, as we showed earlier, is important. Attitude surveys give a work force an opportunity to express their feelings and, if they see the company paying attention demonstrably attributable to these surveys, they see management taking note of the opinions of these feelings.

It must be remembered that attitude towards a particular management action can be adversely affected over time due to no fault of anybody but simply by understanding the full implications of a decision.

Let me illustrate this by another example, this time from the USA. The company found that minority groups, and particularly black employees, were under-represented in their work force and in management. As part of their "Affirmative Action" programme they proposed the introduction of a reverse discrimination programme, whereby the minimum standards for any job would not be changed, but once the minimum specifications had been met, candidates from a minority group would be selected even though candidates with better qualifications were available. The first two or three attitude surveys (conducted every three months on one quarter of the service force) showed a very positive attitude towards this scheme. This deteriorated over the next few surveys until the issue became a problem and was investigated more deeply. It showed that in principle Service Engineers agreed with the approach but when they saw the practical results they had reservations. These practical results were *felt* by the Engineers to show that (a) the quality of intake of new Engineers had been reduced (b) the quality of new Managers was being reduced affecting their own work and (c) perhaps worst of all, their own promotional opportunities were being reduced.

This shows that attitudes can change even though the principle behind the programme was equally valid a year or two later. The crux of attitude surveys is for management to keep their finger on the pulse of the feelings of their staff so that any decision they take (even if it is to do nothing) is taken with the full knowledge of its effect.

Some companies target specific Service Engineer satisfaction parameters as part of the objectives to be achieved by service management – others do not target these areas specifically, as they know that the financial, productivity and level of service targets will not be achieved unless the employees are suitably motivated and managed to demonstrate a positive attitude to their job, their colleagues, their managers and their company.

Summary of Section

It is essential for every Service Department to have clearly stated objectives. The generic philosophical statements are useful only towards developing specific, and wherever possible also quantified, objectives. These objectives can be divided into the prime goals of achieving customer satisfaction at a reasonable cost to the customer and for Service to contribute increasingly to company profits; the indirect goals try to take full advantage of the considerable investment many companies make in their Service Departments by setting objectives for Service to help in building the company's desired image, obtaining market intelligence, feeding back accurate technical information and fully supporting the total marketing and sales activities.

None of these objectives are likely to be achieved efficiently without the full cooperation of the service force which, in turn, requires a satisfied and highly motivated employee.

SECTION II

Forecasting, Planning and Budgeting

Forecasting, planning and budgeting are closely linked and in any organisation these activities are likely to follow each other in the mentioned sequence (see Fig 14). It may well mean, however, that when we have gone through the complete process, the results do not satisfy our targets and we may have to go back to change certain inputs to give us different results. It is obviously necessary to change not only the "numbers" in our calculation, but the new parametes must be achievable and our actions must be aimed at and our resources must be allocated in such a way as to make things happen in the planned way. The whole process is a road-map which leads us from where we are to where we want to be and identifies the means by which we will do so. In the same way as we will need to know the conditions of the roads on our road-map, the speed of the car, the number of stops we will want to take to give us an indication of how long it will take us to travel from 'A' to 'B', we will need to input a wide range of parameters into our plans before we can make a logical approach to our planning activity. Although the end result will be in monetary terms (e.g. dollars) the case has to be built up on a detailed basis. As Service is manpower intensive, the plan would be normally separated into a manpower plan, a materials plan and, where appropriate, a capital plan. The activity plan is the driver of all the other forecasting activities. Let us first examine some of the inputs.

Physical Forecasting Parameters

We need to examine physical factors in a number of different areas to build up a picture of the activity which will be required to be undertaken by a Service

Department. These factors can be grouped into the technical parameters affected by the performance of the products involved, the market parameters identifying the activity case and market conditions, the human parameters concerning the staff involved, and the economic parameters governed by the environment.

Technical Parameters

To establish the manpower plan and materials plan we have to examine in detail the performance forecasts of all the equipments that will be serviced:

Failure Rate and Service Calls

The reliability forecast of each product is based on the mean time between failures (MTBF) of the product which in turn is based on the sum of the MTBFs of the individual components or modules which make up the product. This is a crucial input parameter but not easy to obtain. On an existing product, historical information is available on an absolute basis and trends can be observed. Any known or planned changes need to be considered such as any product modification (engineering change order – ECO) which is retrofitted in the field to improve reliability. Care must be taken to separate MTBF from mean time between service calls (MTBSC) as the latter is affected by other factors in addition to MTBF, such as human factors (see later in this section) which may change the skill mix and experience of the service force, and includes calls generated by the inexperience of customers who may request unnecessary service calls.

On a new product the MTBF is usually established by the Design Engineers who should also input the likely pattern of failure in the early models prior to product maturity. This type of early failure would take into account "infant mortality" of components, learning curve of component sub-contractors and manufacturing assemblers.

MTBF and MTBSC must be carefully monitored for each module, sub-assembly or component which contributes to the MTBF or MTBSC and established whether it conforms to the predicted failure pattern and, if not, to establish the reason for variance, and effect remedial action if appropriate. Here it is important to find the real cause of any problem rather than accept the effect of failure of a component as the real issue. Faulty diagnostic procedures may identify the wrong part of the system as the problem area.

The influence of customers on the apparent MTBSC cannot be overstressed. This has been demonstrated by many manufacturers and is most easily discernible where a company offers an inclusive service contract or service included in the rental of an equipment as well as service carried out against payment on a Time and Materials (T&M) basis. The call rate tends to be much higher where the cost is fixed as compared to customers paying a specific call charge. This has obvious implications on the selling of Service Contracts which we will consider later.

The reliability as perceived by customers tends to be based on the frequency "the machine is down" or "the engineer calls" rather than machine failures which genuinely require the intervention of a Service Engineer. As the perceived reliability is the basis for a manufacturer's reputation for product reliability, a service organisation must strive to affect this perceived reliability as well as improve the MTBF rate by technical changes in the product and by increasing the competence of the Service Engineers. Specific approaches will be covered under Customer Care Programmes.

Preventive Maintenance

One of the physical forecasting parametes which has been highly controversial is preventive maintenance (PM). The controversy arises not so much from the technical efficiency of PMs as from the practical problems of implementing them. The pattern of PM requirements has also changed with the move to a higher electronics content in today's products.

On mechanical components it was relatively easy to establish MTBF for major components and the failure distribution pattern showed a relatively pronounced fall off; the component was changed prior to attaining a peak failure rate. (Fig 6)

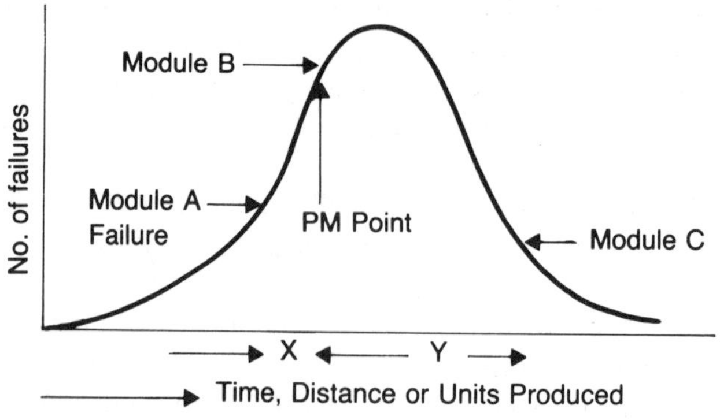

Figure 6. *Normal Distribution of Parts Failure*

On electronic components the curve is reversed, giving a typical "bathtub" shape (Fig 7).

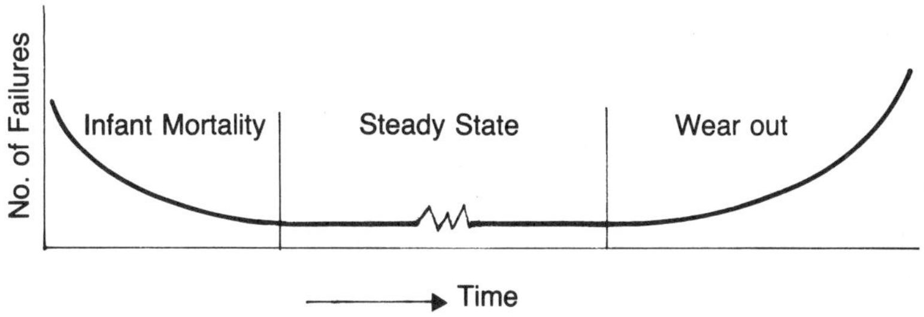

Figure 7. *"Bathtub" Distribution of Parts Failure*

It is typical for the steady state of electronic components to be very long. To reduce failures during the "Infant Mortality" stage, equipment is often "burnt in" by the manufacturer of electronic components. A similar procedure is also adopted in other industries, where, for instance, car engines are "run in" at the factory and aircraft fly a predetermined number of hours prior to use by passengers.

Another difficulty with preventive maintenance decisions is the very fact that modules and components have a different life span, and if PM procedures are to be introduced, certain activities have to be grouped together. This may well mean that some components have exceeded the ideal point for exchange and may therefore have caused a service call, (Module A, figure 6) whilst others still have some time to run before the ideal PM point (Module C, figure 6). In the period marked "X" we are likely to incur additional costs due to module A failing and we could have got additional life from module C, marked "Y", which again incurs a cost. It is a question of establishing the point of least total cost if a purely monetary approach is taken.

Money may not be the main consideration in every case – in some industries safety overrides cost considerations. For instance in an aircraft, redundant systems are built in for critical areas and others are changed well ahead of their anticipated life to minimise the probability of failure.

So far we have concentrated on preventive maintenance at fixed intervals, be they measured in time (years, months, hours, etc.), distance (kilometers, miles, meters, etc.), units (number produced) or other predetermined measures.

Preventive Maintenance intervals can also be detemined in other ways. The simplest deviation from a fixed interval may be the need of operability at a specific time. Many motorists may decide to carry out a maintenance of their car prior to a long holiday journey. Certain industries may be seasonal and would naturally wish to carry out PM activities in the off-peak periods (e.g. power stations) preferably prior to the peak period.

Another approach taken by some service organisations servicing products which require relatively frequent visits to the customer, is to break down the tasks to be undertaken by the Engineer into a number of separate groups and ask him to perform one or more sub-groups of tasks during his normal service calls. Decisions of this nature will depend on the product design (accessibility of the areas requiring PM), the frequency of service calls, the time required to perform these sub-group tasks and the image the manufacturer wishes to project.

An increasingly widely used approach to PMs is the condition monitored maintenance procedure. This approach recognises that identical equipment may perform differently under varying conditions and it awaits "tell-tale" indicators to warn of an impending deterioration of performance. The simplest example is the motorist listening to the "feel" of his engine and its sounds to determine whether to have it "tuned up". Quantitative indicators have been developed in other industries to determine the point at which PMs should be performed. In power stations the temperature change in turbines and vibration give an indication of impending problems. More sophisticated methods employ semi-automatic or automatic indicators of problems which can be built into the product (e.g. a car "low oil" indicator).

Another consideration entering into the PM decision making process is the fact that often problems are caused by an Engineer disturbing a well-running equipment. In a number of industries detailed analyses have shown that the incidence of service calls increases after a preventive maintenance visit by an Engineer. In some industries the "Leave well alone" approach is preferred and equipment is left to run until a service call occurs before even considering PM activities.

I am trying to show that Preventive Maintenance is a complex and emotional subject which has implications beyond the purely technical aspect. However, if employed, it must be included as a time factor in the forecasting and planning process.

Work Time

The other technical parameter needed to establish a reasonable forecast once we know the number of calls that are likely to be made is the time taken to perform these service calls. These are known as the mean time to instal (MTTI) and the mean time to repair (MTTR), which would also include time required to perform preventive maintenance. Obviously, different failures may have very different MTTRs. To enable proper decisions to be taken these MTTRs for different tasks need to be separated but for planning purposes a MTTR per equipment under certain conditions is adequate. This is often "standardised" for "normal" conditions for calculating purposes and can be flexed for different conditions. An example of this approach is a manufacturer of copier/duplicators who may have standardised his calculations for a particular model at, say, 100,000 prints/month. It may well be that the branch dealing with government installations will have an average print volume of 180,000 and another branch working in a provincial city may average only 75,000 prints/month/machine. The input to the forecast would be suitably flexed from the 100,000 prints/month standard for the specific branch for MTBSC, MTTR and possibly other parameters. As in the case of mean time between failures (MTBF), MTTR and MTTI are established from historical data and modified for known changes for existing products and from inputs obtained from Design Engineering for new models. In the case of worktime, the learning curve of Engineers has a particularly strong influence and their experience level must be taken into account (see learning curve under human parameters, later in this section). Service Managers often find it difficult to influence MTTR of their Engineers – if they insist on excessively short MTTRs the job may not be done adequately and generate recalls to the same equipment; if they let MTTRs increase excessively, productivity suffers. They must therefore be able to have the tasks to be performed analysed to develop reasonable standards for MTTRs and MTTIs. This is the area where specialisation often pays off but it must be balanced with other factors such as job satisfaction of the Engineer and flexibility of the service force (see Human Relations in section IV).

An example of the possible advantage that can be gained by specialisation in reducing MTTRs was demonstrated to me during the performance of a major retrofit (modification). My HQ unit had identified a standard for the MTTR for this modification. Soon I had complaints from a number of countries that the indicated standard could not be achieved. I was beginning to believe that my Product Service Engineers who had developed the MTTR had made a mistake. Then I noted that the data fed back from Austria showed that not only were they meeting the standard but their MTTR was only 70% of the standard. As it was an important modification and the suspicion was that the work was not done properly, the Product Service Engineer from London was despatched to Vienna to investigate. He reported that the Austrian Service Engineers had decided to form two small teams of two Engineers to carry out all the modifications throughout Austria. They had developed special skills and although it may have been dull to spend 6 months doing the same job, they got their motivation from the excellent results they were achieving and from the opportunity to travel around the whole country. They were also publicly commended.

The purpose of this example was to show how MTTRs and MTTIs were particularly sensitive to the learning curve for specific activities.

Market Parameters

As with other factors, there is uncertainty about what is likely to occur in the market place over the period of the forecast – typically if it is a one year forecast it will have to look ahead between 15 and 18 months, as the forecast will have to be made well ahead of the commencement date of the period, to enable all planning activities to be completed. The same applies to longer term forecasts, i.e. the period to be considered is 3 to 6 months ahead of the commencement date.

There will therefore often be some reluctance to commit to a forecast of market conditions. Yet someone will have to make the forecast! The logical conclusion is that it should be made by the Department best equipped to do so. When it comes to market parameters, therefore, it is likely to be Marketing which will have the best information on which to base forecasts and the Sales Department will be able to be more specific about individual geographical distribution.

Number of Equipments

To enable a Service Manager to forecast his manpower, materials and other requirements, he will need an input from Marketing and Sales of the number of upgrades, additional installations as well as removals that the plan should be based on. This should be as specific as possible and include not only the models of individual equipments but, where appropriate, also the utilisation of the equipment and the location. Obviously it is difficult to forecast all these parameters but it is likely that Marketing and Sales will make a more accurate forecast than the Service Manager would make if he had to guess at these market parameters. Any opening of new branches or sales territories must also be taken into account by Service in their forecasts.

Response Time

There is growing pressure by customers for a maximum operational availability or "up-time" for their equipment. Our company therefore must try to minimise down-time. Down-time is dependant on the frequency of service calls (MTBSC) multiplied by the mean time to repair (MTTR) plus the time required by our company to respond to the customer's calls plus the frequency of preventive maintenance (PM) calls multiplied by their MTTR. No response time is applicable to PM calls, as the equipment is operational until the Service Engineer arrives to carry out the PM procedure. Response time is normally defined as the time from receipt of customer's telephone call until the arrival of the Service Engineer at the machine. Under normal circumstances, only the standard working hours (e.g. from 8.30 a.m. to 5 p.m.) are calculated and "the clock is stopped" during the night and at weekends. That applies where a single shift service has been agreed with customers. Obviously if 24 hours cover has been arranged, the clock does not stop and the elapsed time then equals response time. Response time can be broken down into travel time (MTTT) to the customer plus the time before the Service Engineer is available to attend to the call from the customer. This is illustrated in Figure 8.

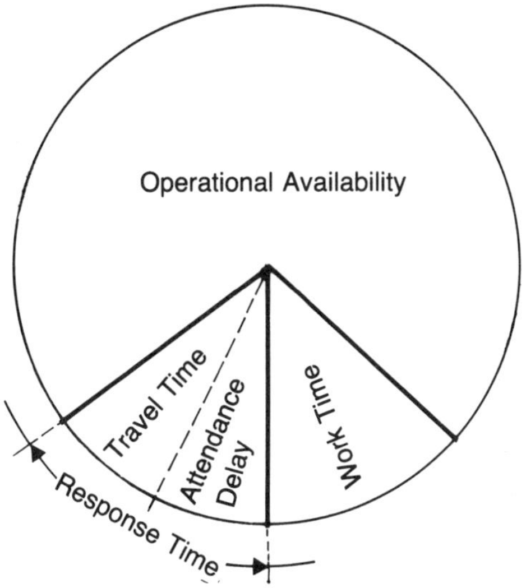

Where:

Work Time	=	$MTBSC \times MTTR_{(SC)} + PM \times MTTR_{(PM)}$
Response Time	=	Travel Time + Attendance Delay
Travel Time	=	$MTBSC \times MTTT$ (PM travel time ignored in calculation of Operational Availability but must be included in calculation of manpower requirements).
Attendance Delay	=	Time elapsed between receipt of customer's call and Service Engineer starting his travel to a customer to repair a failure.

Figure 8. *Division of total machine time*

In consequence the percentage of Operational Availability can be defined as

$$\frac{\text{Nominal Work Hours} - (\text{Work Time} + \text{Response Time})}{\text{Nominal Work Hours}} \times 100$$

For example if the Nominal Work Hours per year are, say, 2000 hours, Work Time (Service and PM calls) per year is, say, 40 hours and Response Time per year is, say, 60 hours then the Percentage Up Time (Operational Availability) is

$$\frac{2000-(40+60)}{2000} \times 100 = 95\%$$

The above example illustrates the dependence of operational availability not only on the reliability of the equipment and its associated repair time but also on the response time.

In fact, response time may play a more important part in the customer's perception of the service given than work time. Psychologically, the customer tends to be less impatient when an engineer is working on his machine than during the period he is waiting for the engineer to arrive.

Another reason why the understanding of response time and the way to plan and control it is so important, is its role in the marketing mix. These aspects will be discussed later – the control of response time in the Service Control Section (Work Control) and the marketing mix implications when we consider Interfunctional Relationships with the Sales and Marketing Functions. In this section we are concerned with its impact on forecasting, planning and budgeting.

We need to understand the relationship of response time, manpower availability, work and travel times of individual calls and territory planning. Response time conforms to the Queuing Theory. The actual numbers of hours and their distribution will vary considerably from industry to industry and often from customer to customer. In modern factories and offices there is an increasing interdependence of various equipments and response time is crucial. In the past, if one of 20 lathes had a breakdown, the plant found it inconvenient but could manage for a day or two until a Service Engineer or a spare part became available. Now that these 20 lathes have been replaced by one or two multi spindle automatics it makes any delay in repair more crucial to the operation of the whole factory. Similar considerations apply to 20 typewriters compared to one computer connected to 10 word processing stations in an office.

For this reason much greater emphasis is being placed by customers, and therefore manufacturers, on response time planning. If no special actions are undertaken, response time will have a normal distibution with a relatively long tail.

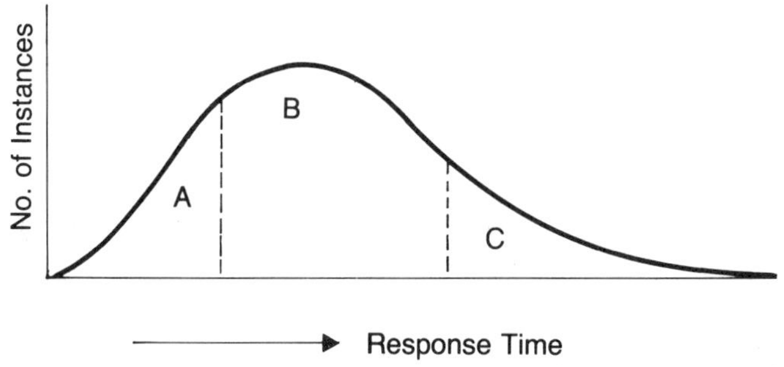

Figure 9. *Response time distribution*

A small number of calls (Area A) will receive relatively fast response time, a large number (Area B) a response time close to the average, but quite a number of calls (Area C) will have long response times which may cause customer dissatisfaction.

There are a number of ways of improving the situation. The simplest but most expensive way is to increase the service force, which will move the whole graph to the left, giving shorter average response times at the penalty of higher costs, lower productivity and possible negative motivational impact on the service force due to excess time on their hands which may lengthen work times per call (MTTR's). Other ways include a more effective Work Control (see Section V), rearranging tasks (e.g. by exchanging modules or sub-assemblies instead of repair in the field to reduce work times), or combining a number of engineer territories into one joint territory (see Territory Planning – Section III) which, for the same manpower availability, will reduce average response times slightly, but substantially cut the tail ('C' in Figure 9) at the expense of increased travel cost. The choice of alternatives will depend on the industry, the geography and road conditions of the territory(ies), density of machine population, management style and degree of specialisation.

For forecasting purposes a planned response time must be agreed by Sales, Service and Marketing to enable a forecast to be made by Service. It may well be that the company decides to allow response times to lengthen to reduce costs or to shorten response times to gain a marketing advantage. Service must be in a position to quantify response time targets in manpower requirements and support needs.

Travel Time

The location of customer installations, both present and additional ones in the forecasting period, will be an important input for determining travel times and arranging engineer or engineer team territories. In addition to the direct impact on travel time and travel costs, there is an impact on response time as we have seen in the foregoing paragraphs. It is obviously important to minimise travel times so that we do not use the time of our skilled engineers in the unskilled task of driving and the associated travel costs which have risen steeply over the past years. On the other hand, travel time savings should not necessarily be allowed to override possible benefits that might be achieved by sharing territories between a number of engineers to improve response times or by increasing specialisation to improve product knowledge and experience which may reduce the number of calls and reduce errors in diagnosis and servicing practices.

Good management practices can be utilised to reduce travel time. These include:

- ☐ Efficient prioritisation of service calls through work control
- ☐ Combining PM activities with corrective service calls provided the duration of the combined call does not become excessive.
- ☐ When carrying out service on a machine in a remote location, look in on other machines in the area to avoid an early call from the same location.
- ☐ Efficient scheduling of installations and retrofit activities. Retrofits may also be combined with either scheduled maintenance (SM=PM) or unscheduled maintenance (UM=CR (customer request)) calls.
- ☐ Good parts planning and replenishment (see Inventory Control – V). This may include radio/telephone controlled spares vehicles, motor cycle messengers, delivery by taxi etc.

In any case, travel time cannot be omitted from forecasting inputs.

Human Parameters

As the human parameters of forecasting are not easily determined and tend to differ between individuals, they are often ignored in the forecasting, planning and budgeting process. We will see, however, that their influence on results can be quite dramatic.

Skill and Knowledge Level

We need to establish the skill and knowledge of the staff we are proposing to employ in servicing our equipment. The effect manifests itself in the time necessary to train an engineer on new equipment, the work time per call, the frequency of making a wrong diagnosis and the consequent increase in call rate and in the tasks we will plan to carry out in the field and consequent structure of the support documentation (service manuals) for the field force.

Let us look at each of these effects a little more closely and examine ways of overcoming deficiencies and how this affects the planning process. In the product specification it is usual to specify the level of engineer who will be servicing the equipment. This will lead to a man specification for the engineers we will employ. In many products this will involve mechanical, electrical and electronic knowledge and often include specific knowledge in, for instance, hydraulic or pneumatic areas. In many companies the existing service force may not have all these skills, yet the company intends to utilise the existing service force on the new products. Similar skill deficiencies may be found when trying to recruit service staff in a new company or for additions to the existing service force. In many companies this is handled by additional basic skill training modules in the areas where deficiencies have been identified. These are normally administered prior to the standard course for the product. Before it is possible to carry out this pre-course training it is necessary to identify the training need (this is covered in greater detail in Section III – Selection Techniques and Service Training). The extra time to administer the additional basic skills and knowledge training modules must be included in the planning process. Some of these basic skills and knowledge modules may be available as standard self-paced training programmes or in other forms of educational material, but others may have to be performed under more tightly supervised training conditions.

Another situation where the different skill and knowledge level of the service force needs to be considered is a relatively sophisticated product designed for service in developed countries and, as an afterthought, it is decided to market the product in developing or under-developed countries as well. It may be neceassary to change the service strategy in some of these markets. A number of alternatives can be considered:

(i) The use of expatriate service staff with the necessary skills, where the local staff start by carrying out only auxiliary tasks and have a long period to learn the full extent of the task. An example of this is in oil installations.

(ii) The extensive training of local service staff in a developed country speaking the same language or locally by expatriate Service Engineers and subsequent field work under expatriate technical supervision. This is often used by manufacturers of agricultural and construction equipment.

(iii) The alternative under (ii) above is sometimes supplemented by telephone advice available from the manufacturer (often referred to as the "hot line") and, if necessary, by a skilled Service Engineer from the manufacturer flying out to repair unusual faults (often referred to as "fire fighters" or "flying screwdrivers"). This is often used by manufacturers of power station equipment to supplement local staff.

(iv) The tasks to be carried out by field service staff are limited to the replacement of complete modules or sub-assemblies in the field and the actual repair of the module is performed at a local workshop under controlled conditions and tighter technical supervision than it is possible to give in the field. An example of this is the office equipment industry.

In all these instances it must be the aim of the manufacturer or supplier to bring the knowledge and skill of local staff up to the required level as quickly as possible to limit the external assistance that needs to be given to the local service force. It is totally unacceptable, and usually also unnecessary, to provide expatriate support on a permanent basis. It should be a clearly stated task for these expatriates to train local replacements for themselves within a specified period.

Manpower Turnover

The rate of turnover of staff may differ by job, from company to company, from country to country and from time to time, but there will be some staff movement. This may be on a planned basis (e.g. promotions and job rotation, retirement, etc.) or on a random basis (e.g. Service Engineers leaving the company) but it needs to be taken into account in the forecasting, planning and budgeting process. It has an impact on manpower availability, which is what enables a service department to give a planned level of service to customers.

(i) For planned personnel movements, replacement staff can be selected, trained and brought up the learning curve prior to moving the experienced Engineer. For random movements, there is seldom enough time to perform all the desired preparations before the experienced Engineer leaves. The time involved may be quite substantial, depending on local conditions. The required period for giving notice varies, the time to find a replacement will depend on the availability of staff of the required calibre at the specific time, the training period will vary with product, number of different products involved, their complexity and the experience of the recruit. The speed with which he ascends the learning curve will also depend on his basic ability and previous experience. A Service Manager must therefore work from his previous experience. (Figure 10).

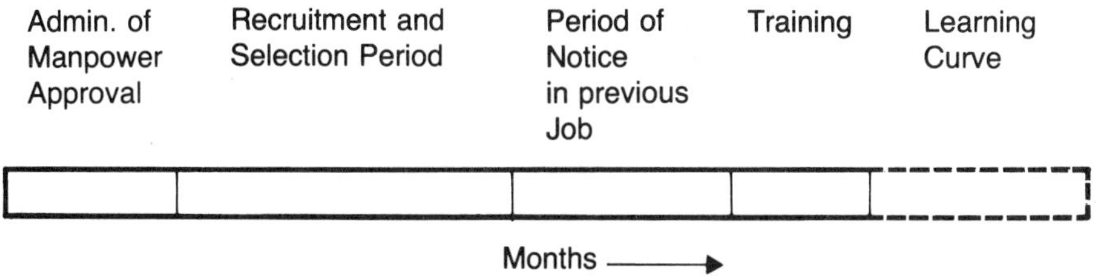

Figure 10. *Time to Replace Experienced Engineer*

(ii) If the existing service force is to be trained on additional product families, a relatively large proportion of Engineers will be out of the field for some weeks of training. If the level of service (LOS) should not deteriorate during this period, additional staff will be required – these are often known as "back-fill" Engineers. If the new product means that the company is increasing its service force, this back-fill will mean earlier recruitment to allow existing Engineers to be replaced during their training by the back-fill Engineers, who will later be absorbed into the service force. Where there is no staff growth envisaged a more difficult situation arises. It will mean either an increase in overtime of Engineers to cover their colleagues while in training, the use of service support engineers or other qualified staff to perform the servicing in the field and/or the early recruitment of back-fill engineers on the assumption of future attrition in the service force. As always, the Service Manager must balance the impact of his actions on the LOS and consequent customer satisfaction and his profit contribution. It is advisable to resolve these issues during the planning cycle rather than after the event.

Learning Curve

Figure 11 illustrates the theoretical learning curve of a Service Engineer. As with many other factors which have to be considered by service management in preparing their forecasts, it will vary from person to person but there is an average slope and shape for the graph which the Service Manager will have to establish for his products and for the staff he normally recruits. Consideration of the learning curve is not only important in the planning process but also as an indication of possible action that may need to be taken to reach peak performance as quickly as possible.

If we assume that peak performance (the distance of the "Steady State" D–E in figure 11 from the horizontal axis) is given by the inherent ability of the Service Engineer and his experience, the Service Manager may be able to influence the time it takes for an engineer to reach 'D'; it must be his aim to reduce this time to a minimum, i.e. to move 'D' as much to the left of the graph as possible. This may be achieved in a number of ways:

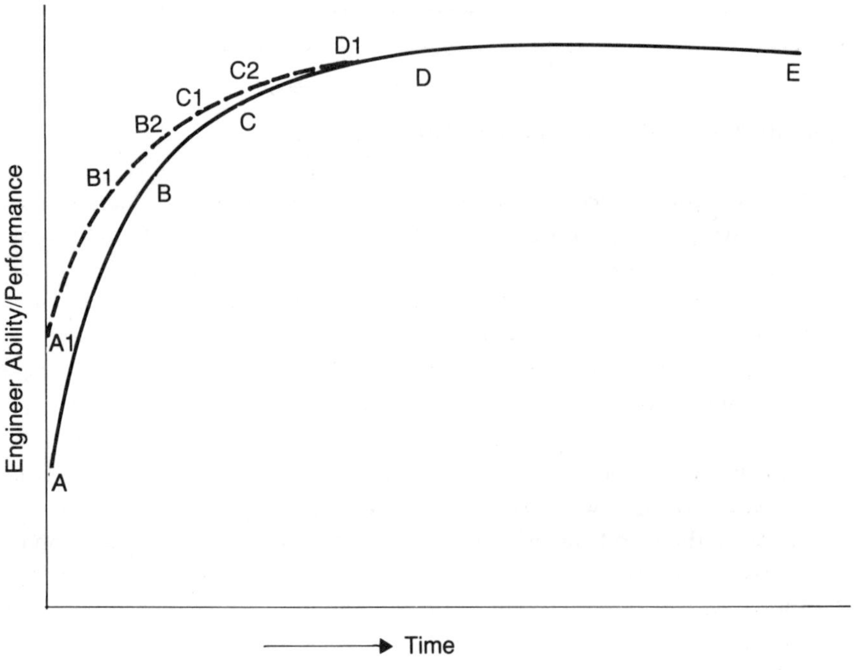

A – Ability at intake
A–B – Formal training
B–C – Steep improvement in early field experience
C–D – Rate of improvement slowing down
D–E – Steady state of performance

A1 – Higher ability at intake
A1–B1 – Shorter training period for same ability an end of course
A1–B2 – Same training period for higher ability at end of course
A1–C1 – Shorter period to achieve certain level of performance
A1–C2 – Same period to achieve higher level of performance
A1–D1 – Shorter period to achieve steady state of performance

Figure 11. *Theoretical Learning Curve*

(i) By recruiting engineers of a higher ability he may be able to move point 'A' higher up on the Engineer Ability axis, which will make it possible to reach 'D' (peak performance) earlier. 'A1' illustrates this on the chart.

(ii) By improving the formal training programme it may be possible to either shorten the training period (bringing 'B'closer to the vertical axis) illustrated by B1) or to improve the ability of the engineer more rapidly (moving 'B'further from the horizontal axis), illustrated by B2.

(iii) By ensuring that the engineer has an early opportunity to reinforce his training experience by practical field experience under professional guidance and supervision, it will either enable performance level 'C' to be reached more quickly (illustrated by 'C1') or to come nearer to peak performance in the same period, illustrated by 'C2'.

(iv) By continuing field experience, effective guidance and interchange of experiences between Service Engineers, peak performance may be reached earlier, illustrated by 'D1'.

In practice it will be difficult to maintain peak performance at the steady state D–E. After working in the field for an extended period, there may be a gradual fall-off of performance. This may be counteracted by Service Managers by effective motivational accompaniment of the Engineer, regular counselling and refresher training.

Economic Parameters

Whereas the Service Manager is not expected to forecast economic trends on a broad basis, he must utilise forecasts on the economy by experts in the planning of his Service Department.

Trends of Industry

These trends will give a Service Manager early warning of impending changes in many areas of his industry. On the purely technical side he might perceive a trend towards different technology and he can prepare his service force for it by suitable basic training in the new technology. Or there may be a discernible trend in the traffic conditions in a city and he may need to plan alternative means of supporting his engineers with spare parts. There may be increased pressure from customers on greater operational availability, which a Service Manager may be able to provide without increasing costs unduly by organisational changes in the service force or better work control procedures. By anticipating competitive actions he may be able to retain the initiative by suitable communication and motivation of the service force.

Inflation

It is not only the rate of inflation that a Service Manager needs to consider in the preparation of his plans – if it were as simple as that it could be done on an across the board calculation for the company as a whole at the end of a planning cycle. Inflation does not affect all areas equally. For instance, the relationship of increasing parts cost and labour costs may be at a very different rate and the Service Manager may be able to adjust his plans accordingly. He may be able to save total costs, for example, by changing modules and sub-assemblies in the field and subsequently repairing them in a batch mode, rather than spend the time of Service Engineers in the field fault-finding down to component level. Another example is the relatively slower rise of communication and data manipulation costs compared to the increase in labour costs. By drawing the right conclusions, a Service Manager may find it advantageous to utilise telephone diagnostic methods before sending an Engineer to a customer's installation. What I intend to stress is that the impact of inflation is not purely a budgeting issue but one for specific changes of approach which must be quantified in the forecasting and planning activities of a Service Manager.

Spare Parts and Materials

The high costs of holding stock, handling it and accounting for it have necessitated the introduction of sophisticated inventory control systems in many companies. This will be discussed in more detail in Section V (Management Tools for Service), sub-section (iii) Inventory Control but it needs to be mentioned here in connection with the forecasting process. The trends in interest rates in comparison with change in transportation costs and parts costs may affect the whole parts support strategy. It may be total cost effective, for instance, to stock fewer expensive items in engineer vehicles and improve the delivery of these items from the local stores to the engineer. It may not be a black and white decision; it may be advantageous to have improved deliveries within a certain radius from the local store but continue stocking the part in the engineer's vehicle outside this area.

The location at which parts and assemblies are repaired may also require to be reconsidered. It may be financially advantageous to effect repairs of smaller batches even at the penalty of lower productivity of the repair if the level of stock is thereby sufficiently reduced. Rarely used expensive items may be more cost-effectively flown from a central store rather than holding them at local level. All these factors must be considered and thought through at the forecasting and planning stage. Service does not want surprises.

Capital

The efficient use of capital within a service organisation also requires careful planning. Capital investments tend to be under much tighter control in many companies than other expenditures. Capital requisitions often require approval at a much higher level than operational expenditures of equivalent magnitude. This usually means a more thoroughly documented case needs to be put forward by the Service Manager for capital expenditure which often makes him more reluctant to consider capital investments to reduce his operational costs. This is accentuated if his first capital requisition has been turned down for whatever reason. The Service Manager must remember that conditions change, and although his case was not accepted at one stage, it may be accepted at another. Typically, Service has not employed capital efficiently and it has been left behind in the investment in modernisation undertaken by many companies in the last half-century. This is now changing and Service Managers must be sensitive to changed conditions. If their investment case makes financial sense, the requisitions should be re-submitted. It may have reached the Capital Investment Review Committee at a time when other priorities were more pressing. There usually are a number of projects vying for a limited amount of funds for capital investment. It is important for Service Managers to present their requisitions in a way identifying clearly not only the cost but also the benefits and the realistic consequences of delaying investment. Benefits should clearly separate directly identifiable savings (e.g. the saving of "A" number of people at a cost of "X" dollars per annum) and the indirect benefits (e.g. improved distribution of response time leading to increased customer satisfaction which will reduce product cancellation in "B" instances at a benefit of "Y" dollars). It is often the indirect benefits which will "sell" a capital investment to a review body which has to choose between projects from various functions.

Let me give you an example from my personal experience in a large multi-national organisation. Over an extended period we established that we would be able to justify the installation of a computer-assisted translation for our service manuals and bulletins, as well as for other service documentation such as training manuals, etc. The financial case of direct savings gave us only marginal benefits. What finally convinced the Capital Investment Review Committee to proceed with the project, was an indirect benefit. The translation of service documentation lay on the critical path of a product launch overseas. The marketing flexibility of being able to launch a new product more quickly, or at shorter notice, in a foreign country was a sufficient benefit to the company (added to the marginal direct benefit) for the project to be allocated the, not inconsiderable, funds required to proceed. Incidentally, for those of you who are interested, the direct benefits were substantially greater than anticipated in the initial proposal, so that the project may have been justified by direct benefits alone. There is a natural reluctance, however, for line managers to commit to substantial savings from a capital investment before it can be shown to be effective.

One other piece of advice to Service Managers when preparing their Capital Requisitions – get the help of your Finance Department in developing your case. A Financial Analyst will be able to present the factual data in such a way that it is easily understood by the Committee considering the various capital investment alternatives. An easily understood proposal is likely to receive more favourable treatment than one couched in vague terms and containing terminology not familiar to those reading the proposal.

Manpower Trends

The trend in manpower changes must also be taken into account when preparing service forecasts, plans and budgets. The economic changes may be on a narrowly geographical basis (e.g. costs in cities rising more steeply than in provincial centres or engineers wanting to work in outlying areas rather than in city centres) or in educational trends (e.g. a move to higher technology subjects like electronics and away from mechanical engineering).

The most important changes in the human resource field have taken place in the social area. This will affect many aspects of the relationship between service management and service staff and will be discussed in detail in Section IV–(i) Managing the Service Force. Here I merely want to stress the need to consider these aspects in the planning process as it will affect aspects such as willingness of engineers to work overtime, team work, leisure time. relationship with colleagues in other functions, the style and level of supervision, speed of being able to introduce new programmes, size of working group, co-determination, communication level and style, etc.

Many of these considerations need to be made well in advance and will be even more applicable to long-range plans (LRP) which will be discussed in the next few paragraphs. As service staff tend to be rather conservative in their attitudes, movements towards the long term goals should be made gradually and there should be no sharp reversals of direction – I have heard Engineers in a number of companies complaining about being "jerked about" which made them somewhat obstreperous and does not tend to make them believe that management has a clear idea of where they are going.

Operating and Long Range Plans

The thoughts just expressed about the need to have a clear longer-term idea of what a company, and within the company the Service Department, wants to achieve, leads us automatically to preparing a plan or plans, outlining how the forecast goals will be achieved. It also acts as a communication vehicle for people in other functions and within the Service Department to indicate that the various activities hang together.

Time Horizon

When a plan is prepared, a decision must be made as to the period it should cover. In almost all companies a short term plan is developed covering perhaps one year (and a second year in less detail) and involving all company functions. This plan, often known as an Operationg Plan, indicates how the targets for the next year are to be reached and each function has, at the time the plan is developed, a clear idea of its tasks and its resources. It is usually developed a few months prior to the end of the current year. If the results achieved in the current year are close to plan, there is a continuity of the current year to the plans now being prepared for the next year. There may, however, be a difference to the current year's plan (be it favourable or unfavourable) and before deciding on the starting point of our plan we must establish, whether the deviation from the current plan will continue to the end of the current year or not. This is particularly important to the Service Department as the manpower is closely linked to the level of service provided to customers, and it also is usually the highest cost factor in a service plan. Let me try and illustrate why this starting point for a plan is more important for a Service Department than, for instance, a Sales Department.

Let us assume that in the first nine months of the current year (let us assume the plan is made in the 10th month) our company has had a shortfall of 10% of new installations. As we have seen earlier in this section, under "Manpower Turnover", it takes a number of months to recruit a new engineer, wait for him to serve his notice at his present employer, go through his initial training with our company and begin his work in the field. The time may vary for the reasons mentioned earlier, but is likely to be in the region of 6 months. It may mean, therefore, that we already have all the staff we had planned for the end of the current year on board in the 10th month. If the starting point for next year's plan calls for a lower number of engineers than we now have on board and we only require the requisite number in, say month 3 of the year, there is nothing the Service Manger can do to bring the number of engineers at the start of the plan down to the required level. In the plan he must start out with an excess of engineers and delay further recruiting. On the Sales side the manpower plan for the next year is unlikely to be affected by the current short-fall of installations.

Although plans may be made for a year at a time, in practice there is no sharp end to one year and beginning of the next. This requires a smoothing effort by management which is achieved by either a "Rolling Plan", where each month the last month becomes history and a new month is added 12 months ahead or by regular outlooks, where the whole company's activities are reviewed in the light of current variance to plan and a decision is made on whether the initial plan will be achieved or whether the outlook for the end of the year will differ from plan. (See Outlooks at the end of this section).

We have seen that greater continuity than a one year Operating Plan is required. At the other extreme is a Long-Range Plan (LRP) which gives long term direction to a company's activity. By the nature of a LRP, its information will be less detailed than an Operating Plan and it will contain more uncertainties. Nevertheless, the LRP does give the whole company a clear indication what to prepare for and in which direction it will move, so that in the short and medium term suitable actions can be taken to align the company for future tasks. Service should take an active part in developing a LRP and to input relevant service information, data and requirements, so that the implications can be evaluated and a meaningful LRP developed. This does not necessarily happen in all companies and the lack of service involvement in the LRP often shows in uncoordinated service programmes.

It is usual for LRP's to be quantified on a year by year basis. Operating Plans most often are developed on a monthly basis for the first year and on a quarterly basis for the second year of the plan. In many companies, they detail 12 months ahead on a monthly basis (rolling 12 months), so that each manager has a full year's plan by month available to him from other functions impacting his department.

Naturally, the Operating Plan and Long-Range Plan are not two separate and divorced activities. The first two years of a LRP are the summary of the Operating Plan. It does not necessarily mean that the same individuals should be involved in the LRP and in the Operating Plan, as that may mean that the pressures of short-term goals divert management from adequate effort on longer term planning.

Utilising the Plan as an Active Management Tool

Plans, be they Operating Plans or Long Range Plans, are not documents that are prepared once a year and then put in a filing cabinet until the next planning cycle begins. They are live indicators of the effectiveness of the company's activities and the realism of their forecasting and planning process. If managers regularly perform much better than plan it may well indicate defensive planning which may be almost as detrimental to company performance as missing targets regularly. It may be preferable to miss an aggressive target by a small margin than to exceed a defensive plan by a large margin.

It must also be remembered that a company's plan gives all functions an integrated approach to achieving goals. If individual functions act in an irresponsible way towards the planning process it may be difficult to ensure achievement of the goals. Let me give you an example:

Let us assume that Sales develops a defensive installation plan and Service prepares a realistic manpower plan based on the defensive installation plan. If Sales now exceeds its installation plan by a wide margin, it is likely that Service will be caught short of trained Service Engineers and the level of service to customers will suffer.

This is where the effective utilisation of a plan for day to day management purposes comes into its own. It is hoped that the favourable variance of installations to the plan will be identified very early in the year and the further installation trend will be queried. Let us examine Figure 12 of an Installation Plan. The line A–Z is the plan.

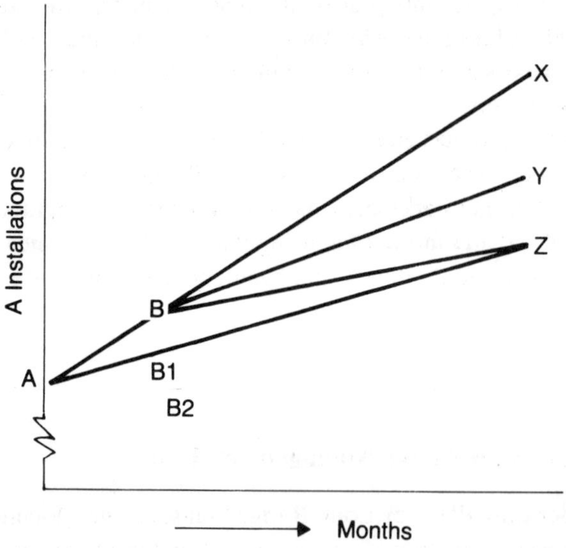

Figure 12. *Installation Plan Variance*

When we examine the situation at point 'B', a realistic view has to be taken by management of further developments. Will the trend A–B continue so that at the end of the year point 'X' will be reached, or will the trend be even more favourable and finish up above the point 'X', or will the advantage gained up to now be maintained but not further increased to reach point 'Y', or will the favourable variance be lost and the end year result finish up at point 'Z' as planned? Any intermediate point or even a level below 'Z' might be forecast but management should carefully examine the reasons for the present variance (B-B1) and whether this variance will continue. Typically, management is likely to examine an unfavourable variance (B1–B2) more thoroughly than a favourable variance (B–B1). This is one of the reasons for a tendency among managers to defensive planning. Both variances have an important impact on Service. This variance naturally also affects other functions; Manufacturing is perhaps even more directly impacted than Service.

A variance analysis is an important tool for Service Managers to identify reasons for over- or under-achievement of the Service Plan. Is the cause of the variance external to his function (as in the example quoted above, where the reason for an unfavourable variance in level of service to the customer was due to over-achievement of the installation plan) or internal? What is the Service Manager going to do about it? In any case, the company must first identify the real *cause* of the variance and not only how it manifests itself (in the example the manifestation of the problem was a worse than planned level of service, the cause was more installations than planned). Once the cause has been identified appropriate action can be taken. In the example given it would imply first of all an investigation of whether the condition of over-plan installations is likely to continue and then to make a decision whether additional staff should be recruited or whether the company is willing to live with a reduced level of service.

This is only one area in which a variance analysis can indicate real or potential problems. Other indicators may highlight other issues requiring action. (See Figure 13.)

	Variance in	Possible Causes	Additional Indicators	Remedial Action
1	Mean Time Between Calls	Intrinsic Reliability Wrong engineer diagnosis Operational faults	Failure Analysis Recall for same fault No product fault found	Modification Training Operator training
2	Mean Time to Repair	Engineer Skill Wrong forecast Over-manning	Variance between Engineers Similar MTTR of Engineers Trend analysis	Training Method Study Improve planning Reduce staff
3	Response Time	Higher Call Rate Higher Work Time/Call Higher Installation Rate Higher Travel Time/Call	MTBSC Analysis MTTR Analysis Installation Analysis Travel Time Analysis	See Above See Above Review Forecasts Review Branch Out
4	Manpower Cost	Excess Manpower Overplan Salaries/Benefits levels	Manpower Analysis Salaries/Benefits Analysis	Depending on cause Depending on cause
5	Parts/Material Cost	Above Plan Usage Above Plan Cost of Items Below Plan Recoveries	Usage Analysis Puchase Cost Analysis Returned & Repaired Parts Analysis	Improve quality Manuf. Training to improve diagnosis Improved buying Improve return disciplines Improve repair planning
6	Logistic Level of Service	Shortage of Parts Wrong Allocation procedures Excessive Usage	Number of back-orders Uneven pattern of back-orders Above plan Usage Analysis	Improve deliveries Improve distribution See Above
7	Travel Cost	Dispersal of Machines Inefficient Call Allocation Above plan petrol prices	Examine Branch Out Plan Study Work Control Allocation Compare Actual/Plan	Negotiate improved planning Re-prioritise Examine alternative transport possibilities.

Figure 13. *Examples of Variance Analysis of Service Plan*

Capital Plan

Here again, Service Managers need to participate actively to ensure adequate resources are planned and made available to service. The type of items included under this heading may vary by company, as some may classify, for instance, tools and test equipment as current expenditure, whereas others may capitalise these expenditures.

The items of importance to Service normally include:

☐ Stores, warehouses, distribution vehicles and associated equipment (e.g. fork-lift trucks, shelving etc).

☐ Workshops and workshop equipment, tools and test equipment.

☐ Service force vehicles.

☐ Equipment for Work Controllers and other Support Staff.

☐ Data Processing equipment.

☐ Printing equipment (manuals, bulletins, etc.)

The Service manager will have to justify the utilisation of the company's capital to improve productivity and service to the customers. We have covered this aspect earlier when we considered the economic parameters of forecasting.

Contingency Plan

An experienced Service Manager knows that even the most carefully considered plans may not materialise for a multiplicity of internal or external reasons. If the fact that a particular planned occurrence does not happen has a major impact on the Service Department, the Service Manager should make contingency plans either within his department only, if only Service is affected (e.g. if a planned investment in data processing equipment is not approved, he will need 'X' additional clerks to do the work) or, more often, encourage the whole company to have a contingency plan in readiness. For example, if the company has planned to introduce a new product which will replace some existing product and there is a likelihood of the product not being brought to the market or substantially delayed, a plan should be ready for implementation if this cancellation or postponement occurs (e.g. upgrade the existing product).

Contingency plans should safeguard a company or department from surprises. It is likely that a better plan will be prepared if the pressure to implement it is not causing damaging shortcuts and omissions.

Service is sensitive to having contingency plans to fall back on, as it is less flexible in many respects than a Sales Department. For instance, if the number of product sales planned for a specific geographical area falls far short of plan but is compensated for above plan sales in another location, it is primarily

Service and Distribution which will be thrown off balance, as manpower and parts will be in the wrong locations. Service Managers therefore need to keep their finger on the pulse of localised forecasts to be able to develop a contingency plan based on possible variations.

Budgets

Once the Service Manager has identified his physical parameters into a forecast predicting what is likely to happen, he develops a plan describing how he will máke the forecast results happen. The budget then quantifies financially all resource requirements and the financial results of the plan. It will now be possible to establish whether the various plans consolidated will meet the specified aim of the company. This is depicted in Figure 14.

If the desired aim is being achieved by the consolidated plans, the budget will be approved and becomes the guide post and measuring instrument for the company and its various divisions and departments.

More often than not, the consolidation of plans falls short of the set target, and certain aspects of the plan will have to be reviewed to come closer to the aims of the company. This review is often a painful process of prioritising certain activities and perhaps postponing others to a more propitious time. Management style is demonstrated in this activity more strongly than in many others. Some top managers will order a specific cut of "X%" across the board from all functions, which will affect those managers adversely, who have planned responsibly, while often leaving managers who have included some "fat" in their plans with all their projects in the budget. Other top managers will critically review the plans of each function and eliminate any "fat" selectively. Obviously, the second alternative is the more effective approach as it will lead to higher efficiency, greater productivity and improved profits. In the first alternative, all managers will start building "fat" into their plans which may lead to some functions being over-resourced for the tasks they have to perform. Top management will be able to produce better results if they have inculcated the need for an honest planning and budgeting process into their functional managers by demonstrating a realistic and selective approach to necessary changes to plans.

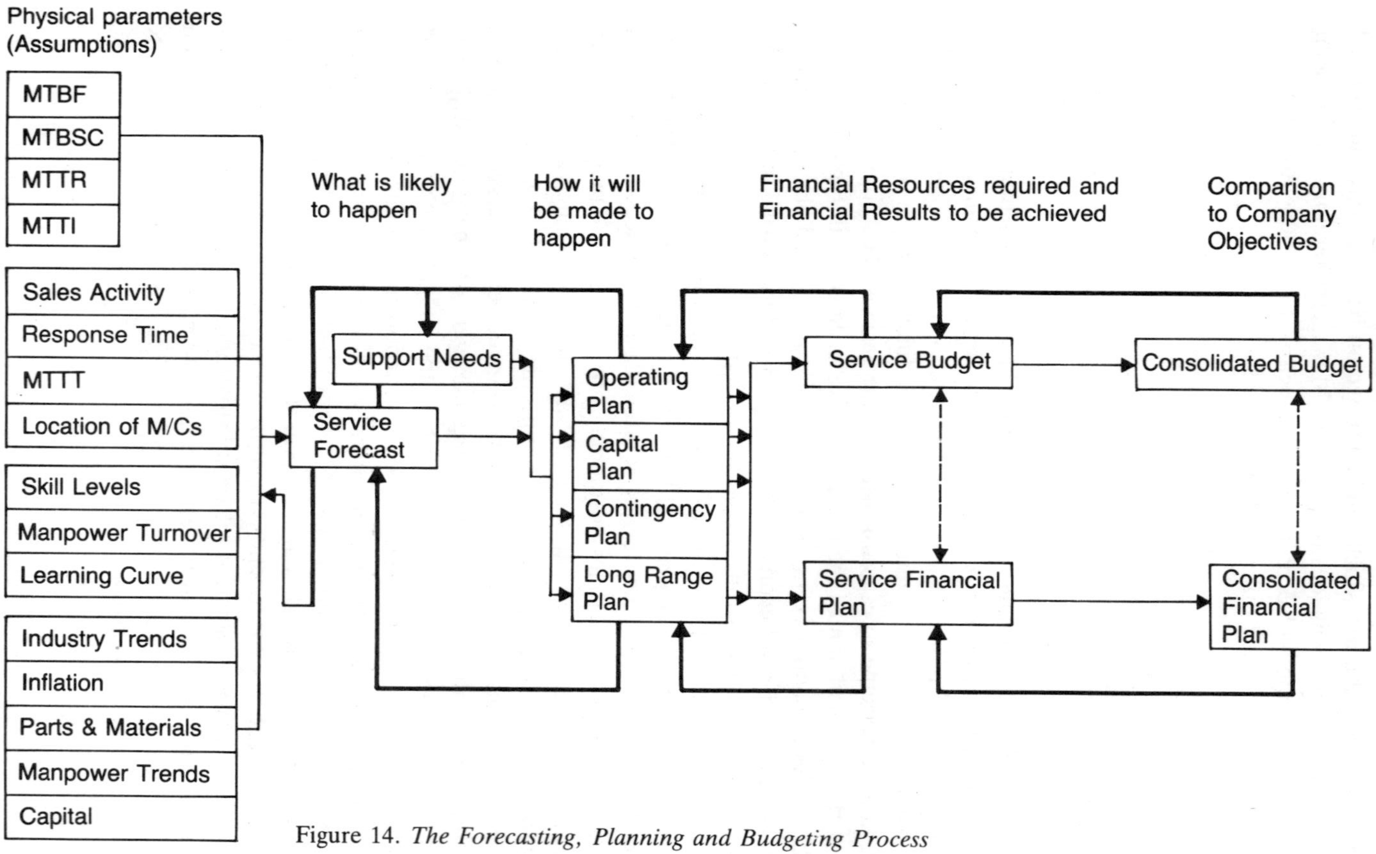

Figure 14. *The Forecasting, Planning and Budgeting Process*

One of the difficulties about the whole planning process is the knowledge of the functional manager that his performance will be judged to a large extent on his achieving the budgeted results. This may lead to defensive budgeting and it is therefore important for the reviewing manager to have a critical appreciation of the needs of the function in question. It is, however, equally important to ensure that the manager responsible for implementing the plan identifies with the budget he had developed and that it does not change to such an extent that he no longer considers it to be "his" budget.

The same applies to a functional budget which may be split into various parts, where different managers carry the responsibility for implementing it. It is advisable for a Service Manager, who may have reporting to him, say, four Branch Service Managers, an Inventory Control Manager, a Workshop Manager and a Service Support Manager, to develop his functional budget and plan in conjunction with his heads of departments, to ensure full commitment to their part of the budget.

The Input

Figure 14 depicts in concept the areas of input – these have been discussed in detail under "Physical Forecasting Parameters" earlier in this Section. Other inputs are often given in the form of guidelines outlining the broad financial goals to be aimed at, quantifying some of the economic parameters and often indicating the likely salary increase to be applied to the current wage bill. These guidelines will also indicate company priorities and capital availability.

Comparison of Actuals to Fixed and Flexed Budget

As we have seen earlier, plans and budgets are useful primarily for identifying whether the planned objectives are likely to be achieved and if not, whether any action by management is needed. It is therefore no use waiting until the end (or near the end) of a budget year before we examine where we stand. As pointed out under Operating Plan, these plans are usually broken down into 12 monthly (or 13 four weekly) periods. The same applies to a budget. It is the responsibility of every Service Manager to examine how he is performing against the budget at every period (e.g. month) so that any changes necessary can be considered and implemented as early as possible. This monthly breakdown of the agreed budget is on a planned activity and cost basis which is known as the Fixed Budget. In practice, however, the various input parameters are unlikely to be exactly as planned.

The main driver in a typical service operation is the activity (sales) plan. In consequence by eliminating the "Volume of Work" variance for the service department indicates to a Service Manager the cost efficiency of his service department by comparing his actual costs against a budget "adjusted" for the variance in volume of work. This is known as a Flexed Budget.

The Flexed Budget is a more realistic guide for a Service Manager than a Fixed Budget but he and his senior managers must understand that some costs are fixed and cannot be altered, whatever the volume variance may be. For example, he would be unable (and it would be impracticable) to change the size of his warehouse if sales fall 20% short of target, but he may wish to reduce his forward orders of spare parts.

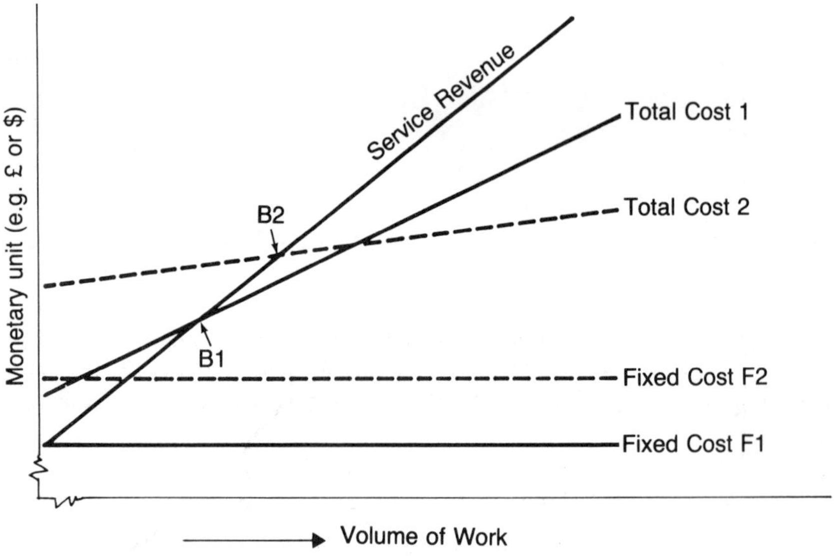

Figure 15. *Simplified Fixed and Variable Cost Structure of a Service Department*

Figure 15 depicts a simplified fixed and variable cost structure of a service department. Irrespective of volume, certain fixed costs will be incurred. The variable costs are directly proportionate (in theory) to the volume of work, and adding the two together gives us the total costs. If we plot the service revenue onto the same graph, the intersection of the service revenue and total cost lines will give us the breakeven point B1. Any volume of work higher than this level will generate a service profit and lower volumes will generate losses. If a Service Manager can reduce his variable costs by increasing his fixed cost (line F2), his breakeven point is likely to be at a higher level, but if his volume of work exceeds the intersection of Total Cost 1 and Total Cost

2, the total profit will be higher. This illustrates the dependence of a Service Plan on the predicted volume of work.

I mentioned at the beginning of the previous paragraph that this works fine in theory. In practice a number of other items enter into the calculation. Fixed costs may also require to be increased if volume of work exceeds a certain level; this tends to be a step function (e.g. the opening of an additional warehouse, bigger training facilities, etc). Variable costs can also not be switched on and off without a reasonable time of adjustment. If there is a shortfall in the volume of work, it is not possible for a Service Manager to temporarily dispose of the service of, say $1^1/_2$ Service Engineers, whom he had trained in anticipation that the budgeted volume of work will be attained. The same applies in reverse, if the volume exceeds the budgeted level, he will be unable to give customers the agreed level of service, as it will take some time to recruit and train the requisite number of staff. It shows that some variable costs are, in fact, only semi-variable. Spare parts, on the other hand, are likely to be genuinely directly variable but even here volume may affect it (see the next example).

If we examine the example of Cost Breakdown of a Service Department in Figure 3, then items 1 to 19 are all likely to vary with volume (except item 16 – rental costs and item 17 depreciation) but items 20–28 are unlikely to be affected in the short term.

Figure 16 looks at an example of a Flexed Budget reflecting new installations at 8000 actuals against 10 000 planned. As in many companies, the service activity in this example is not affected in direct proportion to new installations, as a large part of the activity of Service is governed by existing equipment. But it clearly indicates that urgent action is required.

Service revenue is lower than it should be although the shortfall of installations has not yet filtered through to any large extent except in the warranty area and revenue from outside sources are not only lower than Fixed Budget but also lower than a budget flexed by installation shortfalls.

Direct Labour Costs have not been able to be brought into line with the reduced activity.

To compensate partially for these higher labour costs, more parts were repaired in the field, reducing total Parts Costs. Although this also meant a reduction in Returned Parts Credit, the Net Parts Cost is lower than both Fixed or Flexed Budget. This would indicate that the Service Manager decided to utilise his excess manpower to reduce cost of materials, which is a commendable tactical use of manpower.

Actual new installations 8000 Planned new installations 10000		Actuals £ Mill		Fixed Budget £ Mill		Flexed Budget £ Mill
Revenue						
1. Revenue from Maintenance Contracts		24.7		25.0		24.9
2. Revenue from Time and Material		6.7		7.0		6.9
3. Other Service Revenue from Outside Sources		0.5		0.7		0.6
4. Sub-total – Total Revenue from Outside Sources		31.9		32.7		32.4
5. Imputed Revenue from Warranty		1.5		2.0		1.5
6. Imputed Revenue from Rentals		14.8		15.0		14.8
7. Imputed Revenue from Other Sources		0.3		0.3		0.3
8. Sub-total – Total Imputed Revenues		16.6		17.3		16.6
9. Total Revenues		48.5		50.0		49.0
Expenses – Direct Costs						
10. Variable Labour Costs		12.9		13.0		12.7
11. Semi-Variable Labour Costs		4.0		4.0		3.9
12. Spare Parts Cost	13.5		14.0		13.7	
13. (Returned Parts Credit)	(3.9)		(4.0)		(4.0)	
14. Net Parts Cost		9.6		10.0		9.7
15. Consumable Costs		3.0		3.0		3.0
16. Total Direct Costs		29.5		30.0		29.3
17. Service Contribution		*19.0*		*20.0*		*19.7*
Expenses – Allocated Costs						
18. Selling Costs		1.4		1.5		1.2
19. Service Support Costs		2.0		2.0		2.0
20. Customer Administration		1.2		1.2		1.2
21. General Administration		0.8		0.8		0.8
22. Distribution Costs		2.3		2.5		2.4
23. Other Costs		0.2		0.2		0.2
24. Total Allocated Costs		7.9		8.2		7.8
25. Provisions		0.2		0.4		0.4
26. Total Expenses		37.6		38.6		37.5
27. Profit Before Tax		10.9		11.4		11.5

Figure 16. *Example of a Flexed Budget*

Allocated costs are close to the Flexed Budget. The adverse variance in Selling Costs (to Flexed Budget) is partially compensated by lower Distribution Costs, no doubt due to the lower usage of Spare Parts mentioned earlier.

Once the Service Manager has identified a variance against his Fixed and/or Flexed Budget he will need to study a variance analysis which will identify more closely the cause of the variance. This can be shown in a simple breakdown (Figure 17).

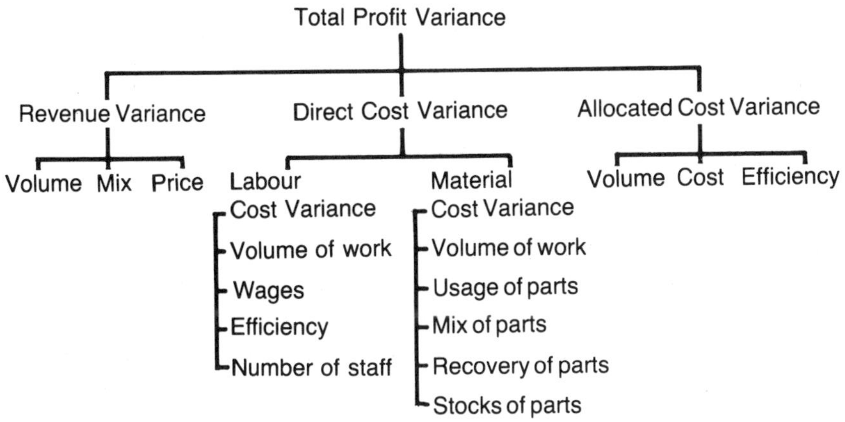

Figure 17. *Service Profit Variance Analysis*

I must come back once more to where we started – comparisons of actuals to fixed or flexed budgets and any variance analysis performed on this data is only useful if the Service Manager utilises the information to consider actions he will take or may consider taking if the trend continues.

Outlooks

As we have just seen, the budget, and the comparison of actual performance against a fixed budget, indicates how effectively we follow the planned course towards our targets. This is also an opportune time to look ahead to see whether we as managers foresee any deviation from budget in future months. This review is called an Outlook. This is important to enable top management to realign priorities, review targets and ensure that effort and resources of the whole company are utilised as effectively as possible. Figure 18 shows a Sales Outlook and the service actions indicated by this outlook.

Sales: Actuals: Budget	Sales: Outlook: Budget	Indicated Service Resource Action
Below	Further Below Same Number Below On Budget	Reduce as soon as possible Consider slight reduction No action
On Budget	Below Budget On Budget Above Budget	Contingency reduction No action Contingency increase
Above	On Budget Same Number Above Further Above	No action Consider slight increase Increase immediately

Figure 18. *Service Action Indicated by Sales Outlook*

Similar decision patterns can be established from the Outlook of other departments. If Manufacturing cannot produce the requisite number of machines, it is no use for Service to plan to maintain the budgeted number and suitable adjustments must be made. If Engineering forecasts reliability to improve substantially due to a clever modification which will take less time to fit than the one used as an input to the Budget, Service will not need all its resources. If Information Systems will be late in developing a programme which was to save considerable Service resources, the shortfall of savings must be reflected in service actions.

As Outlooks are prepared during an operating year and are therefore more recent than the Budget, it must be assumed that they will be more accurate than the Budget and in many companies the performance of departments is compared not only to Budget but also to agreed Outlooks.

Updating and Corrective Actions

As we have just seen, in a changing world many things can happen between the time a budget is established and, say the middle of the operating plan year. This is reflected in showing the actual performance against the flexed budgets and each department will outlook likely trends for the rest of the year. This review of the most likely happenings within the operating plan year will trigger a number of activities commencing with a cumulation of the various departmental outlooks to establish whether:

(i) the outlooks support the planned activities

(ii) the broad company targets are likely to be achieved.

Having established the present position of the company on its path to its targets, a view as to the realism of the outlooks needs to be taken and it may be necessary to update certain aspects of the Plan to ensure any necessary corrective action is taken.

As shown in Figure 14 Service is affected by many functions, particularly by Sales on its activity outlooks and machine location, Manufacturing on the machine availability for installation and its reliability, Purchasing on parts availability, Engineering on timeliness of modification, reliability, and maintainability and by Marketing for predicting the correct level of service requirements. This means that Service is at the end of the planning cycle and may be substantially affected by outlooks of other functions if they happen to have a cumulative effect.

For instance if Sales forecast an above budget order intake, but more dispersed than envisaged, Manufacturing can meet these higher numbers of machines, but at a lower reliability, Purchasing forecast a shortage of spare parts, Engineering will not meet the level of improvements forecast for modifications and Marketing demonstrate that the level of service required by customers is at least as high as in the plan, Service really has a major problem, as all the outlooks indicate the need for higher service activity. This normally requires time to achieve if additional staff is required. Even if productivity programmes may partially bridge this gap, it is unlikely that this can be introduced at short notice. This is when the Service Manager needs to pull out one of the Contingency Plans mentioned earlier and fall back on an alternative tactic to overcome his short term problem. This may consist of a number of actions he can take to bridge the gap until additional staff is trained, e.g.

☐ Postpone cross training of engineers

☐ Utilise qualified support staff (e.g. Product Specialists or Workshop staff) in the field

☐ Utilise contract staff for certain auxiliary tasks to free engineers for more complex duties

☐ Utilise staff from other functions to assist in the field (e.g. have Manufacturing staff pre-instal machines)

☐ Negotiate possible postponement of holidays with his engineers

☐ Encourage more overtime being worked.

None of these approaches are likely to be long-term solutions or should be repeated year after year but may act as an emergency stop-gap.

In companies where the whole planning and outlooking process does not receive adequate coordination and priority, the Service Manager is continually faced by surprises, which is the last thing he wants. The biggest sufferer is likely to be the customer, and in these very competitive days he has a very effective way to demonstrate his dissatisfaction – he'll do so by going to the competition for future needs. Where additional activities are continually piled unexpectedly on the Service Department, the only thing that can give is the planned level of service to customers.

Summary of Section

In this section we have reviewed the parameters used by Service for forecasting what is likely to happen in the service organisation in the period in question. We have seen that many of these inputs will be agreed with other functions to arrive at a list of assumptions on which the forecast is based.

From there the plan is developed, describing how the various activities will come together to give us the desired results and identifying the resource requirements to achieve these goals.

These plans are quantified in financial terms known as budgets or financial plans and consolidated into a total company budget which will be used as an indication of where we are going and the rate at which we are doing so.

These plans and budgets will only be found useful if they are utilised as live documents which are updated by outlooks at regular intervals and which lead to actions by the company or department to take advantage of every opportunity and remedy any problem that may be identified.

SECTION III

The Service Force

In all company activities, the quality of staff is important to the efficient operation of the functions. In few functions is this more important than in Service. There are a number of reasons for this. As we have said before, Service is manpower intensive, so that labour costs are a large part of the total expenditure. Servicing is not process controlled, as many factory and office activities are. Whereas the quantity of work in Service is easily measured, the quality is, in many cases, difficult to measure and often subjective. The service force frequently works on customer premises and is, therefore, not under direct supervision. Service Engineers, Work Controllers and other service staff keep up regular contact with customers.

All these reasons make it even more important than in other functions to be very careful in establishing the real needs for the job, staffing the department with suitable people, training engineers, supervisors, managers and other staff particularly carefully and ensuring that each member of the staff is developed to his/her full capability.

Job and Man Specifications

Before any other decisions are taken on the choice of staff to be employed, each job will have to be carefully analysed. A manager may think that he knows precisely what he is looking for in his Service Engineer, Work Controller, or Product Specialist but until he starts to analyse each task that needs to be performed in some detail and separates tasks that can be influenced by training, example and guidance from those unlikely to be easily affected, he will find it difficult to select the right people for the job, or to establish a meaningful training programme.

In consequence, the Service Manger must carefully determine the individual tasks which make up the job. If he is examining the Service Engineer's tasks he cannot rely on the fact that he established a job requirement some years ago – it may well be that the job of the Service Engineer in the company has changed, and different emphasis needs to be given to the different tasks. The various aspects the Service Manager will need to consider in the preparation of a Job Requirement include:

Skill Requirement

All the tasks that need to be performed need to be established and the various skills, knowledge and experience required to perform each one of them should be analysed in some detail to obtain a full understanding of what is involved in effecting the repair or maintenance. Ideally this type of analysis should be carried out early on in the design of a product, as basic design decisions can be taken based on the knowledge of how the product will be serviced. A well organised company will have generic maintainability and serviceability goals laid down which, among other aspects, would identify the skills and knowledge of the service staff who will maintain the equipment. If not performed before, the latest point at which this analysis must be made is at the spare parts ordering and training programme development stage. It will obviously affect both of these activities. For instance, a decision must be made whether a particular electronic module should be repaired by the Engineer in the field or whether he should merely exchange modules. In the first instance the sparing will have to be done to parts level and the Engineer will require higher diagnostic skills and aids (test equipment) and he will require suitable training; in the latter case the whole module only will have to be made available to the field (individual parts will only be made available at repair centre level, be that in a workshop or back at the factory) and the Engineer will only need to identify which module is faulty. A basic decision of this nature will affect the type of Engineer to be recruited, the whole logistics back up, the depth (and therefore the length) of training, time on customer's premises, service costs, etc. It may even affect the countries where a product can be launched.

The tasks to be performed need to be analysed not only from a technical point of view but also from the customer relations, administrative, and psychological aspect (e.g. tolerance to longer work hours on the machine).

Once the tasks have been analysed, further decisions can be made whether the job needs to be broken down further or whether all tasks can be performed by the same person. This will then lead us into the Man Specification, which outlines the profile of the person from an educational, psychological and human point of view and the experience we expect him to have.

Educational Requirement

(a) Is there a minimum general education standard needed to carry out the job? Here the Service Manager will consider primarily the relationship between the Engineer and the customer's staff, the need to communicate with customers, colleagues in Service and in other functions, the company's need to have some promotable people, the need to be a member of the group and, in some instance, the legal requirements for a certain educational level.

(b) What is the minimum technical education standard needed for the job? Often the technical knowledge required may be in a wide range of differing fields and it may be necessary to identify optimal technical qualifications and enable the applicant to acquire the other job requirements. For instance, if the job being defined is that of a Service Engineer for medical diagnostic equipment, the technical education acceptable might be in electronics or biology, or electro-mechanics, or physics, as the range of equipment to be serviced might well need knowledge in all these areas. It is unlikely for a candidate to have had in depth technical education in all these fields – the Service Manager would identify in which area the technical education necessary for the job could be most easily supplemented by training.

In this context I would warn against establishing excessively high educational requirements for the job in hand. If the job is not found challenging by the Engineer, it will be difficult to motivate him to perform to his optimum capabilities and he is unlikely to stay with the company for a reasonable period. Whereas it may be quite satsifactory to recruit an over qualified applicant with a view to job rotation or promotion, the Job Spcecification should not lay this down as a requirement for ALL applicants. The Job Specification, as the name indicates, should concentrate on the requirements of the job; when it comes to selecting the person for the job we need a Man Specification which may highlight different aspects of the educational requirement.

Experience Requirements

The approach of Service Managers in specifying previous experience necessary to carry out a particular job may vary extensively. The requirement is likely to change with the maturity of the company, its rate of expansion and often with the geographical location. A relatively new company growing rapidly does not have time to develop a Service Engineer with limited or no previous experience from a Junior Engineer to one who is able to work on his own with minimum supervision; this type of company is also unlikely to have the necessary training support to fill the experience deficiency by constant, on the job, training. A more mature company expanding at a slower rate, on the other hand, may prefer to divide their Service Engineers into various grades, depending on experience. They may well prefer to recruit Engineers with limited or no previous experience as Junior Engineers and develop them through the levels; the argument here is that they do not have to "unlearn" bad practices the Engineer may have picked up together with his other job experience.

The implication on the Job Specification therefore is a decision by management whether they want one grade of Engineer with a certain amount of experience or whether they will divide the job into various levels, in which case they will need different Job Specifications for each level, as it is not only the experience of the Engineer which will be different but also the tasks likely to be performed.

The earlier comment on the geographical impact on the job refers to two considerations: it may be that in a rural area, where an Engineer is likely to be more distant from his colleagues and supervisor, an experienced Engineer is required; in an urban area it is possible to give an inexperienced Engineer better support. The other consideration is the specification for staff in different countries – it may well be very difficult or even impossible to recruit an experienced Engineer in some of the under developed or developing countries, and it may therefore be necessary to break the job up into smaller components so that it can be handled by inexperienced Engineers.

This shows that the Job Specification needs to be very specific as it will greatly assist in the recruiting and selection process, and it will also identify precisely to the Engineer what is expected of him.

Psychological and Human Requirements

With the increasing trend (forced by necessity) of team working, the psychological compatibility of the various members of the group needs to be more carefully considered and specified. In an existing service force it is often advisable to examine the psychological factors which distinguish the successful from the less successful Service Engineers to enable the necessary parameters to be included in the Man Specification. It is often possible to limit the number of parameters by excluding those which are shown not to be predictive, i.e. those which are similar in the successful and unsuccessful group of existing Engineers. By careful work in this area it may be possible to find a group of Engineers who will be highly self-motivated.

Service Managers must take full advantage of all the management tools available to assist them in running an efficient operation. All too often Service Managers are loathe to utilise management tools of which they have limited understanding, such as psychological parameter analysis, for which they will need the help of trained psychologists.

The Man Specification should clearly lay down the ideal factors of the human profile of a person.

Selection Techniques

Once we have carried out our task analysis and established the Job and Man Specifications, we have the basic tools for selecting our staff. How are we going to use these tools in our selection process?

Sources of Service Staff

Having identified what needs to be done (Tasks Analysis) and established a profile of the person to carry out these tasks (Man Specification) we need to find suitable candidates.

(a) *Internal*: Wherever possible, internal applicants should be considered for the post that needs to be filled. For certain jobs, e.g. Service Supervisors, it is necessary, or at least highly desirable, to promote from within the company, as the first line Supervisor needs to know a great deal about the work of the Engineers he is leading. He will need to be able to identify strengths and weaknesses of his Engineers and specify individual training needs. If the job is higher up in the management structure, it may be desirable to have a mixture of promotions from within as well as external managers, to ensure that new ideas are generated within the management team and to thus ensure that the company does not become in-bred.

Service Engineers can also, at times, be recruited internally from other sections of Service or from other functions, provided they possess the necessary skills and education previously set out in the specifications. Job rotation of this nature is favoured by many companies, particularly in Japan, where the cross-fertilisation across functions is thought to promote better understanding of each other's problems and which therefore creates a favourable climate for a consensus approach to decision making. It obviously also has drawbacks, as it does not follow that moving a successful Production Engineer into Service will make a good Service Engineer, but we certainly have weakened Production by moving a successful Production Engineer to another function; it also creates the need to train not only an additional Service Engineer but also a new Production Engineer. These issues will be discussed later in this section under "Manpower Development" and in Section IV under "Motivation".

Internal candidates must at least be given the opportunity of applying for a job that becomes available and suitable internal communications need to be set up to ensure that existing staff is kept informed of any opportunities that arise.

(b) *Staff Recommendations*:Another source of candidates is that of existing staff of a company recommending candidates for a job utilising their knowledge of what the job entails and their contact with similarly qualified people in professional or trade associations, educational establishments or on the job. In a number of companies this is encouraged by the management of the company and a small reward is paid to the employee who recommends a candidate who is accepted and who stays with the company a certain minimum period of time.

This approach is said to have the advantage of low cost, usually very suitable candidates (as they were recommended by staff with a detailed knowledge of the job to be done as well as of the candidate) and an easier acceptance of the new person into the Service force due to his acquaintance with an existing member of staff.

(c) *From the Armed Forces*: In some countries the Armed Forced have excellent training programmes for technical personnel and when the time for leaving the Forces draws near, the Forces often use their "out-placement" services to find suitable posts for leavers. Regular contact between a company's recruiting staff and those out-placement units of each of the Armed Forces is a useful source of candidates. The advantage claimed for this approach is again low cost, often a highly skilled and well trained candidate and usually a disciplined approach to the job.

(d) *Direct from Technical Colleges or Schools*: Where a company is looking for a clearly defined educational background and limited or no previous job experience, contact with suitable institutions in the area towards the end of the educational period of a student may lead to finding suitable candidates. The advantage of this source of recruits is said to be a standard basic knowledge on which inhouse company training can be devised and a flexible person with no pre-conceived ideas of how a job should be done, i.e. a person who has not learned "bad habits" in previous jobs which need to be un-learned.

(e) *Advertising*: Insertions in local, national or specialised newspapers, journals and magazines is often employed to reach a wide range of potential applicants. The advantages of this approach is said to be the wide readership of media by candidates who might not be reached by other methods and the side benefit of keeping the name of the company in front of the public and thus influence the image of the advertiser. The disadvantages are the relatively high costs created not only by the advertisement itself but also by the need to screen often a very large number of applicants many of whom may be completely unsuitable.

(f) *Utilising Professional Agencies*: This approach tends to combine the advantages and disadvantages of the various other methods of recruiting. Its advantages are said to be the wide range of candidates that are often approached by these agencies and a certain amount of pre-screening that is carried out by these professionals on behalf of the company. The disadvantage is the high cost of this approach.

The decision as to which method of recruitment should be employed will depend on many factors, and often a combination of a number of methods is used, depending on current conditions.

Selection

Now that we have identified sources of candidates and we have our Job and Man Specifications to hand, we need to make a choice between the various applicants, whatever method we utilised to identify them. This is usually a joint activity between the Human Resource (Personnel) Department and the Service Department, with each function contributing from its fund of professional skill. As the trend in many countries is towards longer term association between the company and the employee, the selection must be undertaken carefully to ensure the right choice is made.

(a) *Initial Screening*: During this stage the unlikely applicants are excluded because for some reason or other, they do not meet the specifications for the job or the personal profile. This can often be done from the written Application Form or an initial short interview.

(b) *Interview*: A number of books have been written on the subject of interviewing techniques: all I would want to say here is to suggest that it must be one which suits the interviewer and can quickly lead him to separate the "possibles" from the "unlikelies".

(c) *Technical Tests*: Where the job entails technical skills and knowledge, it is quite common to put the applicants through a range of short technical tests to establish the level of their current technical knowledge and manual dexterity to perform certain tasks. This is not only useful in aiding the selection process, but also in establishing any potential need for pre-training courses or reading which should be recommended to recruits prior to attending a product training course (see next sub-section on Training).

These technical test batteries can be administered either locally by Service Managers or, wherever possible, by the Technical Training Centre – the tests are usually standard tests which may be supplemented by specific ones added by the company.

(d) *Psychological Tests*: In this instance the test batteries should be designed by psychologists specifically for the job to be filled. The administration of the test can be carried out by either Personnel or Service. The reason why the tests need to be designed on an individual job basis, is the necessity to separate predictive and nonpredictive parameters affecting the performance, relationship and job tenure of the applicant. In one company it was found that recruiting over-qualified applicants adversely affected job tenure.

(e) *Final Decision*: All the preceding activities have been used mainly to ensure that the minimum standards laid down in the Job Specification and the predictive parameters of the Man Specification are being met. Most of these factors have been largely objective. The final stage of selection, the decision, of necessity moves into a more subjective field. It is therefore essential that the candidate's future immediate superior be involved in the final decision, even if he may not have been involved earlier.

The candidate will have to fit into the team his superior is leading and the latter must feel involved in the decision. It is also usual for the next higher level of management (i.e. the superior's superior) to be involved.

(f) *Communication*: The selected candidate must be clearly informed of what is expected of him and be given the details of the conditions of employment. In some countries it is a statutory requirement that these conditions be given to him in writing but even in countries where this is not a legal requirement, it is good company practice. The timing of the candidate's acceptance of the job and his starting date should be clearly stated. There is frequently a certain unease in the new recruit about the company he is joining and his role in its operation – the clearer all these aspects can be made for him, the more relaxed his approach is likely to be.

Service Training

(a) Pre-Course Preparation:

It is important for all participants of a training course to have a minimum knowledge and experience level in a range of subjects which form the basis on which the training programme has been devised. It may happen that an otherwise perfectly acceptable candidate was found to lack some knowledge in a particular field or that he has not kept up with the latest developments in a specific area, as he did not need that specific knowledge in his previous job. It may not be possible to find as good a candidate who has all the knowledge required and it would also be unacceptable for that candidate to come to the training course with a gap in his knowledge which put him at a disadvantage compared to other course participants and therefore impinge on the learning process.

It is therefore preferable to arrange to fill the gap in his knowledge prior to attending the course. This can be done by:

☐ additional background reading

☐ individualised pre-course training sessions in limited areas of knowledge deficiency.

- □ standardised self-paced training modules administered, preferably, under controlled conditions.

(b) Company Initiation Course:

Every employee of the company, including all Service staff, should be given an Initiation course which can be administered on a well planned basis in the local branch office. This course would familiarise the new employee with the company's products, policies and procedures. In companies where video-monitors are available in each branch, part of this programme often is on a video-cassette which enables the new employee to see major company facilities (e.g. factories, headquarters, etc.) and products in operation on customer premises. This approach also tends to break up the monotony of a lecturer talking all day to his group. As an Initiation course often is the first activity of the employee after joining the company, the first impression created by this programme will leave a lasting effect on the new employee. This makes it important for this programme to be well prepared and thoroughly implemented.

(c) Technical Training:

For Service Engineers this tends to be the longest part of the training programme and will also have to be performed on each additional product he may need to be trained on. This part of the training process tends to be very specific and is usually devised for each product by the company itself. It is well worth while to ensure that this training is efficiently designed and implemented as it will affect the learning curve of the Engineer (See Figure 11, Section II, Theoretical Learning Curve).

The servicing methods are likely to be determined by the Field Engineering or Product Service Department with the concurrence of Field Service and Technical Training. At this stage a decision will be made whether to utilise traditional schematic layouts for the service documentation or to employ functionally integrated maintenance systems (FIMS) which show the integration of various systems (e.g. electrical and mechanical, or mechanical and hydraulic). From this basic input the curriculum designer within the Service Training Department will establish a plan for performing the training programme.

The next step in developing a technical product training programme is the analysis of the installation, repair and maintenance tasks that will have to be performed by the Engineer. By comparing these tasks with the task analysis details, on which the Job Specification has been based, will identify any likely deficiency in knowledge or skill that the training programme will have to fill.

Once the gap of basic deficiencies has been filled, the logical way of performing the new product's installation, servicing and maintenance needs can be taught to the Engineers. The Training Department then decides on training methods, training aids, number of equipments required for training and recommends the length of the training course. These aspects are then discussed with Service Management to establish the financial viability, acceptability of time and other factors which will need to be included in the planning process. The training programme will need to be tied closely to the structure of the Service Manual. In many companies the development and production of the Service Manual is part of the Service Training Department's responsibility. The training programmes are linked to the use of the manuals by the Eningeers. We will discuss Service Manuals and their use in the next sub-section.

In designing a service training programme care must be taken to hold the attention of the trainee throughout the course and, in consequence, it will be useful to try and employ a wide range of differing training tools in the programme. This might contain selfpaced training sessions which may or may not be computer assisted, formal lectures, discussion sessions, practical laboratory work and, perhaps, films demonstrating activities difficult to perform in a training centre (e.g. moving heavy equipment by crane) or showing the interaction of various machine functions. Video aids are particularly helpful in role-playing where inter-personal skills need to be demonstrated and the trainee can watch himself improve his performance as he learns new skills (see Customer Relations later in this section).

Now that the preparatory work (curriculum design, task analysis, training method and aids) has been completed, the training manual has to be written, graphics prepared and training aids developed.

Physical facilities will also need to be prepared, these may vary from temporarily rented facilities at a local level to major training centres utilised by some of the large companies, which sometimes include residential facilities resembling a "Company College". An adequate number of machines must also be made available to the Training Department to enable

□ the analysis of the preliminay tasks to be performed

□ the training programme to be developed

□ the trainers to be trained

□ the engineers to be trained

This is often a sensitive issue as there is usually a shortage of pre-production and early production machines on which to carry out the necessary analysis and training. Service Managers will have to make certain that all the equipments requested by Training are really required but then fully support the Service Training Department in obtainig their essential requirements. The Service Manager must remember that it is particularly important for the first engineers on a new product to understand the equipment, as there will be little or no experience to fall back on to supplement any gaps left by the training programme.

The selection of trainers is also very important. Many companies have a system of rotating trainers between the field and the Training Centre to ensure up to date field experience of Technical Trainers. They usually have a nucleus of, perhaps, 10–20% of permanent professional training staff and the remainder are on an 18–36 months assignment from the field (see Manpower Development later in this Section). Obviously, these assignees have to be carefully selected for their teaching ability and have to receive some pedagogic training. This is usually of great benefit to them when they return to the field.

It is recommended to perform the formal training function away from the branch where external pressures may cause interruptions. Training is an important activity and must be seen by the Service Engineers to be regarded as such by the company and its management.

The Service Engineers are likely to receive product training courses a number of times during their stay with the company, as new products are introduced. However, the formal training on a product must not be the end of the training experience on a new product – only its beginning. Certain aspects of technical training can only be learned by hands-on practice (motor skills such as filing or turning a screwdriver). Servicing activities such as installing equipment on customer premises or carrying out preventive maintenance work is best perfected in the field under supervision, after having seen the work done in the formal training on a video monitor or a film screen. This is part of the ongoing OJT (on the job training) which we will discuss in more detail later in this section. OJT is therefore not only a re-enforcement and retraining process but also the completion of the initial product training programme.

(d) Service Manuals:

One of the many issues on which there is considerable disagreement between Service Managers and other service staff at all levels, is the question of service manuals – their structure, form, language and usage.

Taking each of these issues in turn, let us start at the end, i.e. with the usage of manuals. As mentioned earlier (under Technical Training) the training course is likely to have been structured around the manual and the newly trained Service Engineer is probably going to use the manual when he starts servicing equipment on customers' premises. This will be good re-enforcement of his newly gained knowledge. On many products, however, faults tend to be repetitive and as the engineer gains experience, he will probably need to refer to his service manual less and less, except for spare part numbers and for the setting of certain tolerances. This may encourage an engineer not to carry his service manual with him on every call which will make him guess at certain numbers or relationships and this in turn may cause repeat calls (re-calls) for the same fault. The situation is made worse where a Service Engineer services a wide range of products each with its own manual – the bulk of literature is likely to be substantial. Some Service Managers may insist that his engineers carry the relevant service manual to every call, whereas others accept that this may not be necessary and have resorted to other means to encourage their engineers to use the documentation when needed (see below). Another issue on the usage of manuals is the need to keep them continually updated for every machine configuration likely to be serviced. The only way to encourage an engineer to utilise his manuals is to make the information useful to him and produce the data in a palatable format.

Let us then look at the form in which manuals are made available to Service Engineers. The most common approach is still through a full sized, printed manual which is either loose-leaf or bound. Obviously, in the case of a loose-leaf manual the updating is achieved by sending engineers replacement and additional pages but management relies on the engineer to replace the relevant pages and possibly lose any annotations he may have made for himself on the original page. Due to the cost involved it is usually not feasible to reprint bound manuals frequently as changes in the product occur or modifications are introduced. This usually means keeping the engineer advised of changes by issuing service bulletins and relying on the engineer to cross reference or annotate his manual, until a new service manual is printed. The advantage of both these formats is easy legibility but it has the disadvantage of having to rely on the engineer to carry heavy manuals and updating the information.

A number of companies have changed their approach by producing the service manual on microfiche, whereby a single fiche of A–6 size (148 mm × 105 mm) contains a large number of pages (depending on the reduction ratio used in filming) and a whole service and spare parts manual can be reproduced on one or two fiches. Portable very light microfiche viewers have been developed for engineers to read the fiche. It is easy to update the information, as microfiche is easy and cheap to reproduce and much less expensive to distribute than hard copy manuals and bulletins. It is therefore feasible to have up-to-date manuals with every engineer. The disadvantage is primarily the inconvenient way of reading data on a portable microfiche viewer and the initial cost of supplying a viewer to each engineer. It is also not possible for engineers to scribble notes or otherwise annotate microfiche.

A compromise approach is used by some firms, They issue an engineer with a full sized manual on the training course and it is likely to be used by the engineer during the first few weeks or months after returning to the field. They also supply him with a portable microfiche viewer and the relevant fiche containing all the information from the manual. In addition they provide the engineer with a diary size pocket manual which contains only the most important and frequently used data such as tolerances, part numbers etc. In practice the experienced engineer would only carry the pocket manual and the microfiche and viewer. The pocket manual is likely to satisfy the great majority of calls and only where unusual problems occur would he need to refer to the fiche. This approach is said to combine the advantages of both systems.

As audio coupled devices are becoming more widely available, it is now possible to obtain service information through portable terminals carried by engineers, although the writer admits he has not seen this application in the field, even where portable terminals were utilised for reporting purposes. On some customer installations there is a hard wired access to the Service Engineer's company which would also enable him to obtain the necessary information from the database.

Some companies also keep service manuals on customer sites to obviate the need for engineers to carry a wide range of manuals. This is particularly popular in the heavy industrial equipment field where service manuals tend to be kept with the equipment. Configuration control and up-dating of manuals needs to be carefully controlled.

The next incentive for an engineer to utilise his manual is to produce it in his mother tongue. It is naturally expensive to translate manuals into a number of languages and to print them in these languages. But is it less expensive to give Service Engineers manuals which they do not use? Typically, the length of service training courses is decided centrally, based on the experience of engineers who are being taught in their own language and who use manuals in their mother tongue. Is it reasonable to expect engineers in other countries to be equally effective if they are being trained in a foreign language and have manuals in a language in which they have more limited knowledge? These considerations have led to a number of different approaches:

(i) Use of foreign language manual.

(ii) Use of foreign language manual but translate important sections.

(iii) Translate and print manuals in own language.

(iv) Develop "minimum vocabulary", ensure the manual uses only the identified terms, and expect engineers to learn only these terms in the foreign language.

(v) Develop "minimum vocabulary" and translate into engineers' own language.

Solutions (i)–(iii) are self explanatory so let me concentrate on the last two. Let us first discuss the "minimum vocabulary" concept.

It is believed that the first company to use the minimum vocabulary approach was Caterpiller Tractor. In their case an 800 word vocabulary was developed to cover the total number of words to be utilised in writing any service manual on their products. This obviously does not include the name of spare parts, where the original English word is acceptable. Each word has only one, clearly defined meaning (e.g. lift could mean either "raise" or "elevator" but not both). All overseas mechanics then had to learn only these 800 words and can also be issued with a very simple "dictionary". Equally, it is then much easier to translate manuals written in this convention.

A further development has been pioneered by another multinational company where their interpretation of a minimum vocabulary (around 1400 words) was then translated with the aid of a computer. The intention was to reduce the translation time by two thirds by giving the translators a computer translated document which they would edit. It was soon found that translators' time could be reduced by 80% (i.e. much better than target) and even without any editing the manuals were clearly intelligible. In fact, the biggest problem was found to be the writing of the manuals rather than the translation. The Technical Authors were not easily persuaded to give up their beautiful prose for a somewhat staccato document only using minimum vocabulary and more illustrations. An unexpected benefit was the preference of English speaking engineers for the new, more precise and more concise document – they were not interested in reading the author's beautiful prose, what they wanted was information. An important benefit to the company and one which justified the initial investment, was the substantial saving in elapsed time for translating a manual which increased marketing flexibility, as the translation and production of manuals lies on the critical path of a product introduction. The process was further streamlined by linking the computer assisted development of the service manual and its graphics to the computer assisted design and manufacturing systems (CAD/CAM) so that identical information was being used throughout the system.

Some of these translation programmes are now available as standard software packages from a number of suppliers.

The decision on which is the most advantageous approach must be taken on a case by case review of all relevant factors, such as number of Service Engineers, number of different products being serviced, the limitations on recruiting staff caused by a single language manual, complexity of product and other parameters.

There is a general trend toward DIY (do it yourself) in the service industry as well. This trend obviously affects not only the design of the product but also the design of the service manual – it must assume a lower level of basic knowledge and must lead the DIY enthusiast through the tasks in greater detail, as there has not been a specific product service training of the amateur repairman. He may not necessarily have to be able to resolve all problems.

(e) Administrative Training:

It is often assumed by management that Service Engineers do not need to receive any training in this area and management is then surprised if the information received from the field is not of the required standard. The position is made worse by the fact that the majority of Service Engineers dislike administrative tasks.

The Service Manager's job is therefore fairly self evident. The first essential requirement is to question the need of every adminstrative task we ask an engineer to perform. Is the information necessary? Can it be performed more effectively by someone else? Is the information really used? For example, it has been found that service reports are seldom reviewed and information that was important to collect two years ago may no longer be needed. Furthermore, information which is still needed may be more easily obtained through the Work Controller rather than asking the Service Engineer to complete a report (see Section V, Service Reporting).

If it is found that a particular administrative task needs to be performed by the Service Engineer (be it a written task or by telephone or verbally), it should be made very clear to the engineer what is expected of him and it must not be forgotten to tell him precisely why we require him to perform the task in question and explain to him what we will do with the collected data.

Administrative procedures and policies should be set out clearly and given to all service staff involved in a written form to enable them to refer to the procedure if and when required.

The very fact that administrative tasks are not popular with engineers makes inclusion of a short but informative training session essential. The one administrative task that is seldom neglected by Service Engineers is the completion and timely submission of Expense Sheets! It is not unusual to require the submission of less popular administrative forms at the same time.

(f) Customer Relations Training:

The increasing importance of maintaining good customer relations by every member of the company in direct contact with customers has led to a wide range of training programmes to be developed. These programmes can be standardised to a large extent, as the basic Customer Handling Skills are common to most industries, services and professions. It is usual to add specific points pertaining to individual companies to the standard programme. This is an area of training, where role playing is used as an effective tool to teach students how to communicate with customers, deal with their problems and handle difficult issues.

Service Engineers are usually much more perceptive about their technical short-comings than they are about their lack of customer handling skills. It is, therefore, all the more important for the training programme to be professionally designed.

Customers want their equipments to be operational and any interruption in this activity is a loss of productivity, be it for corrective service or for preventive maintenance. If it is a PM that is being performed, some companies encourage their engineers to agree a mutually convenient time with the customer and for a sign to be put on the machine indicating that a preventive maintenance is taking place, so as not to indicate to casual observers that the machine is unreliable.

The relationship of the engineer and the machine operator can influence the customer's perception of the reliability of the equipment and the image of our company. Using the same situation as on page 26, the same information is communicated by a remark such as "Sorry, Mr Decisionmaker, I cannot do the work you requested, the machine is down again" as by "I will do the work shortly, Mr Decisionmaker, as soon as the preventive maintenance has been completed", but the impression created is very different. The operator's attitude to an engineer and to the product will influence the unconsciously chosen wording.

May I tell you a true story here, indicating that one can overdo customer relations. I was visiting the Italian service organisation and requested to see a customer's installation. The Service Manager asked me to select a customer and, not unnaturally, I selected a user who had had more than his fair share of visits from the company's Service Engineer. We went to the machine and examined it, and its service record, carefully under the watchful eyes of a pretty operator. We could find nothing wrong with the machine and I was therefore surprised, when the Italian Service Manager told the operator that he was going to change the Service Engineer as he had to call so frequently at the machine. The operator immediately remonstrated that the engineer was doing a good job, and so the Service Manager agreed to let the Service Engineer continue working on that machine. As we went out of the customer's door I asked why he had suggested changing the engineer when the condition of the machine indicated that the engineer was doing a good job. The manager laughed in his relaxed way and said: "We will not have too many calls on that machine in the future. The Service Engineer servicing this machine is a very handsome and personable man and from the machine record it is obvious the operator called the engineer out for no better reason than that she wanted to have a talk with him". It turned out that he was right and the number of calls received from this customer dropped dramatically.

To come back to the issue we are discussing, the danger of an excessively friendly engineer is much smaller than the danger of the engineer appearing unfriendly to a customer in the rush of his pressure of work. An engineer should be taught that a minute or two spent explaining what he has been doing will be time well spent.

Often it is not the Service Engineer but other company staff who create an unfavourable relationship between customers and the company. Telephones that are not answered promptly, letters which take a long time to be replied to, staff who is not concentrating on the customer's issues, "passing the buck", promises not kept without an explanation of the reason, all contribute to leaving an unfavourable impression on the customer.

Specific actions that a Service Engineer may consider to improve further his relationship with the customer include:

□ Telephone the customer if there is an undue delay between receipt of the call from the customer and the engineer's arrival.

□ Patiently perform any customer training requirements.

□ Honestly respond to customer's questions but

- don't guess at the answer; if the answer is not known, say so and arrange for someone else in the company to respond to the customer's query
- never blame another department in the company or a colleague
- be positive

- ☐ Never leave the machine dirty or dirt around the machine.
- ☐ Get the customer's positive agreement that the problem has been resolved.
- ☐ Don't "blind the customer with science".
- ☐ Keep the customer informed.
- ☐ Show interest in the customer's problem.

There are different ways to present information to a customer and a positive attitude is always recommended. If, for instance, there has been a need to replace a number of parts which will make the bill for the repair quite high it is preferable to say: "I changed these parts to ensure that your equipment will again work perfectly and produce high quality products" rather than "I'll have to throw all these expensive components away; they are all faulty".

Lastly, but not least, remember that we, as a company, require customers more than the customer needs us! Service Engineers are the front line troops who can demonstrate to the customer that we care.

(g) Refresher Training:

It is difficult for a Service Engineer (or for his manager) to realise that he may require refresher training on a product on which he works regularly. There are, however, a number of causes which make this desirable.

A very common cause which makes re-training necessary is the fact that all of us tend to drift into bad habits and we need to be reminded of the correct approach. This may be in any of the areas of trainig mentioned earlier. For instance, an engineer may be performing preventive maintenance tasks very frequently but he is not approaching the job in a systematic way so that he may cause himself excessive work. In the copier/duplicator servicing organisation of a major office equipment manufacturer I saw an engineer vacuum cleaning the machine, but instead of doing the job as taught from the top of the machine downward, he worked from left to right which meant that he had to clean certain low parts of the machine repeatedly which, of course, was unnecessary and time consuming labour. The same issues can arise by approaching fault finding in a haphazard way – it is not unusual for Service Engineers to jump to a conclusion ("It solved the problem on my last call") instead of analysing the existing problem systematically.

Another reason for refresher training is for seldom performed activities which may nevertheless be crucial. The most obvious example is from the airlines industry, where probably the most frequently performed refresher training is for emergency situations. It is hoped that the crew will never need to use these emergency procedures in a live situation, but they must nevertheless be almost automatic to each member of the crew, just in case they may, one day, be needed. Many airlines provide emergency procedure refresher training every six months.

Where improved methods or modifications are involved, additional training may also be required.

Customer relation skills need to be re-enforced at regular intervals and the ability to show an engineer on a video monitor how he is performing under simulated stress situations is naturally of great help to him.

Refresher training has specific training problems of its own. Whereas on a new product course Service Engineers will tend to be attentive, it will be difficult to run them through a retraining programme and hold their attention for the limited areas where retraining of the individual engineer is necessary. In consequence different methods and techniques for refresher training have been developed. Where formal courses are necessary refresher training is often carried out on a very small group (or even individual basis) after a specific area of weakness has been identified in a Service Engineer. Typically, the training packages are short and to the point. It is important that different material from the original training programme be used.

A very effective way of performing refresher training is on the job (OJT). In this case, a Senior Engineer, Technical Specialist, Service Supervisor or Service Manager develops the skills of the Service Engineer during normal accompaniment. This can be in technical, administrative or human relations areas. This is a particularly effective training method as it can be repeated from time to time, if necessary. If the person accompanying the engineer is unable to perform the training himself, he must at least be able to identify the training need and ensure subsequently that it be filled.

If a Service Manager identifies a deficiency in, let us assume, mechanical setting of an assembly by one of his engineers, there is no need for him to perform the remedial training himself, if he is not qualified to do so. He can get someone else in the organisation to do so. If he has another Service Engineer on his team who is good at these mechanical settings, he could ask him to give a talk with demonstration at the next team meeting. This will achieve a number of goals:

(i) The Service Engineer will read up and practice for this demonstration and will become even better

(ii) Other engineers will benefit from the talk and demonstration – they will listen carefully to one of their own peers.

(iii) Team spirit is likely to be fostered.

(iv) It will build up the engineer giving the talk in the eyes of his colleagues, and recognition is a highly motivating factor for the engineer (see Section IV – Human Relations).

(v) If engineers have further problems they are likely to be more ready to ask a colleague who has the knowledge for information than ask their line manager, who will review their performance.

We will discuss mini-teams (3–5 engineers) in some detail under Manpower and Territory Planning later in this section (also see reference to it in Figure 9, Section II – Response Time). Here I want to mention the benefit that a mini-team, working as a subgroup within the Supervisor's or Service Manager's team, has on the mutual training support of each other. Service Engineers working in the same mini-team are dependent on each other's performance and quickly learn the strengths and weaknesses of each member of the team. Whereas engineers working individual territories have no real interest to help each other perform better, those working together in a mini-team in a larger territory have a vested interest to bring the performance of the weaker ones up to standard. Any defective work of one member of the team means the others will have to work harder to make up for his faults. In consequence, they have a genuine and personal interest to improve each others' performance as well as their own.

Another aspect of field training I want to mention here is the planned and supervised performance of specifically identified tasks which cannot easily be taught in the training centre. Activities such as performing PM tasks would fall into this area, as the machines at the training centre do not require preventive maintenance activities to be performed as often as Service Engineers need to be trained.

(h) Cross Training

Cross training is the training of a Service Engineer trained on one company product on one or more additional products. In theory, there should be no special issue arising from this activity but in practice, a number of problems tend to occur. Let us examine some of them.

Let us look at the training programme itself. It may well be necessary to devise more than one training programme for a particular new product, depending on whether it is designed for an engineer with no prior knowledge of any of our company's products or for an engineer who may be familiar with some parts of the new equipment.

For the Field Service Manager there are other issues that arise. Will he be able to provide the requisite LOS (level of service) to his customers while one or more of his Service Engineers is on a training course? Consideration may have to be given to utilising back-up or relief engineers to temporarily fill the gap left by the absence of the original Service Engineer on a training course.

A basic decision will have to be taken by the Service Manager whether the new products, which may form an additional work-load on the service force, should be serviced by experienced Service Engineers who have been trained on other company products or by newly recruited additional engineers. A number of aspects need to be considered, including the geographical area covered, similarity of products, need for specialisation, complexity of products, rate of growth and a number of others. One important issue the Service Manager will need to take into account is the preference of the present Service Engineers. Some might have been working a considerable time on the "old" products and would like a change (particularly if the new product is more sophisticated). Usually there is pressure from the Service Engineers to move to the new product in the very early days of its installation in a particular country or branch as each engineer wants to be the most knowledgeable one on the new product. Once a number of Service Engineers have been trained in a locality, there is some reluctance of existing engineers to move to the new product; they know they are the experienced engineers on the old product but on the new product they are the "new boys" and some of their colleagues, who have been cross trained earlier, are more experienced. The Service Manager must also ensure that he does not weaken the old product support too much. This is not only a question of the number of Service Engineers but also one of experience (see Learning Curve, Fig 11, Section II).

All these considerations show that cross-training has to be carefully examined and all alternatives explored. It can be a very expensive approach to train all existing Service Engineers on the new products and then train new engineers on the old products to take the workload of the experienced engineers who have moved to the new products. The motivational and development needs of the Service Engineer (see next sub section) must also be considered. Like most other decisions a Service Manager must take, his alternatives are seldom black and white and he must balance various shades of grey instead.

Manpower Development and Career Planning

I am frequently asked by Service Managers: "Who in my organisation should be developed?" My invariable answer is just one word "Everyone" with a little addendum, "Everyone, to the limit of his capabilities". Development does not necessarily mean change of job or promotion, it can equally mean development in his present job. In fact, the emphasis of the professionalism of the Service Engineer's job is an important part of the development process of engineers.

Manpower development is a question of utilising all of a person's skills and capabilities and, as we will see when we discuss motivation in Section IV, this means broadening his horizon and considering his natural talents and ambitions.

In all too many companies the whole question of manpower development and career planning does not receive the attention of management which it deserves. It is often regarded by managers as a once or twice a year paper exercise instead of a continuous management process. In fact, managers play lip service to the whole management development issue without realising that a thorough and coherent approach to it would make the management of their function much simpler and more effective.

It is often said that a Service Engineers's job is a "dead end" job – nothing could be further from the truth! The number of career opportunities are virtually limitless, although in practice some career outlets are more frequent areas for developing Service Engineers than others. I can quote real-life situations where a person who started life as a Service Engineer developed into each of the directions indicated in Figure 19, often rising to management positions in the new career. Let us look at some of the alternatives from a practical point of view, both within Service and in other functions.

The most obvious development for a Service Engineer will be up the promotional ladder – through Senior Engineer, Service Supervisor, to various levels of Service Management; the sky's the limit here.

Not every engineer has the desire or the leadership qualities to move along the direct line management path – many may develop into technical specialisation. There are usually a number of levels of Technical Specialist and Product Service Management positions towards which an engineer can be developed.

An important career path leads along the Service Training and Publication route for either a permanent career or for development assignments. Many companies feel that great benefit can be achieved both for the development of the individual and for the company as a whole in that type of assignement. The individual adds pedagogic knowledge to his field experience which will serve him well if he returns to the field in a more senior position and the company also benefits by the fact that Service Engineers being trained by a Service Trainer with recent field experience are likely to accept his teaching more readily than if they believe that he has not been at the sharp end servicing a customer's machine for a long time.

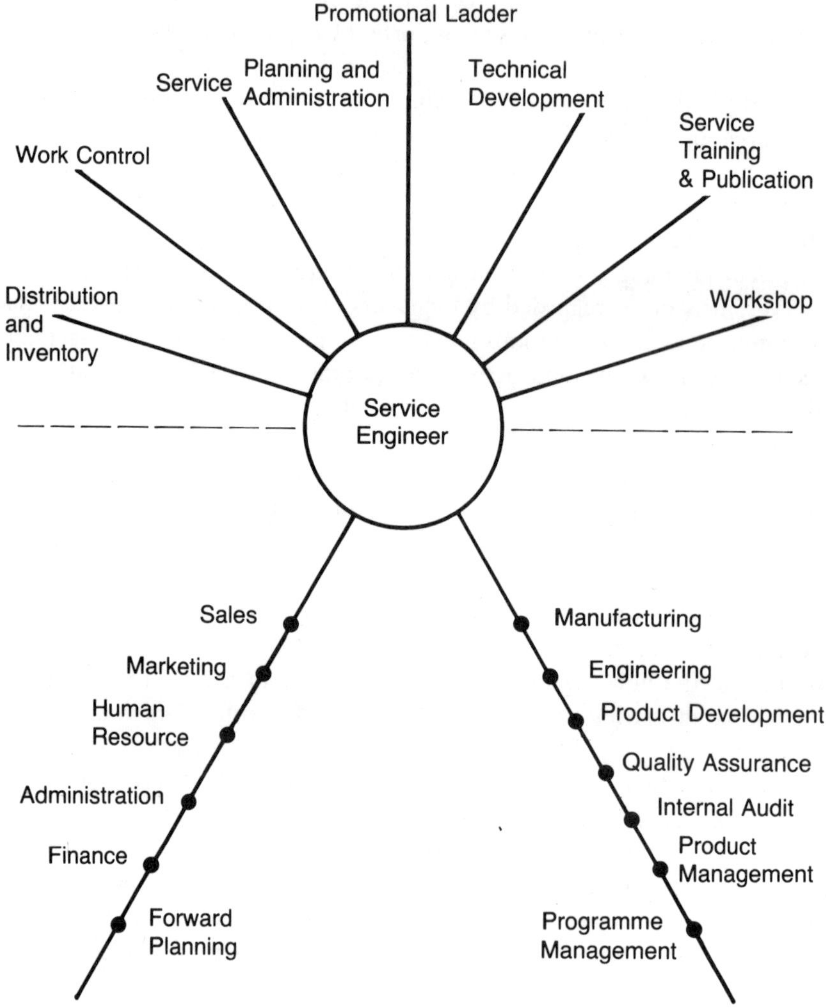

Figure 19. *Career Path Opportunities for a Service Engineer*

In many companies a career path also exists through the Workshops, repairing faulty assemblies or refurbishing machines. This can be used to sharpen specific technical skills of an engineer (e.g. developing his diagnostic abilities under controlled conditions) and the fullest understanding of field requirements will be useful to the workshop.

Development within service need not be in the technical areas described above. It can also be in the Service Planning and Administration area, where his previous field experience can be very useful and, for himself, may help his development to a management position.

Work Control is an area of Service requiring increasing attention and support. An engineer may well be able to organise this activity effectively and also "talk" a customer (or even another Service Engineer) through a reported problem. His understanding of field conditions should be very helpful within the Work Control Centre.

The supply and control of spare parts and supplies often is a major issue to the whole Service function. Development of Service Engineers in the Distribution and/or Inventory Control function often helps to highlight the issues and to relieve conflict.

Before leaving the development of a Service Engineer within the Service function let me stress perhaps the most important development – to help the engineer to become a better Service Engineer which will give him a great deal of job satisfaction and through this job satisfaction, he will perform even better which is of advantage not only to the customer and the company but creates further job satisfaction to himself.

Outside Service a Service Engineer can develop through almost any other function, both utilising his technical skills, knowledge and experience (e.g. Manufacturing, Engineering, etc) or his field experience (e.g. Sales, Marketing, etc.).

Obviously, moves of the nature described above are not in one direction only – there is also movement into Service from any other function with suitable knowledge, experience and skill. These moves in either direction can be permanent or temporary. Job rotation is often regarded as a useful way of cross-fertilising the experience of various functions and as a motivational tool for the employee. Western companies who practice job rotation to a substantial extent have some aspects in common with Japanese companies – they tend to keep their employees for a long period and often operate in a genuinely decentralised manner. This is not accidental. If a company has a high turnover of staff they cannot afford to rotate jobs frequently as they fear that the training will be wasted when the employee leaves. Equally, from the employee's point of view, in companies with a high turnover of staff he would not wish to leave his professional skill in his chosen field, as this is "saleable" if he left the company, whereas his broader "company knowledge" is unlikely to be of much use to him outside the company. The reason why genuine decentralisation is more easily achieved by companies with a well planned job rotation programme is also easily understood. It is not the quantifiable decisions that managers, in general, are loath to delegate – those are likely to be as effectively decided by their juniors. It is the decision with a philosophical implication which senior managers feel uncomfortable to delegate, because each manager has had a different background and experience. In Japanese (and Japanese style) companies the junior managers all tended to go through very similar experiences and have become indoctrinated by similar company philosophies in a number of departments – this gives the senior manager some confidence that the decision that will be taken by his junior is likely to be the same as his own. Naturally, this also has its disadvantages, such as an excessive conformity and lack of creativity.

Care must also be taken by management to ensure not to develop an engineer in unsuitable directions. This applies not only to promotion (Peter's principle – Promote to level of incompetence) but also to development into other functions. It is not much use to a company or to the individual, if we lose a good Service Engineer and gain a mediocre or below standard Salesman or Design Engineer. Manpower development and career planning is one of the most important activities in a company. It must be professionally managed and line managers and reviewers need to be suitably trained in this field.

Manpower Planning – Territory Planning

When we talked about Forecasting, Planning and Budgeting in Section II we discussed the parameters without looking at the detail of how a manpower plan is developed. As we are now examining the Service Force, the time appears appropriate to cover the manpower planning activity. Let us look at how a Service Engineer spends his time. Let us assume, for simplicity's sake, that he works 40 hours a week; in consequence in a year he is paid for 40×52 hours, i.e. 2080 hours. As we all know, the only really useful hours an engineer employs on behalf of the company are those he spends working on customers' premises or repairing items elsewhere. As the the gap of hours between these two figures and 2080 hours is considerable, we need to understand what goes into them and how we, as Service Managers, can influence them.

Let us look at the breakdown of hours illustrated in Figure 20. We will see that the "Total Hours" consist of the "Standard Paid Hours" plus "Overtime". Overtime is usually a very small proportion of the "Standard Paid Hours" and allows for a certain amount of unplanned overload which might have many causes such as above plan installations, above plan sickness, work load fluctuations, below plan reliability, climatic problems and many others.

A certain amount of time can be excluded right from the beginning. We know that the Service Engineer's holiday entitlement (varies by country and company but is often a substantial part of the year, often 4 or even 5 weeks, i.e. 160-200 hours) is not available to the company and must therefore be excluded from the hours available for servicing customer's equipment. In some countries (e.g. Switzerland) the military duties an engineer is obliged to perform must also be taken into account. Both of these items can be easily established, as both the holiday entitlement and military training time is known when establishing the plan.

TOTAL HOURS		
Standard paid hours		Overtime
Non-available hours	Available hours	
	Indirect time	Direct time
Holidays Sickness Formal training	Response availability Informal training Parts collection time Admin. time Meetings	CM Work hours PM Work hours Customers training hours Installation work hours ECO time Parts repair off customer premises Call associated travel time Call reporting time
Non-controllable hours (Engineer not in branch)	Partially controllable hours (Engineer in branch)	Active hours

Figure 20. *Breakdown of service engineer hours*

There are other hours which are not available to the Service Manager and which therefore must be excluded from the plan, as they are completely uncontrollable or only very marginally controllable. Even Service Engineers fall sick from time to time and, from previous experience, a Service Manager must make suitable allowance for this in his manpower plan. This will vary from company to company and often from season to season. The other hours which are not available to a Service Manager are those when his engineers are on formal training courses. It is often possible to calculate the hours a branch will lose due to formal training courses, as these are frequently governed by new product introductions, cross training needs or expansion of the service force.

All the above hours are lost to the branch and not controllable by the Service Manager – these hours are usually known as "Non-Available Hours".

The other hours are controllable by company decisions and actions – they are known as "Available Hours". Available hours are usually subdivided into two groups – the first called "Direct Hours" which are the effective work hours of the engineer and the associated travel and reporting hours and the other group, known as "Indirect Hours" which is the time necessary to povide the agreed "Response Time", "Informal Training Time", "Parts Collection Time", "Administration Time" and "Meetings Time".

A few words on the logic of some of these allocations. There will be little disagreement on the placing of "Corrective Maintenance Hours", "Preventive Maintenance Hours", "Customer Training Hours", "Installation Hours" and "Modification (ECO) Hours" into Direct Time or Active Time. "Parts Repair Hours off Customers' Premises" should also be included here, as it is equally active time on behalf of the company. The two items which may require some discussion in this group are "Call Associated Travel Hours" and "Call Reporting Time". The reason it is suggested it should be included under Direct Time is the direct link of the work carried out to the need to travel to the work and report on what has been done. Travel and reporting are the direct cause of the need to visit the customer. The need for breaking out each of the above factors as accurately as possible is to enable Service Managers to plan future activities and, just as important, to identify areas of their operation where remedial action is needed or where they might be able to learn from an engineer, a team or a branch how to improve certain activities. For instance, if it is found that work hours per call are running higher than anticipated, a more detailed analysis will show whether this phenomenon happens throughout the operation. If this is the case, the problem is likely to be either in the serviceability of the design or the training programme or manuals of the service force. If work hours are longer in specific geographical areas or engineer territories only, the issue is more likely to be the management of that area or the lack of experience of engineers or the selection, support and OJT of the engineers. If travel time is high, it is likely to require re-examination of Service Engineer (or mini-team) territories, the degree of specialisation or the spread of customer equipments. It may also indicate a need for changing Work Control prioritisation or the approach to PM work could be reviewed (e.g. combining corrective and preventive maintenance into a combined call). Similar deductions from the other factors can be made to lead to action orientated re-examination of management directions.

Let us now look at the group most difficult to calculate precisely, namely "Indirect Time", the time the Service Engineer is in the Branch but when the way he spends his time is only partially controllable by management. In the other groups most of the factors are dictated to the Service Manager by either the law, local practices, equipment, customer or geography. If there is a 4 weeks contractual holiday period, for example, the Service Manager knows this and can include this factor in his calculations. Equally, he knows that when a customer requests a call, his department needs to respond, with the automatic impact on work time, travel time and reporting time. "Non-Available Hours" and "Direct Hours" are relatively inflexible in the short term and any overload or underload is likely to be reflected by parameters in the "Indirect Hours" group.

In consequence, Service Managers must clearly understand how these factors are linked to the LOS (level of service) the Service Department provides to the customer and how he, as Service Manager, can affect the final results. All of these factors are likely to require engineer hours but the manager can, in some instances, decide on their timing. The factors in the "Indirect Time" grouping most directly linked to the service call and its associated work, travel and reporting hours is "Response Availability Hours". This is the time an engineer cannot be assigned to active work as the Service Department could then not meet the planned response time. In theory, if an engineer's "Direct Time" equalled "Available Hours", response time for an additional call would be infinite. The ratio of "Direct Hours" to "Available Hours" is often defined as the Utilisation Ratio and is expressed in percentage terms.

$$\frac{\text{Direct Hours}}{\text{Available Hours}} \times 100\% = \text{Utilisation } \%$$

In some companies, the ratio is calculated as a percentage of "Direct Hours" to "Standard Paid Hours" or even "Total Hours". It is not recommended to include "Non-Available Hours" into this calculation for two main reasons. Firstly, "Non Available Hours" can be determined fairly precisely in advance (holiday entitlement is known, formal training depends on product introductions and manpower growth) and are largely outside the control of the Service Manager; the Service Engineer is not available to the local service operation. "Available Hours", by definition are available to local Service Managers to provide the necessary service and therefore this is the utilisation factor on which the effectiveness of his management can be judged. Secondly, non-service management frequently find it difficult to understand a utilisation factor of relatively low percentage points which results from the latter calculation.

When we look at response time we automatically move into the implications of Territory Planning. We have covered some part of this in Section II – Figure 8 and 9. Figure 9 shows the Distribution of Response Time in a single engineer territory. If the geographical distribution of our machines is such that travel time does not rise excessively by putting two, three of four engineer territories together, then the average response time and its distribution around the mean can be favourably affected by joining these individual territories together into a larger mini-team territory. The reason for this is the fluctuation of work load. This fluctuation is greatest in a single engineer territory and joining territories has a smoothing effect on this fluctuation.

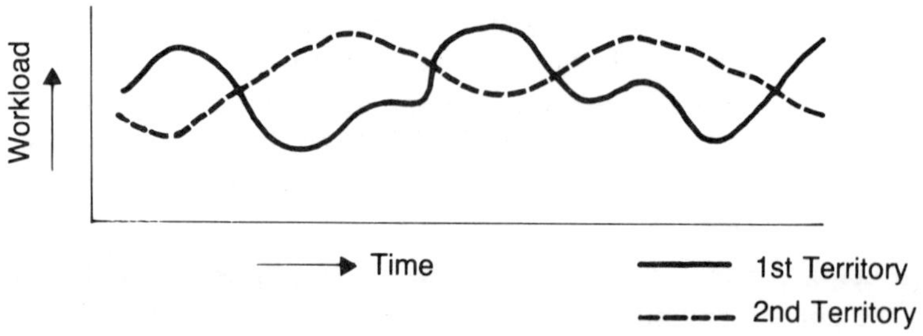

Figure 21. *Workload Fluctuation*

From the simplified two territories graphical illustration in Figure 21 it will be clear that the likelihood of both territories having peaks or valleys at the same time are smaller than if we have to cope with one territory only. Obviously if we overlaid another one or two territories, there would be an even greater smoothing effect of the combined load of 3 or 4 Service Engineers. This combining of territories must not be taken too far, as this may then have adverse effects on travel time, and the inability of too many engineers to build up a good relationship with a customer. Another prerequisite of combining a number of territories is an efficient Work Control or Dispatch function to co-ordinate the activities in the field (see Service Control, Section V (ii).

In consequence, by suitable Territory Planning we can achieve a better response time with the same number of Service Engineers, or the same number of engineers can accept a higher workload without adversely affecting response time, which means a higher utilisation factor of the service force.

The relationship of utilisation and response time is illustrated in Figure 22. It shows that where the utilisation factor is already high a further slight increase will extend response time very considerably (Area A in figure 22).

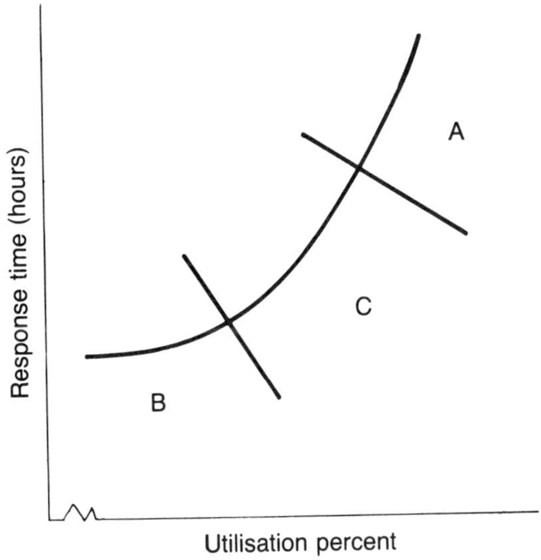

Figure 22. *Response time/utilisation*

At the other extreme, at very low utilisation, a further slight reduction in utilisation will make no difference to response time, and even a relatively substantial reduction of utilisaton will reduce response time only slightly (Area B). The Service manager will therefore try and operate on the middle part of the curve (Area C). This graph has been constructed on the assumption that all other factors (except the two parametes plotted) remain the same.

We need to consider these other factors, however, because the Service Manager may have to influence them if, for instance, he needs to achieve very short response times and cannot afford the very low utilisation necessary to achieve this without changing some of the other factors. The most important ones of these are the length of the individual call (plus travel), the length of the workday and the efficiency of the Work Control. The last of these we will discuss in Section V. Let us now consider the first two, i.e. duration of call and length of workday.

The shorter the duration of the call (work time plus travel time plus reporting time) the more flexible the work force will be to respond quickly to customer calls. To take an extreme situation. Let us assume two different products serviced by different Service Engineers; product A is relatively simple and the MTTR is 0.5 hours, there are many of these products and they are therefore close together and MTTT is 0.2 hours and reporting time is 0.1 hours. The Total unit of time for an average call on product A is therefore 0.8 hours. Product B, on the other hand, is a complex product, MTTR is 4.0 hours, MTTT is 0.4 hours and reporting time is the same as before, i.e. 0.1 hours. The unit of time for an average call is therefore 4.5 hours. Even if we compare, say, 6 calls a day for Product A (total Direct Hours $6\times0.8=4.8$ hours) against 1 call a day for Product B (4.5 hours Direct Time), the utilisation factor for Product A will be higher (say for an 8 hour day $4.8/8.0\times100=60\%$) than for Product B ($4.5/8.0\times100\%=56.25\%$) but the average response time for Product A is likely to be very much shorter. The probability that all calls for Product A will be received shortly after the Service Engineer starts on his first call is very low whereas for Product B the second call could come in at any time.

The action of a Service Manager, therefore, may well be to try to reduce work time on Product B (e.g. by more exchange of assemblies or modules and less repair on customer's premises) whereas on Product A he may consider combining preventive maintenance with corrective maintenance, as the ratio of travel time plus reporting time to work time $0.2+0.1/0.5\times100=60\%$ is high and therefore the impact of travel + reporting time needs to be reduced. On Product B, travel + reporting represents only $12^1/_2\%$ ($0.4+0.1/4.0\times100$) and therefore the work time needs to be reduced if possible. Team working will also be more important in the case of Product B, as with long call duration the smoothing effect of combined territories becomes more pronounced.

The most beneficial impact could be made by the Service Manager if the products and the skills of the work force would allow him to train at least some of the Service Engineers on both Products A and B which would allow Work Control to balance work loads and response time needs of the whole product range. Consideration must be given to the additional training cost, the carrying of spare parts and manuals for both products and the reduced specialised knowledge of the Service Engineers trained on both products. It may be possible to identify a group of engineers who will perform effectively under this multi-product approach (generalists) whereas others will perform better as one product specialists. The skill of Service Managers is to identify the motivational factors of each individual engineer (see Section IV-i) and match these to the operational requirements.

From the above considerations it will also be obvious that the longer each workday, the higher the utilisation can be for a given response time. If everything else stayed the same, we could work more effectively on four 10 hour days than on five 8 hour days. The difficulty is that everything else does not remain the same. Fatigue may set in, customers' premises may not be open, family life of the engineers might be affected and other similar considerations need to be taken into account.

In this connection I would like to put a partial fallacy into perspective. We are often told by the financial community that "Overtime" is very expensive. This is only partially true, because in a well run Service Department overtime is only used at a time of temporary overload and it will tend to be at 100% utilisation – it is likely to be used to complete a call or to satisfy response time requirements and is invariably "Direct Time" with no waiting or "Indirect Hours".

We have spent a great deal of time on "Response Availability". Let us quickly examine the other factors of "Indirect Time". "Informal Training" is on the job or in-branch training, where a Service Engineer is instructed by his Supervisor, Product Specialist, Field Trainer or by a self-paced training programme. It is usually separated from "Formal Training" because it is in shorter units, it is local and, therefore, in case of need, the Service Manager can postpone the "Informal Training" to a more convenient period.

"Part Collection Time" is the time needed for the standard replenishment of the Service Engineer's parts stock in his vehicle. Depending on the number of engineers and the distance involved, Service Managers can reduce this time by suitable actions. In some companies all replenishment parts are sent to the Service Engineer to a predetermined address (could be his home, or a customer with whom special arrangements have been made, or a post-office or railway station). In others, replenishment parts are prepared by the local stores in an individualised locker for each Engineer so that it is ready for him to be picked up during a less busy period. In major cities some companies deliver replenishment parts overnight to a room where a number of Service Engineers have their lockers; yet others use radio-controlled spares vehicles to rendez-vous with engineers to supply them with spare parts.

"Administrative Time" includes the time spent in preparing all non-call related reports and forms, the maintenance of vehicle and similar activities; it must be the aim of every Service Manager to minimise and simplify these tasks as much as possible.

"Meetings" are essential to keep Service Engineers in touch with the company and with each other. Service Managers must ensure that this time is used as effectively as possible by planning the meetings carefully, allow free discussion without permitting it to drift away from the subject and clearly identifying the objective of the meeting. The subject of planning and running of meetings is one which must be included in the training programme of Service Managers and Supervisors. It is almost identical to running meetings for any other function except that the timing needs to be more carefully considered (customers are waiting to be serviced) and the Service Engineers need to be involved more positively than in other functions – Salesmen, for example, are by nature more extrovert and are usually more willing to take an active part in a meeting.

We have now considered Service Engineer "Manpower and Territory Planning" factors. The simple next step would be to calculate the product requirements (see Section II – Forecasting, Planning and Budgeting) and divide by the "Direct Hours" to give us our Service Engineer requirements. This is reasonable in theory, but the Service Manager also needs to consider seasonal fluctuation of product performance, customer usage, engineer holiday preferences, peak sickness periods, timing of new product introductions and others. He will therefore need to make a month by month calculation and establish his manpower requirement from the results. Here he will again have to make judgemental decisions. It will probably emerge that there will be a workload fluctuation as shown in Figure 23. If he recruits to peak load (line A in illustration) he will be overstaffed for most of the year; if he recruits to minimum workload (line B) he will be short of staff. The judgement, therefore, needs to be exercised on where to put line C, which will be his Service Engineer manpower plan. He will try and cover his overload situations by trying to arrange his engineers' holidays in the trough periods, working some overtime in peak periods, trying to arrange formal training in non-peak periods and re-arranging non-urgent or non-time sensitive activities.

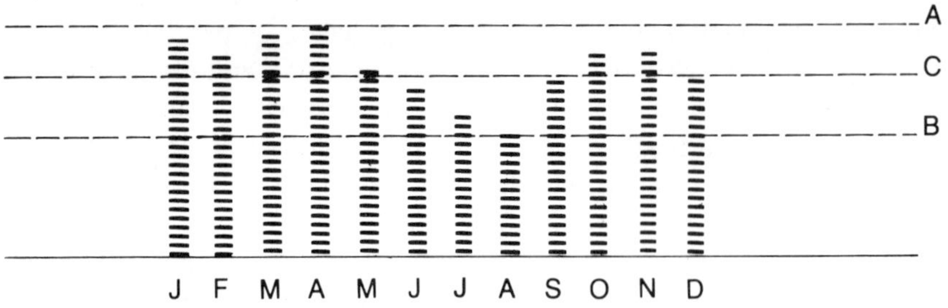

Figure 23. *Variance in Workload*

Once the Service Manager knows his required number of Service Engineers, he needs to decide on the level of support needed. Some of it will be dictated by organisation (e.g. if a company decides to have a Branch Manager in each branch, then the number of Branch Service Managers is dictated by the organisation) or by the number and types of products, or by geography. Other support numbers are discretionary such as the span of control of Service Supervisors. In any case, the number and location of Service Engineers is the basis for all subsequent decisions. In many cases, the Service Manager must work from previous experience, rather than by any quantifiable method of calculation. It may vary from time to time. For instance, if a service force expands very rapidly, the span of control of each Service Supervisor may have to be reduced, as inexperienced new Service Engineers are likely to require more assistance and guidance than more experienced engineers, and, in any case, a number of the Supervisors themselves are likely to be relatively inexperienced and therefore should not be given too many Service Engineers to lead. A stable and mature service force may not require as much help from service management and the span of control could well be increased.

One area of the company which should never be understaffed is Work Control – it is in contact with the customer and he should not be required to wait a long time before the telephone is answered. Also it is a waste of engineers' time if they have to wait too long for the Work Controller to deal with them. As we will see in Section V, there are ways of balancing uneven workloads in the Work Control Department without staff being idle.

Summary of Section

☐ Before we can even start thinking about the service force we need, we must examine the job which needs to be done.

☐ We then analyse each task, identify the specific skills, education, experience and psychological profile of the person we are looking for.

☐ Having built up a model of the job and a profile of the person we need, we proceed with the selection of the requisite staff and try and ensure that he complies as far as possible with the specification we have created. It may be necessary to make some compromise, provided we can compensate the shortcomings by additional training.

☐ The training process is usually the first activity of the company with which a new recruit will become deeply involved; the impression created on him will have a lasting impact on his attitude to the company and to other company employees. He must therefore receive not only technical training, but also get a good understanding of the philosophy of the company during his initiation and he must also be trained in customer relations and administrative procedures. The training process only begins with this initial training – it must continue by regular on-the-job training, refresher training and cross training on other products.

- ☐ During the whole life of an employee with the company, he must be developed to the limit of his capabilities. This development can take many forms and should be part of a well thought through career path adjusted to each individual's aspirations and ability. For some it will mean becoming better at their chosen job and getting their satisfaction from knowing they are doing a good job and being recognised as good performers; others will be promoted along the hierarchical structure; yet others may develop along technical, pedagogic or administrative paths or in functions outside of service.

- ☐ Finally, we examined the whole area of Manpower Planning. We defined our terminology and discussed why a complete understanding of the underlying factors will help a Service Manager with his action orientated decisions. We concentrated on the response to customer calls and the effect territory planning can have on manpower requirements and response time. We then identified a range of alternatives a Service Manager has at hand to affect the efficiency of his operation linked to manpower and territory planning issues.

SECTION IV

Service management

Managing the Service Force

Although I have said it before, I do not apologise for saying it again. The service force is highly manpower intensive and Service Engineers frequently work away from their base, alone in the field, and represent the company on customers' premises – the efficient management of the service force is therefore at least as important as that of any other function, if not more so.

Human Relations

The attitude of the Service Engineer to the customer, to his job, to his colleagues, to his management and to his company will be an important factor in achieving a positive approach to his work and, through it, to meet the generic service goals of customer satisfaction, service profitability and a happy employee.

I will not endeavour to summarise the reams that have been written by behavioural scientists such as Frederick Herzberg, William Dowling, David Mc Clelland, Peter Drucker, Chris Argyris, B F Skinner, Douglas McGregor, Rensis Likert, Fritz Roethlisberger, Warren Bennis, George Homans, and others on the subject of motivation. Instead, I will try and show, how their findings can be put to effective use by Service Managers.

The first lesson a Service Manager must learn is to be consistent in his management approach. He cannot say one thing and act in a contradictory manner to this message. Secondly, the Service Manager must build on the individual strengths of each of his subordinates and utilise all their capabilities. This may mean considering suggestions from Service Engineers on any aspect of the company, i.e. not only on the subject of servicing equipment but also in other areas, such as proposals for improving the product, methods of more efficient management, simplifying the administration and others. This obviously does not mean accepting every suggestion, but it does mean careful analysis of each proposal and information to be passed back to the proposer on what further action is being taken or, if no further action is proposed, why the decision has been taken not to pursue the suggestion. It may be a time consuming task for management but nonetheless essential to demonstrate to every employee that we recognize that he may generate ideas useful to the company where he spends a large part of his day.

Although each of us is different and has dissimilar ambitions in life, there are certain motivators that apply to all of us to a greater or lesser extent.

- ☐ We all want to know that our work is successful.
- ☐ We all want our achievements to be recognised.
- ☐ We all want adequate reward for our work.
- ☐ We all enjoy working if it is made palatable.
- ☐ We are all willing to accept a reasonable amount of responsibility.
- ☐ We all want to know precisely what is expected of us and where this fits into the total business.
- ☐ We all like to feel important.

The usual division of these factors is into "Motivators" and "Demotivators" or "Hygiene" factors. Let us first look at the hygiene factors as they are much easier to identify and influence. They are those factors which are satisfying the basic needs of an individual – their absence or inadequacy are detrimental to the job but their existence does not positively motivate an individual. In a service operation these Hygiene factors would include:

- ☐ *Appropriate Pay*. Above the rate for the job may keep a Service Engineer with a company but it will not motivate him to do better work. Inadequate pay for the job will, however, act as a demotivator.
- ☐ *Logical organisation*. The structure should facilitate the work of an engineer and ensure that his goals and the organisational structure reinforce each other.
- ☐ *Opportunity to affiliate with peers*. In a service force, engineers need the feeling of belonging to a team, as they are working on their own a great deal of the time.
- ☐ *Company policies and administrative practices*. These should be seen to be reasonable and equitable.

These Hygiene factors will merely ensure that a climate exists in which the service force can be motivated.

Let us examine a few practical ways of motivating Service Engineers.

Clearly establish what you, as a Service Manager, expect of your Service Engineer.

This sounds simple but in all too many companies there is no clearly laid down objective for the engineers. Ideally, those objectives should be worked out jointly by the manager and the engineer. These objectives and the likelihood of their achievement should be regularly reviewed between the Service Manager and the engineer (not just once a year). Wherever possible, these objectives should be quantified. A number of methods exist of establishing these goals in a systematic way and Management by Objectives (MBO) is one of the best known of these methods.

Recognise achievement

In many other functions the achievements of the employee are easily recognised and appreciation is shown (e.g. salesman exceeding his target). In the service force achievement is not so obvious and even where the manager recognises it, he may not let the engineer and his colleagues know about it. Service Manager should work on the principle of "Criticise in private and praise in public". Company journals, magazines and news sheets as well as team meetings are useful for publicising outstanding achievements.

Expanding job content

Within the service function, there are a number of ways of expanding the Service Engineer's job, let me mention just a few:

- ☐ cross-training on additional products (needs to be balanced against possible loss of expertise)
- ☐ greater involvement in customer training and management
- ☐ encouraging suggestions and ensuring feed-back

☐ training reponsibility for junior engineers

☐ participation in customer audits

☐ involvement in planning sessions for team

☐ selling maintenance contracts (see Service Revenue).

Provide reasonable support

There are few aspects of a Service Engineer's job that are likely to make him feel more dissatisfied with his job than receiving inadequate support. This may manifest itself by a chronic shortage of spare parts, unsuitable or clumsy tools and test equipment, badly designed or late documentation or inadequate technical or administrative support. The Service Manager cannot reasonably ask an engineer to be highly productive without ensuring adequate support from other company activities.

Communication

As Service Engineers are likely to be away from their base for a good deal of the time, it is even more important to keep them well informed of what is happening in the company. This applies not only to events which have occurred but also to future activities. It is for example, annoying to an engineer if the customer knows more about a product being launched by the company than the Service Engineer, who, after all, is a company representative in the eyes of the customer. It demonstrates a lack of trust and thoughtfulness by the company towards the engineer – without this trust we cannot expect loyalty from the Service Engineer. Communication also encompasses the feed-back of information to the engineer on how his inputs are used by the company (be it to the reporting system, the suggestion scheme or whatever).

Broaden opportunities

Opportunities should be made available to Service Engineers for promotion within the Service Department as well as for broadening experiences outside it. Service Engineers are often stereo-typed in the minds of management who do not consider them for certain posts for which they may be well qualified.

Allow contributions to the decision making process

It is often thought to be difficult to arrange for Service Engineers to contribute to decisions affecting the department; this is only a question of management attitude. If the Service Manager is determined to involve his Engineers, he will find ways of doing so. Let me give you an example I saw in a Japanese company's service function. Work time (MTTR – mean time to repair) is one of the most difficult service tasks to be affected by the actions of a Service Manager, as he does not wish to encourage engineers to carry out incomplete calls simply because he pressurises them on MTTR. In this particular company the Service Manager felt that he could reduce MTTR by 20 minutes per call. He got his Field Engineering Department to identify improvements which would save about 12 minutes. He then arranged for his Field Engineers from headquarters to visit each branch in turn and talk to the Service Engineers at Branch Meetings. At these meetings the problem was identified as a joint issue for all concerned, i.e. "We" have to find a saving of 20 minutes. Field Engineering can only find 12 minutes savings. Service Engineers then went into individual team sessions to find additional ways of saving time without affecting quality. The results of the suggestions from all teams were analysed and an action programme developed. This programme was rigorously implemented throughout the company with the fullest cooperation of the Service Engineers, as they felt that they themselves had been fully involved in "our" problem of saving 20 minutes on the MTTR. The total saving turned out to be 25 minutes. True, this was a slow process taking many months but it more than achieved the objectives of the programme and, instead of upsetting Service Engineers by being "pushed" too hard, it motivated them by the trust the company showed in them to be able to come up with good suggestions.

Disciplined operation

As much as it may surprise some managers, most Service Engineers welcome the opportunity to work for a disciplined company and resent a lack of supervision. Service Engineers often feel that their job cannot be thought by the company to be very important if they are not reasonably tightly supervised and discipline enforced. We all prefer to work under an efficient manager and lax discipline is not an indication of good management. This does not mean going to the other extreme of an autocratic ("X") style of management – there is no contradiction in having a consensus style ("Y") of management and reasonable discipline and tight supervision.

Frequent counselling

It is far preferable to have frequent, short, informal couselling sessions with one's Service Engineers than to save the counselling to the once or twice a year formal review sessions. The latter will, by nature, appear to be an adversary style of discussion whereas regular informal counselling will be viewed much more constructively. In addition, it is much easier for the manager to be constructively critical at the time of an incident rather than saving up the issue for the occasion of a performance review.

To summarise the foregoing, I would advise Service Managers to motivate their Service Engineers by listening carefully and utilising the consensus approach to resolving issues.

The question of monetary incentives often arises. This is an issue which must be considered from case to case on its own merits. In Service, incentives are not usual and even in other fields there is some movement away from incentives linked directly to production – the quality of the work needs to be included in the equation. It is getting much more usual to have group incentives rather than individual incentives.

On the other hand, where a joint field force of Salesmen and Service Engineers are working together, it would be demotivating to the service force to see the Salesmen receiving special incentives in addition to their normal salaries plus commissions such as "Par Club" (100% Club) trips etc, without some equivalent reward to the Service Engineers. As one Managing Director put it to me: "If a Salesman exceeds his target by a substantial margin, the commissions he earns will be far higher than for an average Salesman; a far above average Service Engineer will receive only a marginally higher income than the average Engineer and therefore inclusion of Service Engineers in a Par Club is more important than for Salesmen, where the high earners could well afford to pay for the trip themselves".

My own opinion is that incentives are not highly motivational to the service force but having incentives for one part of the field force would make it highly demotivational to Service if they were not included – it would encourage the feeling of "second class citizenship" in the service force.

We have touched on the question of Career Planning when we discussed "Manpower and Career Planning" at the end of Section III. Here I would only like to stress its impact on the motivation of service staff in general and Service Engineers in particular. Like any other human being, Service Engineers want to know what alternatives are available to them in their further development in the comapny. To achieve this it is not sufficient to publish openings for promotions or possible transfers to other departments, although obviously this is also essential. The most meaningful approach is personalised career counselling both by the Service Engineer's manager and by a professional from the Human Resource Department. This counselling is not a single-directional lecture to the engineer on career prospects within the company but a genuine review of the aspirations of the Service Engineer and a joint exploration of his suitability (or otherwise) for the job. These may be long term aims, the achievement of which may require a combination of training by the company, self-development by the engineer and experience opportunities to be made available to him. It may, on the other hand, involve the counsellors explaining honestly and frankly to the Service Engineer why they believe that his aims appear unrealistic to them and perhaps try and steer him in another direction. Career planning must be seen by the employee to be regarded as a genuine development of the individual and not just a paper exercise to comply to some procedural practice laid down by the company.

In this connection the professionalism of the Service Engineer's job should be stressed. Career planning for many Service Engineers is likely to mean getting better at their chosen profession of servicing customers and equipments. Management must ensure that the professional approach to this aim is facilitated and fostered and the contribution to the firm publicly recognised. Companies have developed specific programmes to publicise the professionalism of the Service Engineer's job throughout the company but these programmes will only succeed if top management demonstrate by their actions that they really mean what the programme propagates.

I would like to give you an example of a programme developed by a large multinational company for use in a number of countries and how the support from the national top managers influenced the effectiveness of the programme. First let me explain the programme, entitled "The Professional Service Engineer". An advertising agency developed a symbol for the campaign – a modern, high quality object, aspiring to the skies. The actual shape was interpreted differently by different people. Its practical purpose was a very attractive table lighter that any engineer would be happy to put on his sitting-room table. This lighter was sent by the General Manager of each country to the home of each engineer with a suitable letter. This letter thanked the Service Engineer for his past contributions to the not inconsiderable achievements of the company, explaining the difficulty of a General Manager to show his appreciation personally to the engineers and stressing the prefessionalism of the Service Engineer's job and recognising the difficulties under which he was operating and the satisfaction he must feel in resolving problems.

The symbol was adopted for all service letters, literature and documentation and a poster programme was started using the symbol. For instance, the first poster appeared in all company premises just showing the symbol with a headline: "What's this?" "If you don't know, ask the Service Engineer". This was timed to coincide with the letter from the General Manager to the engineers, where the symbol of "The Perfect Engineer" was explained to the Service Engineer. This gave the image of the Service Engineer a boost in all countries.

In countries where the General Manager fully supported the programme and followed it up effectively with additional posters on specific subjects (e.g. "Spare a Thought for Spares") the motivational benefit lasted a long time. In others, the impact was short-term. The re-emphasising of the programme by some General Managers would take the form of suitable remarks in his speeches to other managers and staff, "personal" letters prepared by the Service Manager for the signature of the General Manager for special achievements and occasional attendance by the General Manager at Service Engineer meetings. The Service Manager in some countries used the symbol to recognise Service Engineers' contributions (e.g. all service staff would get a tie pin in polished steel, whereas high achievers would receive it in silver or gold).

The reason I spent some time on this example is to show that motivational programmes, if wholeheartedly supported by senior management by their actions, can have a fairly long-term motivational impact on the service force by making everyone realise the importance of the function and, at the same time, promote the professionalism of the Service Engineer's job. The range of programmes is only limited by the imagination of the management.

The last (but not least) aspect of motivation I want to mention is the consensus approach as a motivator. We have mentioned this once or twice before in other contexts. Nothing is likely to motivate any of us more than to be involved in the decisions concerning our work. Even if the final decision is contrary to our voiced opinion, as long as we understand why our advice was not heeded and know that it has been genuinely considered and listened to, we will be much more wholehearted in implementing a decision to which we have contributed.

Service Department Structures

The structure of a Service Department will depend on a multitude of factors, some of which might be controllable by Service Managers, wheareas many will be outside his control. The ones most likely to have a serious impact on the structure of his department include: type of product and customer, portability and transportability of product, density of machine population, state of development of the company, method of product distribution, desired market image, future trends, etc. The structure in turn, will decide the type, level and location of support activities.

The all important aspect of structure is that it must facilitate and support the management of the service force by clear lines of responsibility and authority.

Field Organisation.

There are two prevalent ways a field force is organised – either on a functional basis whereby the responsibility and authority is vested in the functions themselves (Sales and Service) or on a geographical basis, where the sales and service functions report to a Branch Manager, who is responsible for the total field operation. (Figure 24).

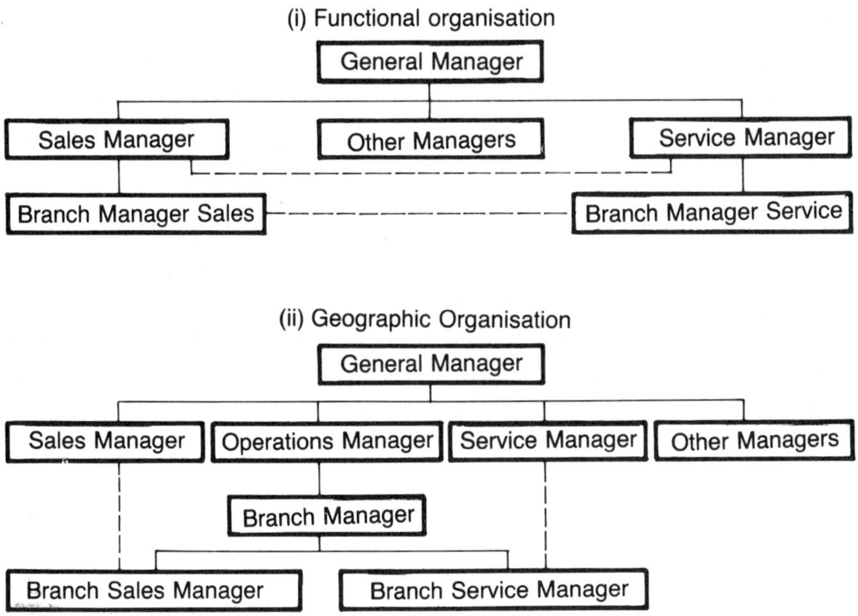

Figure 24. *Organisational alternatives*

With the trend towards establishing Service Profit Centres there has been a movement towards functional organisation structures, as they make the allocation of responsibilities and authorities more clear cut. There is nevertheless a need for a close communication link between functional managers in each location. This organisation enables each function to structure its operation in a most cost-effective way to satisfy customer requirements and contribute to company profits. It also enables the Service Profit Centre more easily to provide service to a number of company divisions or even to third parties (outside companies) without accusations of preferential treatment to one division or the need for multiple service organisations with multiple overheads.

The geographical organisation is often used when a company is new in the market and requires a clearly identifiable "one face to the customer" manager with responsibilities for the whole local field operation. It is likely to be very flexible often at the expense of by-passing (or "bending") the company's functional policies and procedures. The Branch Service Manager may have divided loyalties if his line manager's instructions contravene his functional manager's procedures.

Field Service Structure

At customer level the main alternatives open to the Service Manager will be limited by the density of installations. For power plants or major paper making machinery there may be no choice – there is usually one or more Service Engineer per installation. We really need to consider only such industries where the Service Manager does have a choice, i.e. where there is a relatively high concentration of installations with relatively many service calls of short duration. In that circumstance the Service Manager has the choice of structuring his Service Engineers into individual territories with reponsibility for customer service in that territory or the joining of a number of engineer territories into one, larger, mini-team territory in which between two and five engineers work together. Let us consider both alternatives.

In an individual territory the main advantage is the clear responsibility of one Service Engineer for servicing his customers and the consequent personal relationship that can be developed between the customer and the engineer. The engineer can also be clearly measured on his performance. But if we consider that out of every 52 weeks a Service Engineer will be out of his territory for 4 weeks for holidays, perhaps another week for sickness, and two weeks for training, we already have 7 weeks out of 52 when another engineer needs to assist the customer if he requires service. That is more than 1/8th of the time. In addition, the workload in an individual territory will fluctuate steeply but if a number of territories are joined, there will be a smoothing effect.

It is often not the consideration for customers, engineers or the company that make Service Managers want to implement individual engineer territories; it is, instead, for the Service Manager's own convenience, as he finds it easier to manage Service Engineers when he can get specific quantified data on the performance of individual engineers. However, management is not so simple, the figures will not manage for a manager – they are just one of the tools of management. Trying to manage Service Engineers "by the numbers" will only achieve manipulation of input data and a de-motivated service force, because it is an unjust way of judging engineers. For instance, one territory can have much more demanding customers than another which will affect the quantified evaluation of the engineer although he is not able to influence the result.

Let me give you a specific example in one tightly packed city. An office equipment manufacturer regularly measured the copy quality produced by his copiers and also asked the customers to express their level of satisfaction with copy quality. These evaluations regularly showed that the copy quality in Mid-Town Manhattan (part of New York) was high but customers were dissatisfied with it. On West-side Manhattan the opposite was true – copy quality was low but customers were highly satisfied with it. That is not surprising as in Mid-Town the headquarters of many companies are located and the quality of the copies must be such that it is presentable to customers. On the West-Side, where many of the warehouses are located, the main criteria was legibility. Can we really review engineers by numerical results only or does the subjective judgement of the manager also need to be considered?

In practice there are various alternatives in between the two extremes mentioned. In some companies a specific customer is allocated to a Service Engineer for all routine activities which are not very time sensitive (e.g. preventive maintenance calls, modification calls etc.) whereas corrective maintenance calls are shared between a small group of engineers. The members of the group should, as far as possible, be compatible, as their cooperation will be more harmonious.

National Organisation

At national level Service Managers will concentrate those activities which cannot be carried out as efficiently in the field. As a matter of principle, any support activity should be located as close to the field as is economically and operationally possible. Certain activities, however, will benefit by centralisation. In most companies it will not be economical to carry out formalised training in the field and this will need to be done nationally or even for a number of countries jointly. We will discuss this more fully in the next sub-section.

Other activities which often require some degree of centralisation include:

- □ Strategic decisions
- □ Asset management decisions including inventory policies
- □ Systems development (with end-user's input)
- □ Forward planning activities

In some companies, the time horizon will detemine where certain decisions will be made. The field will make the short term decisions (perhaps 0–3 months), at national level medium term decisions are made (say, 3 months – 2 years) at the corporate level the longer term decisions are made (2 years plus). The cut-off points are arbitrary and there must be involvement across these boundaries to ensure continuity.

International Co-operation

We have mentioned that certain activities may require greater centralisation than is possible in a national operation. A corporation should not let artificial barriers impede an efficient operation and ways should be found to utilise facilities to the full. In an European context it may not make sense to train German speaking Service Engineers from Austria or Switzerland separate from those coming from Germany. The training of Engineers for all three countries is likely to be identical from the technical point of view, although some of the administrative procedures may differ. These considerations do not necessarily apply to other functions – for instance, a different competitive or pricing situation may require a different approach by the Salesmen in the various countries. The expensive process of developing service documentation should also be made once only, even if the material needs to be translated.

In many companies re-charging procedures have been developed between Service Departments in different countries if this will give better support to customers or improve total profits. In this way customers in the north of Sweden may be supported by Service Engineers from Finland. The most efficient approach for Service Managers it to establish the best way of doing a particular task, initially ignoring artificial frontiers, and then establishing ways of overcoming any issues arising from the fact that these frontiers do exist.

As far as the structure of an international service operation is concerned, it is usual to have only minimal functional staff management at international level with the line management at national level being responsible to a country manager. This should not stop the National Service Manager from optimising the service operation in his own as well as in other countries, even if it means "buying" or "selling" certain services.

Minimising Sales/Service Conflict

As the sales and service force are working in the field together, yet have very different task assignments, there are frequently areas of conflict which management must try to minimise. Before management can do so, it must identify the likely areas of conflict, and only then will it be able to take appropriate actions.

Many issues arise from:

☐ lack of understanding of each other's problems

☐ unwillingness to adhere to company policies

☐ lack of understanding of the income structure and rewards

☐ short-term priorities by senior managers

Once the cause of the problem has been identified, management is in a position to consider remedial action. Let us examine the above mentioned issues:

Lack of understanding of each other's problems

The Salesman views the Service Engineer as a welcome "guest" at the customer, who goes there at the latter's invitation, repairs the fault and leaves a satisfied customer. He knows little about the pressure an Engineer works under when the customer needs the equipment urgently, and breathes down his neck to get it operational whilst the Engineer has not yet diagnosed the problem or, having diagnosed it, does not have the necessary tool or spare part to fix it. The Salesmen does not realise the difficulty of planning a Service Engineer's route to satisfy customers at different corners of a territory because, as a Salesman, he is used to being able to plan to spend most of the day in one corner of his territory and go to the other next day – he does not usually have response time pressures.

The Service Engineer, on the other hand, will tend to view the Salesman's job as an easy way of making a lot of money, he sees the Salesman as giving away extra warranty periods and free service and spending a good part of his time wineing and dining customers and potential customers. The Service Engineer knows little about cold canvassing and knocking on customers' doors, of pressure by the Sales Manager to get quick results or of the disappointment of losing an order, on which the Salesman has worked for some time, to a competitor.

Management can help a great deal by ensuring that there is a better understanding of each other's jobs by actions such as:

- ☐ Having a Sales Trainer spend two hours or so on service courses explaining the sales issues and a similar participation of a Service Trainer on sales courses.
- ☐ Having a representative of the other function at team meetings.
- ☐ Ensuring that information gained is propagated throughout the sales and service force.
- ☐ Creating a climate in which informal contact between Salesmen and Service Engineers can take place.
- ☐ Arranging for a formal communication channel for passing information from one function to the other and ensuring suitable feedback of resulting actions.
- ☐ Joint customer audits.
- ☐ Early warning to each other of likely problems (e.g. informing a Salesman if one of his customers has had a lot of calls on his machine, or warning Service of a peak load at a customer).

Unwillingness to adhere to company policies

All of us tend to take short-cuts to make our own job easier without realising the problems we cause other people. In one company, for instance, it was the duty of the Salesman to sell and arrange operator training at the time of selling the equipment. The average success rate was under 60%. In one Branch, however, the reported success rate was regularly in excess of 90%. I went to investigate – it had nothing to do with geography, transportation facilities or better premises. It was due entirely to the Sales Manager's attitude. He was convinced that operator training was beneficial so he made this clear to each Salesman by stating that he could accept orders only if they either included operator training details or had a statement from the Salesman explaining why he was unable to sell the operator training concept.

You will note, he did not refuse any order. In fact what he did was to clearly demonstrate to all Salesmen that he wanted them to sell operator training and they found that it was no big problem once they knew the manager meant business.

The answer, therefore, for company policies and procedures is either to enforce them in a disciplined way or, alternatively, to arrange for them to be changed or withdrawn. The alternative of simply ignoring them should not exist, as that makes it difficult for any employee to know which policies need to be followed and which can be ignored with impunity.

One of the frequent complaints in this context is overselling the capabilities of the equipment. This does not often occur with experienced Salesmen who have found that they are not doing themselves or their company any favour by overselling – it is much more prevalent in less experienced Salesmen who find it difficult to sell the positive benefits of their products. A quiet word by the Service Manager usually suffices to bring an errant Salesman into line – if not, then the Sales Manager must be involved.

Lack of understanding of the income structure and rewards

This tends to be a point of issue for Service Engineers who at times do not understand that Salesmen's commissions are an integral part of their income structure. It is part of the job of a Service Manager to make it clear to his force that no cross-functional comparisons are valid. The Service Engineer should examine whether he is reasonably paid for the job that he is doing. He has the option of applying for a Salesman's job if he has the capabilities and is willing to live with the greater fluctuation of income and the insecurity of the job.

What the Service Manager should ensure, however, is that the positioning of incomes within the industry is the same for both functions. If the company decides it wants to pay its Salesmen, say, in the second quartile of the industry's income structure, then the Service Engineers should be in a similar position in comparison with Service Engineers in other companies in the industry. What is much more difficult to explain is a different approach to "extra-ordinary" rewards, such as "Par Club" or 100% achievement trips which does not include Service Engineers as well. A good case can be made to offer similar benefits to the whole field force – as mentioned earlier, it may not be highly motivational to the bulk of the service force, but it is demotivational if part of the field force are eligible for special rewards and another part is not.

Short-term priorities by senior managers

This issue is difficult to surface but it tends to make managers at a lower level act irrationally which may cause conflict between Sales and Service. Let me illustrate by an example. The company in question had tight targets for both Sales and Service and both Salesmen and Service Engineers were working towards achieving these targets. Sales targets are usually apparent in the short term, i.e. often at the end of the month. Service targets are usually more medium term targets, as many aspects (such as Level of Service, Customer Satisfaction, etc.) become meaningless on a short term basis. In an endeavour to "help" the operation, senior management put pressure on the local manager to instal additional equipment by the end of the month. By doing so, support from Service to existing customers was reduced to free more Engineers to "crash" in a few more machines. Service Engineers interpreted this as pressure from Sales and it reflected on their attitude to Sales. It demonstrated to the Service Engineers a lack of recognition of the importance of their activity, re-enforcing the "second-class citizen" feeling.

The lesson to be learned may well be that conflict between Sales and Service can be minimised by:

☐ thinking through the effect of any action.

☐ understanding each other's problems.

☐ good communication.

☐ disciplined approach.

☐ stressing the interdependence on each other.

Service Productivity

Productivity in this context is not only the quantity of work performed but also its quality. This close link between quantity and quality is more evident in a service function than in many others, as a service call badly performed gives rise to an additional call. The measure of productivity will have to be different for each industry, as it cannot be tied to any universal parameter. Even in the same industry there may be a need for different standards of measurement both within a company (e.g. due to distance between equipments) and between companies (e.g. due to different reliability or serviceability). To understand productivity each Service Manager must appreciate what factors will affect it:

Factors affecting Productivity

We can divide these into various groups:

- □ Technical factors. These will include the basic reliability of the product, serviceability, tools and test equipment and similar aspects which a Service Manager cannot influence in the short term.
- □ Skill factors. These can be influenced by Service Managers by proper selection, training and OJT as well as by ensuring suitable back up.
- □ Logistic factors. These consist of the dispersion of equipments, ability to support the Engineer with spare parts and materials and the transportation available to him.
- □ Planning factors. Here the Service Manager plays a vital role in assuring adequate staffing, parts availability and proper territory and call planning procedures.
- □ Human factors. Even with the best product and well organised service operation, the Service Engineer's attitude and motivation will, to a large extent, determine productivity. In Service, which is not process driven, the willingness of the Engineer to give of his best will be of crucial importance to productivity.

Although I agree with the implication of the statement that we should stop measuring productivity and get on with inducing it, (i.e. that measurement without action will not improve productivity) I nevertheless believe that we need to measure it to show us where we are going and to help us plan the future. It is important to realise that the measurement of productivity to an excessive accuracy may detract us from developing programmes to increase productivity.

Optimising Utilisation

We have examined the relationship of utilisation to response time in Section III (Figure 22). Here we will look more closely at the way a Service Manager can optimise the utilisation of his service force. The most crucial aspect is to smooth the inevitable fluctuations of workload and to balance it with availability of service time.

It is most helpful if there are certain jobs which a Service Engineer needs to perform which are not highly time sensitive. This is where preventive maintenance (PM) activities are useful with certain provisos – the PM activity must not be delayed too long as it would then defeat the purpose of the PM procedure (i.e. prevent a breakdown), it must conform to the intervals agreed with the customer and individual PM calls should not last too long. One way used by some companies to ensure the first two of these three conditions are complied with is by suitable procedures in Work Control, e.g. one which lays down that if a PM call which has been scheduled has not been fitted in during the last, say, three days, it gets upgraded to the priority of a corrective maintenance call.

Other tasks which can be carried out during less busy times are routine car maintenance, fetching spare parts, off customer premises repair of modules, parts or assemblies, the completion of administrative reports etc.

Another aspect a Service Manager needs to establish is the pattern in which calls are received as this may enable him to predict peak demand and he can plan accordingly. We have mentioned the "Monday morning syndrome" in many service organisations, where a peak load often coincides with a valley in manpower availability – by re-scheduling controllable activities, these two factors can be brought more closely into balance (e.g. no meetings, no PM's, no installations, discourage days off, etc.).

Here we should mention again the smoothing effect a Service Manager can achieve by grouping his engineers into mini-teams wherever possible, to enable him to achieve a relatively high utilisation without detrimental effect on customers.

Even in a very efficient service organisation, there will be a need to accept that in a field operation there will be unproductive time and the task of the Service Manager is to balance the need for a certain level of service to customers with a reasonable utilisation of manpower.

Customer Care Programmes

The above activities to optimise the productivity of the Service Force must not be made at the expense of support to customers. They are intended to improve productivity whilst maintaining the real level of service (LOS) to customers.

In addition to the real LOS we can try and influence the customer's perception. One of the most important aspects of this is to show him that you, as a company, care. This can be achieved by the simple technique of asking him whether you are providing what he wants; we can do this through occasional questionnaires or, particularly with important customers, by having well planned customer audits. During these audits the departments most closely involved with the customer (usually Sales and Service) hold a joint meeting with relevant customer's personnel. The level of this review will depend on the importance of the customer.

Another important way of keeping customers happy is to keep them fully informed of planned changes. If, for example, you are planning to change from a single Engineer territory to a miniteam concept, tell the customer and explain the reason for the change, i.e. to give even better service to him. If you are establishing a new Work Control procedure, tell the customer how it will affect him and perhaps invite the relevant staff from the more important customers to look at it, demonstrating that your company is in the vanguard of service support and "selling" your company to the customer.

In some companies they have established User Associations where customers are invited to exchange ideas and help spread information on applications. In other companies they have Operator Clubs to enable Service to put across new concepts to a large audience.

Judgement must be used on which customer care programmes are going to favourably influence customers' perception. The same programme may have a different effect on different customers. If we are introducing a more frequent PM procedure to reduce corrective maintenance calls, some customers will see it as a positive approach to reduce breakdowns while others may simply see it as more frequent calls by the Service Engineer. The first customer will perceive an improved reliablility whereas the second one may see it as a deterioration. Often a careful explanation may bring more customers into the former group.

Training the Service Supervisor and Manager

Too often in the past, the best Service Engineer was told on a Friday afternoon that as from next Monday morning he would be the Service Supervisor, and no training was given to him to perform his entirely different job. If he was lucky, he had a good Supervisor himself and was observant enough to be able to follow the example, and, as the new Supervisor, he had an understanding Service Manager who would give him adequate on the job instruction.

More recently management has realised that the biggest step in a person's career path is the first step on the promotional ladder – this is the first time the person does not do the work himself but works through others. His individualistic skills as an Engineer may be of only limited use to him in his Service Supervisor's role. Having come to this conclusion, preparations for this major change in role will have to be made.

The training for a Service Supervisor falls into two separate areas. The first group are general management skills which are very similar in many functions, be it Sales, Service or Manufacturing. These skills are concerned with leadership, motivation of people, management concepts and techniques. The second one is the specific application of the general skills to the service function and to the job of Service Supervisor or Manager in that particular company.

General Management Skills

The most usual way of teaching this type of skills is in public or in-house courses where Supervisors and potential Supervisors from a number of functions are instructed together. The advantage of this approach is a broad background of experience and the consequent cross-fertilisation of functional knowledge. It is also of advantage to run these courses for potential managers and supervisors, i.e. prior to making a firm decision on promotion. It will give the candidate an opportunity to establish whether a managerial career is the right path for him and will also enable the company to observe his adaptability to different tasks and to colleagues from other disciplines. It can also be motivational for an Engineer to realise that he has not been forgotten and, even if he is not promoted, he learns something of the job of his manager.

Specific Service Management Skills

It is often difficult for a newly appointed Service Supervisor or Manager to know how to adapt the general skills of management to the Service Manager's job and to develop additional skills specific to Service. Some of the larger companies have therefore developed in-house training courses for the basic skills of Service Managers or they arrange for this type of course to be implemented in-house by outside specialists. Alternatively, there are now an increasing number of public courses being arranged in serveral countries for Service Supervisors/Managers from different companies and industries. In this latter case the course cannot be specific to the practices of any individual company or industry – it has a compensatory benefit, however, namely the possibility to learn how service management tasks are being performed in other industries and thus, perhaps, find ways of improved practices in your own industry. The specific skills are discussed throughout this book.

Human Relations Skills

This aspect of the manager's job is probably the most important area where the new Service Manager needs to change his approach. Obviously, human relation skills needed to be practiced by him when he was a Service Engineer but the way they are practiced now that he is a manager and their implication on the company is much greater. It is not the purpose of this book to go into details of human relationships as this subject has been written about extensively by Behavioural Scientists. I just want to stress the importance of this area in the service management field where the Service Engineer is often away from his base for extended periods. In the Service Supervisor's or Manager's role, his relationships with customers is also of increased importance, as, by the very fact of his new position, he is likely to talk to customers at a higher level and with greater authority. He must, therefore, be very adept at customer handling skills.

Service Revenue

The revenue generated by Service represents an increasing proportion of company revenues and profits. This is creating greater visibility of the Service function and its professional approach to the whole Service Business. Some companies are trying to highlight this increased importance by the creation of a Service Profit Centre or upgrading the level of service management.

In this context we will ignore the role of Service in the marketing of the company's product, but concentrate instead on the direct profit and revenue generated by Service.

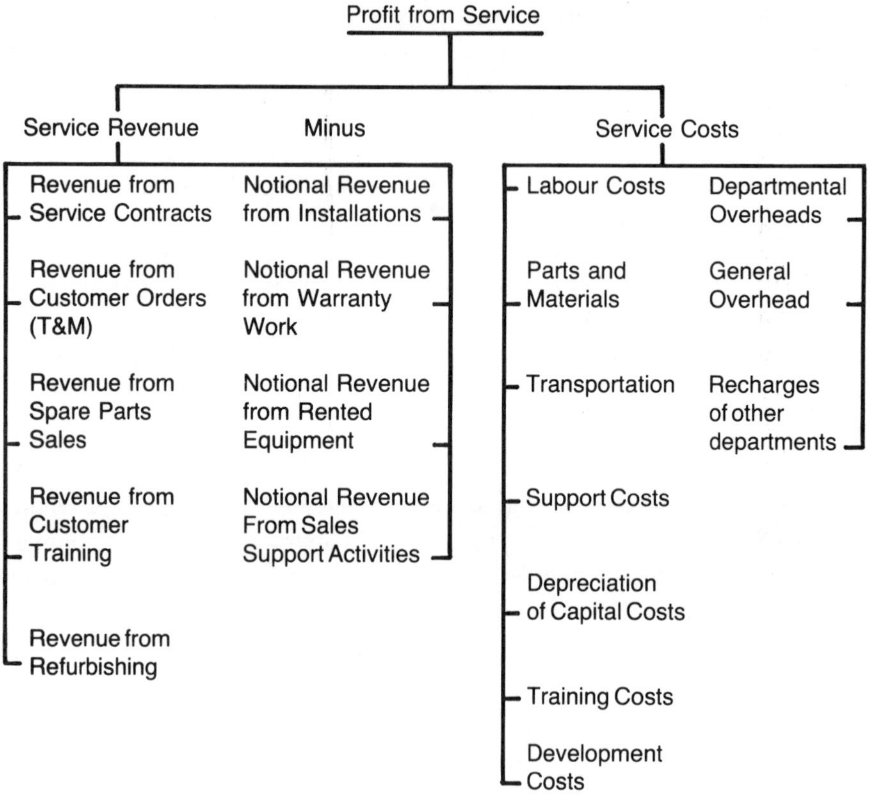

Figure 25. *Major Service Revenues and Costs.*

Income From Customers

The divison into income direct from customers and notional revenues, where the customer buys service as part of a bigger package (rental or warranty), is somewhat artificial. All companies will tend to attribute the direct revenue to the Service function but only some of them will make notional transfers for service work bought by customers together with the product or other services. It is considered good management practice to identify costs and revenues to the function that is responsible for causing the costs and generating the revenues.

Revenue from Service Contracts

Service contracts are usually the most efficient and profitable way of dealing with the provision of service to customers. The advantages to the manufacturer or dealer include:

- ☐ Simpler planning as workload and parts requirements are more predictable,
- ☐ Assured revenue, often in advance,
- ☐ Regular contact with the customer (upgrades, additions)
- ☐ Balancing of workload with PM and other activities
- ☐ Simpler administration as there are fewer orders and invoices.

The customer also has advantages from Service Contracts:

- ☐ No need to place rush orders when equipment breaks down
- ☐ Maintenance of company assets due to regular PM's
- ☐ Reduction in administrative costs (fewer orders and invoices)
- ☐ Known cost (insurance factor).

Due to the many advantages to both parties to the contract we should examine their pricing and effective selling more closely.

Most Service Managers have a good idea of the average cost of servicing a particular product configuration in a customer's location or at the company's own base. How should this be used in determining the price of a Service Contract? In the past it was often the only basis on which a price was determined. The average cost was uplifted by a certain percentage for "profit" and often prices were not reviewed for long periods of time nor their real profitability examined. This was due to the relative lack of interest of top management in Service and the lack of business acumen of Service Managers. It should not have surprised anyone to find that many contracts were not as profitable as assumed, as labour cost increases could not all be absorbed in higher productivity or improved product reliability, and some overheads were often not included in the cost base.

More recently, it has become the practice for the pricing of Service Contracts to be determined by the same method as other company pricing, i.e. by establishing what the market place was willing and able to pay for the service. It has become part of the total pricing strategy of the company. Once the value the market place puts on the Service Contract has been established, it is necessary to examine whether the total cost to provide the agreed service gives the company the desired margins. In some cases this may not be the case and it becomes necessary to examine what factors should be changed to achieve the desired margins (e.g. reduce the LOS, spread the overheads over more revenue by selling more contracts or taking on additional service commitments, reducing the cost base, examining whether a higher price could be justified to customers due to some unique feature of our service, etc.) If this is not possible, the decision needs to be taken by the company whether, as part of its total marketing strategy, it is willing to accept lower margins or whether to pull out of servicing completely and allow third parties to provide the support.

In some industries it is still usual to charge a certain percentage of the sales price of the equipment for an annual contract. With the changing of technology and of the market-place, this is becoming a less meaningful approach. High margins by the manufacturers and dealers in some industries have attracted a number of third party service companies into the business. These companies are often able to offer a good service at a reasonable price, as they are able to pick the most attractive contracts (e.g. in concentrated urban areas) and may not carry the same overheads as the manufacturer. The advantage of lower prices for the customer are often counterbalanced by a higher risk in dealing with third-party companies and the implied effect on retaining the value of the assets.

Once a pricing structure for Service Contracts has been established, the active selling of these contracts will be necessary. I am saying pricing structure (rather than price) advisedly, as it is likely to differentiate between various types of customers and customer needs (e.g. by distance from base, by LOS required by individual customers, by number of contracts, or other meaningful factors). Answers will have to be found to questions such as who should sell the contract, when should it be sold, what incentives should be given? Clearly, it will depend on the type of product we are talking about which will determine the answers. For instance the selling of a Service Contract for a paper mill will be a different kind of selling project than selling a Service Contract for typewriters. A few thoughts on the subject may help in finding the right answer in your case.

There are a number of good reasons why a Service Contract should be sold at the time of selling the product. A skilled Salesman is negotiating with the company's decision makers, who will be interested to insure that the value of the asset they just bought, be maintained. The Salesman is on customer's premises and therefore no additional time needs to be devoted to selling the contract. The continuity from installation through warranty period to the Service Contract is ensured.

The next best occasion is at the end of the Warranty period. The continuity of maintenance is assured, protecting the customer and enabling the company to plan the service. It will, however, require an additional negotiating session.

The next opportunity for trying to sell a contract arises the first time a Service Engineer is called out on a corrective service call. There has, by now, been a break in the continuity, a special visit has to be made by a Salesman, or a Service Engineer, who is not a specialist in selling, and he has to try and convince the company's decision maker to enter into a Service Contract.

It does appear, therefore, that trying to sell a contract at the time of selling the product has a number of advantages. The difficulty, in some cases, is to encourage a Salesman to do so. If commissions are on a proportionate basis of product price and contract price, the differential is often not sufficient to encourage a Salesman to sell a Service Contract. Some companies have, therefore, taken a different approach. They establish that the total package being sold to the customer is the product plus the Service Contract, for which a certain commission is paid. If only part of the package (i.e. the product only or the Service Contract only) is sold, the commission payable becomes considerably lower. At first these companies were concerned that their product sales activity may become adversely affected by this approach, but they found that once the Salesman understood that the company really wanted him to sell the total package, it did not act as an obstacle to the total sales effort, but was used by the Salesman as an additional sales aid.

The question of incentives to Service Engineers who sell Service Contracts needs to be treated with some care. On the one hand, the same incentive should be given to a Service Engineer who sells a Service Contract as to a Salesman who does so. On the other hand, care must be taken not to divert too much of a Service Engineer's time into a selling task and away from servicing, and the fact that for one of the tasks (selling) the Service Engineer receives a commission and for the other (servicing) he does not, may encourage him to spend a disproportionate amount of time on the former. In some companies a compromise has been reached by which the incentives for selling a Service Contract by the service force are shared by the whole service team which ensures a more balanced approach.

Revenue from Customers' Orders (T&M)

In addition to offering Service Contracts, most companies also provide service to customers on a Time and Materials (T&M) basis. In this case planning is very much more difficult and the customer may often have to wait until the Service Department's contractual obligations have been fulfilled before T&M

requests can be attended to. It also means that the customer has to generate an order for each call and invoices for relatively small amounts will have to be handled by both the company and the customer. Also, in many products of modern design, the cost of individual modules may be quite high, and although the failure occurs in few instances only, the customer who does have the failure may incur high costs. In calculating the costs of a Service Contract, these rare but high parts costs are spread across the total population whereas in a T&M service call each customer is charged for the individual items (either new or refurbished).

Nevertheless, a proportion of customers will prefer to carry out a part of the servicing and maintenance activities themselves and call in the manufacturer only where his special knowledge, skill or tool is required. In some industries there has been a trend for increasing customer servicing activity on a do-it-yourself (DIY) basis and the design of some products is catering for this trend. The revenue and profit from Service for the manufacturer is generated by the sale of spare parts, tools, test equipment, service manuals and training programmes.

Revenue from Spare Parts

We have just mentioned that in some industries there is a carefully planned trend to encourage customers to do their own servicing and to make the profit from spare parts and associated items. Spare parts can provide a good source of revenue and profit for a company. In the motor car industry, for instance, the manufacturer of the initial part used by the car producer makes little profit on his sale to the car manufacturer but he makes it from subsequent sales for replacement purposes.

Pricing policies vary substantially and often provide for higher margins on unique items manufactured to the maker's specification whereas generic items carry a lower mark-up.

The cost of parts must include a suitable allowance for spare parts holding and handling costs, the high cost of money and the danger of obsolescence. All these costs are frequently underestimated – we will discuss this more fully in the next section, Section V, Inventory Control.

Revenue from Customer Training

This revenue arises not only from the training of customers to service their own equipment, but also from the training of customers in the operation or handling of the product and its accessories. It also includes the sale of instruction manuals and similar documentation. All these aspects have become big business in some industries.

In some companies, revenue is also generated by training staff from third-party service organisations who will compete with the company's own staff in the field. In many countries it would be illegal to refuse training to third-party organisations if such training is offered to customers.

Revenue from Refurbishing

Another area where Service is generating revenues and profits for the company is in refurbishing machines, modules or parts. In some instances Service carries out the repair work, whereas in others it acts as an intermediary between the customer and Manufacturing or the initial supplier of the components, or it subcontracts the repair work. In all instances this should be a lucrative source of income for Service.

The location of the repair facility must depend on the complexity of the work involved, the tools, spares, test equipment and skills required for the repair and on distances involved. In many instances adequate repair can only be effected where a certain batch size is handled – some countries put restrictions on the importation and exportation of second-hand items.

There is a trend in the design of products to change whole modules either by the customer or by the Service Engineer and to repair them with the aid of specialised equipment (e.g. automated test equipment (ATE) in the case of printed circuit boards). It is a tedious operation to locate the fault by other means, except where a fault pattern has been established.

Notional Revenue from Installations and Warranties

The expense of installing a new product and service it during the warranty period is usually included as part of the sales price of the product, where applicable (in some instances no installation by the manufacturer/dealer is necessary). Service Managers need to keep records of the installation and warranty work carried out so that they can ensure that the transfers into service revenues adequately compensate them for the work the department performs.

These notional revenues are just as real a part of service income as revenues collected direct from customers. Certain expenses associated with revenues direct from customers do not arise from these activities, i.e. selling, invoicing and collection expenses.

Warranties are increasingly used as marketing tools by some companies (e.g. 3 year unlimited warranties on cars or TV sets). The principles mentioned in the preceding paragraph again need to be applied by Service Managers, as the cost of this marketing approach needs to be cleraly identified and costed. If the costs are submerged in a pile of other costs, the implications to the company may not be so easily identifiable.

Notional Revenue from Rented Equipment

The same considerations apply in this case as in the previous paragraphs on installations and warranties. The difference for rented equipment is that it is a permanent arrangement, whereas both installations and warranties occur only once, when the customer buys the equipment.

Notional revenue from rented equipment is, in most companies, treated like a Service Contract for sold equipment, although some may calculate an allowance for the reduced cost of not having to sell or administer the Contract. With equipment on rental the Service Manager has the added alternative of being able to change a customer's machine if it turns out that the performance of the equipment is below standard or its age and usage make continued service too expensive.

Notional Revenues from Sales Support Activities

Any specific support given by Service to Sales for activities such as exhibitions, demonstrations or special events should be recharged to ensure proper control of these activities. It will help Sales Managers to establish the net benefit of these activities to the company with the full knowledge of expenses incurred which, in turn, will lead to better management decisions.

These notional revenues will also ensure the whole-hearted support from Service to these activities, particularly if they were included in the initial planning process.

Service Costs

Although Figure 25 shows a rough breakdown of these costs, we need not enter into detailed discussions on this subject here as they are covered in other parts of this book. They need to be borne in mind when we consider Service profitability, as there are few, if any, opportunities for service revenues which do not also generate service costs. We must never forget that profit contribution is one of the basic goals of Service.

Marketing Service

Elsewhere, we are talking about Service as an integral part of the package marketed by a company. Here we will discuss the Marketing of Service.

Service is as much part of the offering of a company as the product or its consumable materials (e.g. film for cameras). In the past, companies have marketed the product and its consumables very forcefully, but the marketing of Service is a relatively new phenomenon. Among the reasons for this recent increase in the marketing of Service has been the realisation of its revenue and profit potential, its particularly attractive return on assets and the increased competition from other companies who have recognised this lucrative source of profit and who want a slice of it.

This publication will not discuss marketing techniques as these are similar for the "Service Package" and for other products or services being marketed, and a wealth of literature is available on this subject. The only recommendation I would extend in these pages is for Service Managers to be fully involved in the creation and implementation of marketing programmes for Service and to examine its implications thoroughly.

Summary of Section IV

- ☐ In this Section we dealt with the complex subject of Service Management, covering the broad area of managing the service force, identifying and optimising service productivity, the training of Service Supervisors and Managers and, ultimately, the increasing emphasis being placed by top management on service profits and market share by increasing service revenues.

- ☐ We covered the human factors in a service group, the motivation of individuals and the help a well-structured organisation can provide. We also discussed the external human relationships with customers and with Sales.

- ☐ We identified the need for understanding the individual parameters which affect service productivity and how Service Managers can positively influence them.

- □ We established that the first step on the management ladder has most changes in approach attached to it which will necessitate suitable preparation of new candidates through well designed training programmes. This education can be provided partially by generic management and potential management courses and seminars, and partially by specific service orientated programmes.

- □ During our examination of service revenues and profits we established the increasing proportion of company profits in many industries being generated by Service and the consequent increased need in the professional approach to handling financial matters. This created the need to examine different methods of generating service revenues, and of accounting for notional revenues hidden within other company charges to the customer. This has also necessitated a more aggressive marketing and selling of Service.

SECTION V

Management Tools for Service Management

Service Reporting

Identifying Need and Resulting Actions

One of the difficulties in developing a reporting system is the decision as to the detail to which service information needs to be reported. There is a tendency to either endeavour to collect and analyse every bit of detailed information or to go to the other extreme and not record any data.

The decision must clearly depend on the purpose for which the data is being collected and what actions will be generated from their analysis. If we are servicing aircraft, for instance, then it will be essential to report every detail of the activities we perform as there is a firm requirement to keep detailed logs of all changes. If, on the other hand, we service bicycles, then the level of reporting will not need to be as detailed, or can be eliminated completely.

It is good practice for Service Managers to examine their reporting procedures and practices at regular intervals, as the needs of every organisation will change with time. Reports which may be essential during a particular phase of the company's development (or that of a specific product's), may not be needed at a later date and vice versa.

The crux of a decision to collect and store service data must be made on the use that will be made of each of piece of data, and the frequency of its utilisation. Whereas the manipulation of data has become relatively inexpensive due to the wider use of computers and the reduction of cost per bit of information, the collection and inputting of this data is an expensive process. The conclusion from this technological fact must be:

(a) collect only information which will be needed for action oriented decisions.

(b) collect that information only to the level required (e.g. in some cases sampling may be quite adequate).

(c) utilise the same information as widely as possible i.e. do not input the same data more than once (e.g. the spare parts usage report can be utilised for restocking Engineer vehicles, interface with Distribution and Inventory systems, and initiate billing and accounting actions).

Although all the above statements may seem self – evident, I am always surprised to find that, in practice, issues arise from not applying them consistently. This may mean that some essential information is not available to management, that other data is collected to an unnecessary degree of detail, and not used by management, or that the same data is input in different formats to various functional systems and management then wastes time in resolving the difference.

We established that reporting can be quite costly and the affordability of developing the system needs to be established. The other face of the same coin must also be examined, i.e. the likely cost of not having the information when required.

Data Collection

The method of collecting information can also vary depending on the volume of data, the speed with which it is needed and the dispersion of the Engineers. The information to be collected consists usually of certain fixed information such as

(i) Customer name and address

(ii) Machine type, serial number, configuration

(iii) Operator name, machine location

and variable information such as

(iv) Date and time of customer request for call

(v) Reported fault

(vi) Time Engineer dispatched

(vii) Time Engineer arrived at customer

(viii) Work time and travel time and mileage

(ix) Fault found and cause of failure

(x) Other work perfomed (e.g. PM, modifications)

(xi) Parts used and location of stock

(xii) Meter reading (mileage, time, units etc)

The level of detail will depend on the use being made of the information.

It is not unusual for certain parts of the information to be provided for each service call whereas detailed data is only made available on a sample of the population.

Many of the input parameters are often coded to make it easier for the Engineer to pass the information to base and for the data to be encoded.

The information can be in a variety of formats

- ☐ Written document
- ☐ Coded punch card which can be encoded manually or by an optical character reader (OCR)
- ☐ Over the telephone to be input by work control (see below)
- ☐ Direct input by Engineer through a portable, audio coupled, terminal.

The layout of each form must be made to suit the industry involved.

It will be evident that the fixed information has already been recorded when the call from the customer was received by the Work Controller or Dispatcher or Telephonist, as well as some of the variable information. If we refer to the 12 items enumerated at the beginning of this sub-section, items (i) to (vi) are available to the Work Controller. It is therefore wasteful to record the same information again by the Engineer in his report and it is therefore recommended to investigate the feasibility of reporting through Work Control (see pages 143–150 later in this section).

Administrative Needs

LOTS OF CUPS OF TEA!

This need can usually be broken down into three areas utilising the same or similar information.

- ☐ For control purposes
- ☐ For planning purposes
- ☐ For marketing purposes

Control purposes

To enable a company to offer a customer a certain level of service (LOS), the company must be able to establish where it stands at the moment, what parameters affect the LOS and how management can influence these parameters. Once a specific LOS has been agreed with the customer, the company must be in a position to measure the achievement of this LOS to satisfy iteself as well as the customer. This usually involves an analysis of items (iv) to (viii) of the above list. It is also a useful tool to identify strengths and weaknesses in the performance of individual Engineers or groups of Engineers.

Planning purposes

It will be difficult for any company to make realistic plans for the future without a knowledge of what is happening out in the field at the present time. Current trends may need extrapolation and the anticipated results of action programmes must be superimposed. The effectiveness of the plans, in turn, are measured by comparing actual reported results with the plan.

Marketing purposes

The after-sales service support a company provides has become an integral part of the marketing mix offered to a customer. To enable a Salesman to offer a particular LOS to the customer, he needs to have the confidence of knowing what current LOS is being delivered. It also enables marketing management to decide, together with Service, what any change of LOS would add or subtract from the cost base and what benefit could be gained in the market-place by this change. This enables the company to offer flexible LOS and associated contract terms to the customer. For all these activities a reliable reporting basis is required.

Technical needs

In this case, also, the information from the reports is required for current and future product purposes. The areas of particular interest will be item (ix) of the collected information (Fault found and cause of failure), its associated

Work time (item viii), a comparison of (v) (Reported fault) with item (ix), item (x) (other work performed), (xi) (Parts used) and (xii) (meter reading). Obviously this will be of interest in relationship to item (ii), (machine type, serial number and configuration).

Suitable analysis of the reported information in conjunction with the product specification will identify priority areas for technical improvement. In the instance of a mature product the depth of technical reporting and analysis can frequently be reduced, as further changes are unlikely to be introduced, although some overall trends need to be followed to establish the time a product should no longer be supported. (see also under sampling, pages 137 and 141).

The problem areas of current products also give a good indication to technical management on the design and manufacture of future products.

In some companies it is standard practice for technical management, consisting of Design, Manufacturing, Service, and Quality Assurance to meet at regular intervals to review technical issues highlighted by the reports or by suggestions from the field. This group decides whether action will be taken on the current model in the field (e.g. modification or different component), on future production of the current model, or on future models only. This decision needs to be carefully recorded and progressed to ensure that the relevant decisions have been appropriately implemented by the function concerned.

Parts Needs

The service report not only provides Distribution and Inventory Control with usage details of a part but frequently also with information from where the part was obtained (customer's stock, Engineer's own imprest stock, local store, main warehouse).

This will enable Service and Distribution to jointly determine the echelon at which parts should be held. We will discuss this more fully under Inventory Control.

The basis of the whole inventory planning system must be the usage of parts in the field rather than the issues from stores and this is where the information provided by the Service Engineer's report is essential.

It also enables the company to establish the relative performance of new versus reconditioned parts and, if suitably coded, parts from different plants or suppliers. It must be remembered that the failure applies to the part in the machine and not to the part now being installed. Provided this information is used to take some action, it is a useful tool for management to run an efficient organisation.

Expense and Mileage Reports

There is usually no difficulty in getting an Engineer to write out an Expense Sheet (unless, of course he has had expenses in advance). For this reason, some companies tie the submission of Expense Reports to the submission of other, less popular, reports. The Expense Report is an essential tool for the Service Manager to keep his costs under control and the Mileage Reports may well indicate to him the need to review engineer or team territories or to discuss the placement of equipments with his colleagues in Sales.

Special Reports

If we have decided to limit regular reporting to the essentials and have coded the information which will be reported, we may need special reports for specific occasions to enable Service Engineers to communicate useful information to their own management and to other functions.

(i) Launch Reporting

At the time of launching a new product it is desirable to have more detailed reports from the field on the performance of the new equipment and encourage suggestions for improvements. At this stage it may also be more difficult to establish a meaningful coding of faults, as the fault pattern is not yet established.

The reporting cycle may need to be short-cut to make reports on the performance of new products available as quickly as possible to the whole technical community of the company. This may mean analysing reports on a weekly, instead of a monthly basis, analysing them in greater depth, and giving rapid access for Service Engineers from the field to HQ Service and/or Design staff ("Hot Line" – direct 24 hour telephone access).

(ii) Installation Reports

Any faults found during the installation of an equipment need to be fed back immediately and specifically to Manufacturing and Distribution, so as to safeguard against the same problem re-curring on the production line or in transport and handling.

The trend in the number of faults found during an installation are a more meaningful measure of manufacturing quality than the acceptance rate by Quality Control. The service reports reflect the "real life" situation and Quality Assurance procedures should be adapted to the critical acceptance of the product by the customer and the Service Engineer.

(iii) Defect Reports

Any component which reaches the field in a faulty condition requires a similar approach as a faulty new machine. A short-circuit report back to Service HQ and from there to Manufacturing, Quality Assurance and Distribution should ensure a minimum period before the problem is corrected to limit the number of defective components produced.

(iv) Sampling

Once a sufficient number of equipments are in the field and the product is fairly mature, it may not be necessary to have full technical reporting from the whole product population. Nevertheless it may be desirable to continue monitoring the technical performance of, at least, a statistically representative sample. The method of selection may vary – for instance, one can choose a geographical area or a serial number of product (e.g. every installation whose serial number ends with an "8") or other suitable alternatives.

It is advisable not to choose the whole sample in one area, as the quality of an individual manager may influence the reported problems.

Validity of Reports

The usefulness of reports is dependent on the quality of the input – hence the adage of "GIGO" (garbage in – garbage out). It is therefore essential for service management to ensure that the data provided by the Service Engineers is as factual as possible.

This is not as easy a task as it might at first appear, particularly if the Service Manager uses the output of the reporting system to beat the Service Engineer about the head. As we have seen earlier, inexperienced managers sometimes believe that figures can manage for them. They must realise that reports are only one (even though an important one) of the tools in the service management kit.

There are various ways to encourage accurate reporting:

- ☐ Make it clear to the Service Engineer why we require the information and how it is used to improve the operation.
- ☐ Give the Engineer feed-back from his reports.
- ☐ Utilise reports for the purposes for which they are intended and do not try to "manage by the numbers".
- ☐ Use the report for frequent counselling of the Service Engineer and pick up any problems immediately to show him your genuine interest in improving his performance.
- ☐ Arrange reporting through Work Control as this minimises or completely eliminates written reports by Engineers and, in addition, ensures that a part of the input is outside the area of manipulation by the Engineer.

Finally, do not expect excessive precision from a report. If, for instance, we require an Engineer to report the time spent on each of a number of activities he carried out at a customer, we cannot expect him to keep looking at his watch and record each action. He will probably know when he started work and when he finished work at a customer, but a break down of individual activities will only make him guess at the individual periods of time.

Service Control

The control of the service force through an efficient telephone centre is probably the most crucial administrative area of Service to enable it to satisfy customer needs effectively without incurring excessively high costs for the company. This is particularly true for companies who have a relatively large number of Engineers working in a reasonably tight geographical area – if there is only one Engineer in a city, the telephone centre is merely a message transmission unit. Where a number of Service Engineers are dispatched from the centre, it becomes the nerve centre of the local operation and is usually referred to as Work Control.

Work Control

Thus the task of Work Control is to

(i) receive customer requests for service

(ii) check customer status

(iii) record the relevant information

(iv) prioritise Service Engineer activities

(v) pass the request for service to the Service Engineer

(vi) note the time the call has been passed to the Engineer

(vii) receive Engineer information of call completion (and allocate his next call)

(viii) update customer records

(ix) send reports to computer centre.

Figure 26 illustrates these tasks graphically.

The aids available to Work Control will vary from company to company depending on the size of the operation and its sophistication.

In its simplest form, the records are just slips of paper stored in a customer record file. The more usual way of keeping these records in a summarised form is on customer record cards which are stored in a suitable system either alphabetically or by customer number. This preprinted card usually has fixed information at the top where it is easily visible to the Work Controller and the variable call information is entered on each line of the card. The more sophisticated service organisations have a fully computerised Work Control Centre; this does not necessitate a very large company, some medium sized companies utilise a fully computerised Work Control Centre, but instead of controlling the operation of one or two branches only, or of a country, they control the activity of a much larger area. For instance, one medium sized company I know controls the activities of all their Western European Service Engineers from one computerised Work Control Centre in Germany.

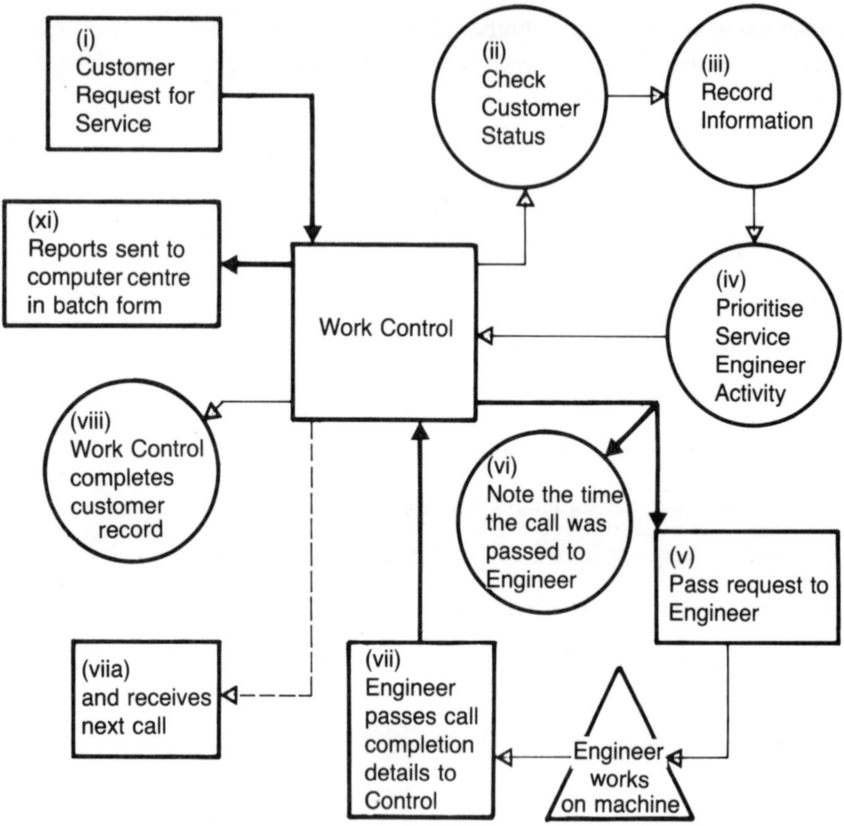

Figure 26. *Work Control Function*

The actual information recorded and tasks performed are identical for the manual or the computerised system – in most companies Work Controllers or service management have the opportunity to override the calculated priority if this is considered desirable. The amount of pre-planning of calls will differ from system to system, and I have seen both manual and computerised systems which indicate an overload which may arise, well in advance of it occuring which is, of course, the essential information for Service Managers to act on. If they wait until the overload happens, management can only sweep up the debris.

Let me describe a simple manual system which enables a Work Controller to foretell that he will not be able to meet his response time commitment. Customer records are maintained in alphabetical order on narrow cards with the slots at the bottom offsetting each card by the width of the "Name" column (see Fig 27), and a number of cards fit into each section of the cabinet. Each cabinet contains perhaps 2000 customer cards.

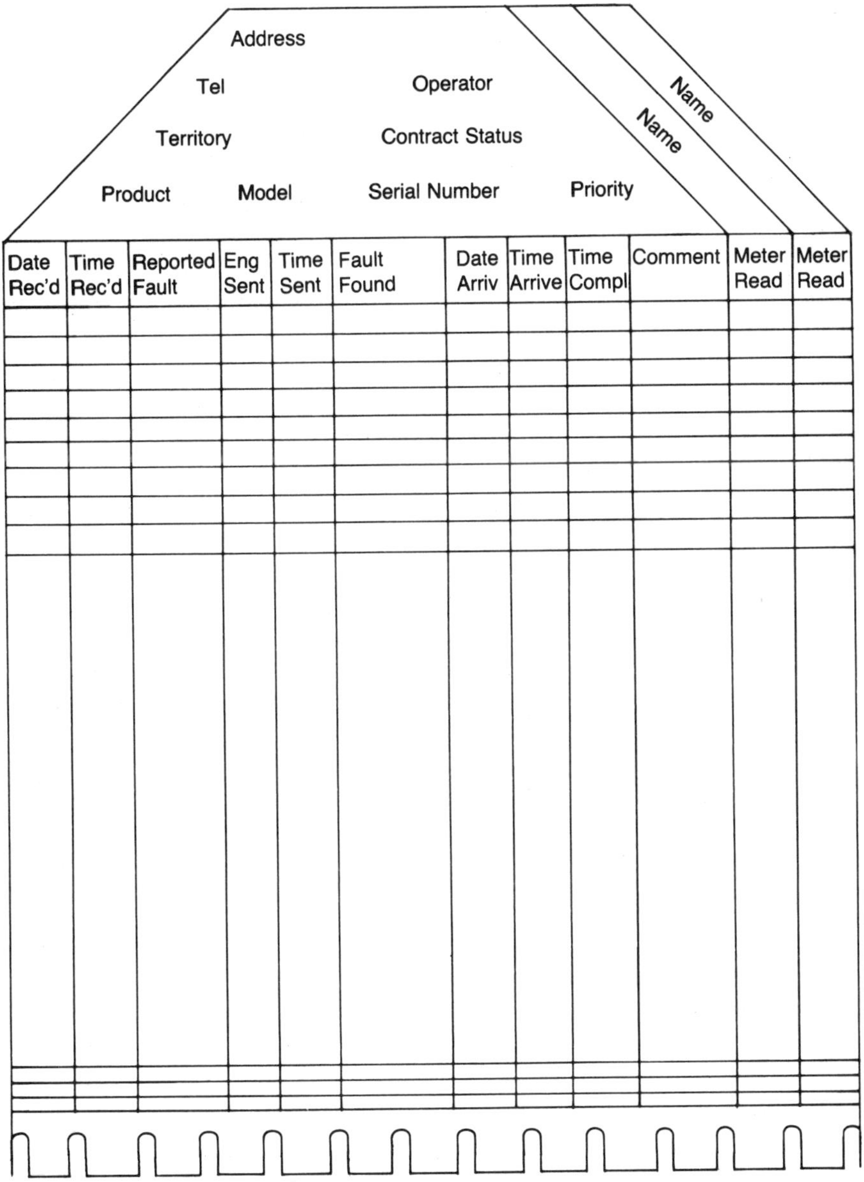

Figure 27. *Two Record Cards (example)*

When the customer telephones, the relevant card is located and withdrawn from the cabinet, the serial number of the equipment checked with the customer, the machine status is noted and the time and the reported reason for the service call entered (in coded form) on the next line of the record card. The static information on the card indicates the territory in which the equipment is located and the card is allocated to a particular rack which displays the activities of this particular team. The card also indicates the response time priority of this particular installation.

An example of a display rack is shown in Figure 28. The top of the rack is divided into hourly or half hourly columns showing today and tomorrow (today's "Tomorrow" becomes tomorrow's "Today" and today's "Today" becomes tomorrow's "Tomorrow" so that the sequence of the two days changes from the left to the right of the display every day). Let us now assume that the call is received at 9 a.m. and the response time requirement is 3 hours. The card is then inserted into the slot at 12 mid-day (9 a.m. + 3 hours).

When the call is allocated to a Service Engineer, a magnetic disc marked with the Engineer's name is attached to the card, indicating that the Engineer is working on (or travelling to) the machine.

The Work Controller, the Service Manager and any other authorised person entering the area can therefore see at a glance whether any cards without a disc are in the display unit on the left of the present time which indicate that planned response time has been exceeded.

The planning area of the display unit consists of a number of magnetic strips indicating the total time available to each mini-team. The standard time for a service call of the type reported by the customer plus average travel time is represented by a length of magnetic block. As the card is put into a particular slot on the display, the Work Controller selects a length of block (representing the standard time required for the work for the reported fault plus travel) and adds it to the strip. By comparing the length of strip (mini-team time available) with the lengths of bars representing the time committed to work and travel, the Work Controller can forecast overloads in any area and alert service management to take action before response time promises have not been met (e.g. by moving a "floater" into the mini-team area, postponing PM's or modification work, getting assistance from other mini-teams etc.). Early warning enables an action to be initiated.

If the time at present is 11 a.m. and all response time targets are being met, there should be no cards on the board without an Engineer's disc attached to it on the left of 11 a.m.

When the Engineer completes his customer call he will phone his Work Control, give the relevant information on time travelled, time worked, fault

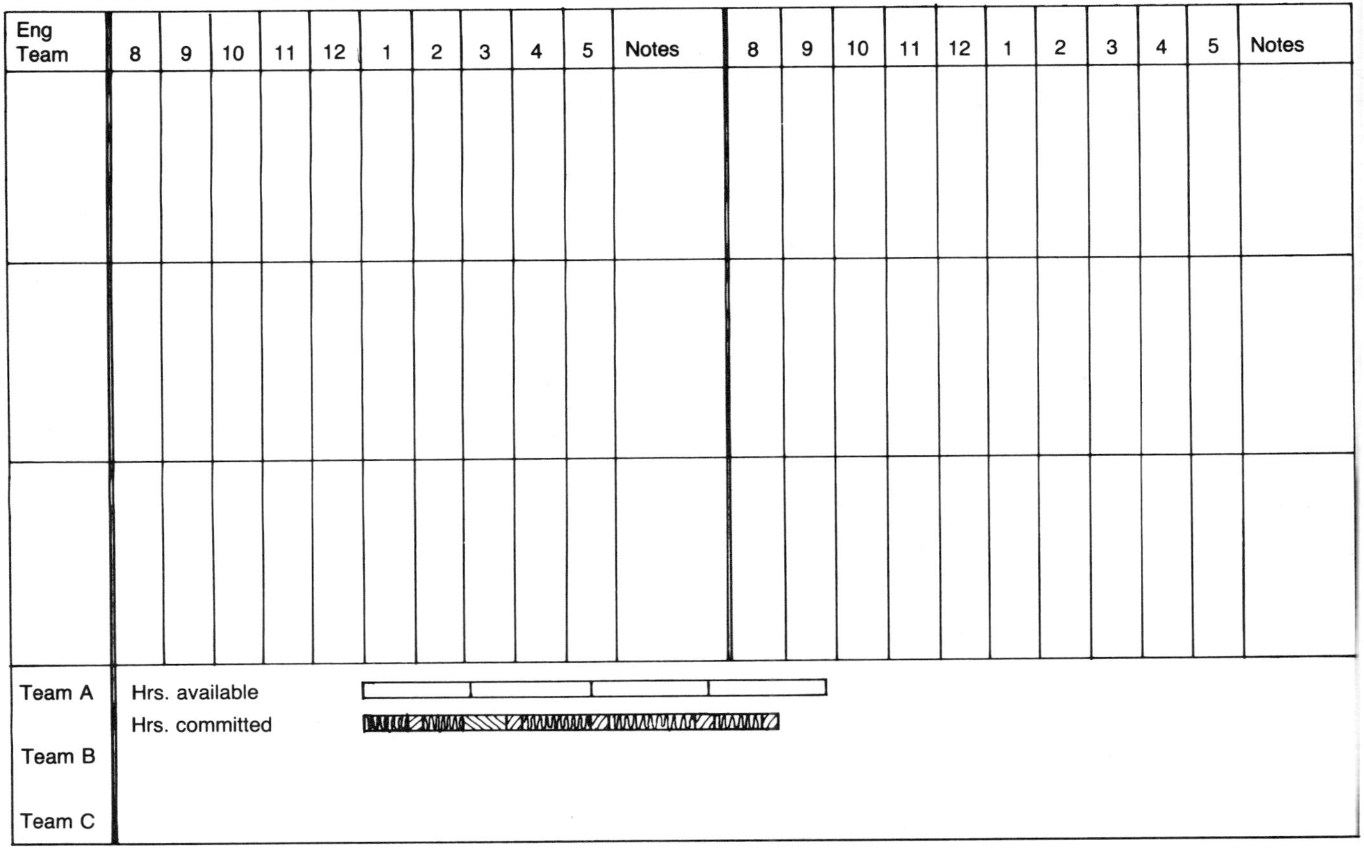

Figure 28. *Example of display unit*

found and meter reading to the Work Controller who will complete his record card which he has removed from the rack. He will also note any spare part used which will be notified to the warehouse for replenishment purposes as well as to the reporting system for Accounting, Service and Engineering needs. At the same time the Service Engineer is given his next service call and the whole process starts again.

Various refinements in the system can be introduced by, for example, colour coding products, using tags to indicate due time for PM's or Contract renewal, modification status indication etc.

In a computerised Work Control system the identical process takes place except that no writing is necessary. The Work Controller calls up the customers records on his VDU screen and adds the new call on his keyboard. He then has the choice of a number of displays on the screen which will show him the prioritisation calculated by the computer from the predetermined prioritisation criteria. This does not preclude the Work Controller from overriding the calculated priority based on his own knowledge and experience. The computer would also "know" the products on which an Engineer is trained and holds a list of spare parts currently in the Engineer's vehicle stock. Every time a part from this stock is used the system updates this information; replenishment details are also input, so that the data is always up to date. The computerised Work Control is linked to the Inventory Control system so that each bit of information is input only once to satisfy all (Service, Inventory, Accounting) systems.

Many computerised Work Control systems also have diagnostic facilities programmed in to enable telephone "Call Avoidance" to be performed by Work Control or to indicate to the Engineer the likely cause of the fault and any spare part he will need to resolve the problem.

Both manual and computerised Work Control systems are also used for giving service management rapid information on crucial aspects of the operation, such as distribution of response times around the average. In a manual system, all that is needed is for the Work Controller to put a cross into the relevant column of response time duration when the Service engineer reports his call completion details (Figure 29). Response time can be read direct from the card by calculating the number of work hours between the "Time Arrived" and "Time Received". This will automatically generate a distribution curve.

In a computerised work control system this information is generated automatically. Some companies, who do not have a computerised work control system, provide the response time distribution to their management through a very simple program on a micro-computer.

Due to the importance of minimising waiting time of customers (and engineers) when telephoning Work Control, there are instruments available on the market which will measure and print out on demand, a wide range of information on how long customers and engineers have been waiting before the call has been answered, the time of day the call was received, duration of call, etc., which enables service management to plan their activities more effectively. For instance, if it is found that first thing in the morning more calls are received and therefore waiting time is longest, management can arrange for Service Engineers to telephone the previous night for their first call to leave more Work Controllers to answer customers' calls, to ensure full manning of all work control stations first thing in the morning and, if necessary, draft other staff into Work Control at that time. In some companies customers have different telephone numbers from Service Engineers to call Work Control.

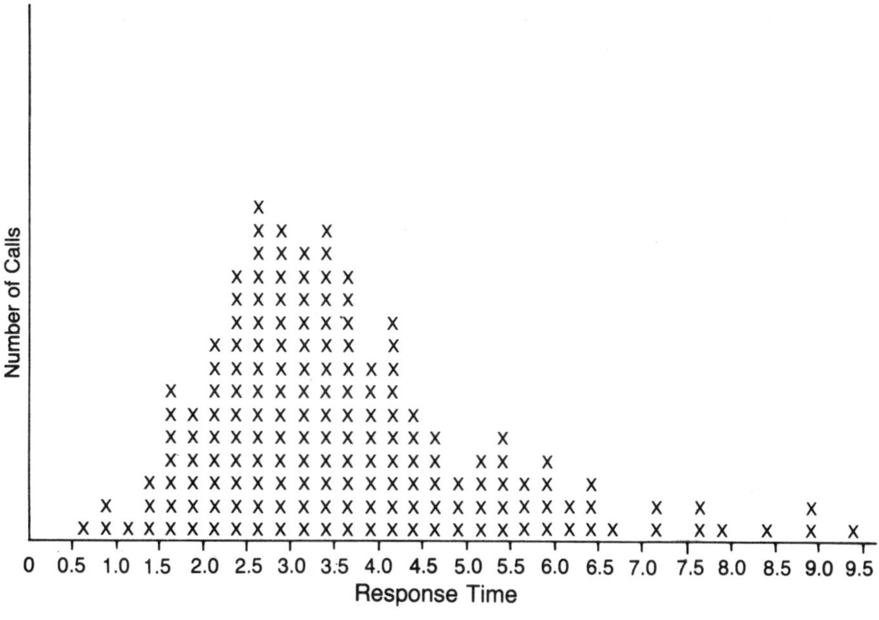

Figure 29. *Example of a Response Time Distribution Curve (Average 3.5 hours approx.)*

As you will see, the Work Control Centre is an essential tool for service management in every size of company to plan the work and stay in touch with its Service Engineers in the field. Service Managers should make it a habit to spend a few minutes in Work Control a number of times every day when they are in the office. When they are out of the office, Work Control should always be aware where the Service Manager can be reached.

Reporting through Work Control

We have covered this subject in an earlier sub-section in operational terms. The clear advantage of this approach is the immediate availability of the data at the base location, the elimination (or at least reduction) of the need for Service Engineers to write reports on their visits, the completion of the reports by personnel at a desk and the consequent increased legibility which is particularly important where OCR (optical character reading) techniques are used for inputting the data, the more accurate input of time related information and other associated benefits.

The only time an Engineer may have to complete a written report is on Time and Material calls, where the customer pays for the specific service rendered and parts supplied. In these cases a written report from the Service Engineer may be necessary which usually needs to be countersigned by the customer. This may be an incentive to an Engineer to sell a Maintenance Contract as he is unlikely to cherish the idea of writing reports.

The opportunity of ensuring that all data is captured and in some instances also validated makes the reporting through Work Control an attractive proposition.

Where a computerised Work Control system is in operation the program will validate a certain amount of the input data on line, so that correction can immediately be requested. For instance, if an Engineer reports that he used a certain part number while servicing a product but that part is not used on that particular product, the system will not accept the information and the Work Controller will query the input with the engineer prior to passing on to the next input parameter. The same applies if usage of a part is reported which is not shown in the Engineer's inventory.

In most automated systems the information collected during the day on the local mini-computer is sent in batch form overnight to the central computer from where reports are generated. The information is updated and next morning all information in the Branch is completely up-to-date.

The combination of an efficient Service Reporting system and a well organised Work Control is a powerful management tool for Field Service Managers.

Management use of Data

The danger of having such a powerful tool in the field is the excessive reliance by field service management on the reporting system to manage their operation. The manager must always remember that the reporting and work control systems are only tools for him to use. He must never forget that he is dealing with individuals both in his negotiations with his customers and in his guidance of his Engineers. This does not mean he should ignore the information gained through the reports but the very opposite – the information should encourage him to look more deeply into the issues raised.

The modern techniques tend to be built up in such a way as to make a balanced approach feasible. In the past the company had the alternative of providing a great deal of information to its Field Service Managers or to give them only limited reports. In the former case, Service Managers were flooded with information which they either ignored, spent a disproportionate amount of time analysing or they only read selected parts of the total report.

In present systems it is usual for summarised information to be printed at regular intervals and drawing managers' attention to a statistically significant deviation from either standard or average. If there is no clear understanding by the Service Manager why this deviation has occurred (e.g. he might know that his branch had been hit by a 'flu epidemic and that is why his Engineers worked an excessive amount of overtime), he has the opportunity of accessing the system and to obtain data in greater depth on any part of his operation.

It is not recommended to link the results shown by the reporting system directly with Service Engineer Performance Reviews – it is preferable to deal immediately with the issues arising from reporting with the engineer concerned in a constructive counselling discussion rather than storing the information for the relatively rare review times.

Service Managers should use the information from the reporting and work control systems to identify

☐ Areas of imbalance in customer support

☐ Variance in Service Engineer performance

☐ Deviations from financial, manpower or reliability plans.

I would stress, again, that these reports are only useful if they are utilised to generate action. This action may be to find out what a successful Engineer or team of Engineers does differently from others, introduce changes in approach or procedures, counsel weaker performers, arrange training programmes, rearrange territories, establish causes for shortfalls in reliability or profits and introduce remedial activities.

Frequent issues arising in Work Control are

□ Variations in load between days of the week and hours of the day

□ Reluctance of Engineers to take calls in the latter part of the afternoon

□ Complaints of delays.

Once the pattern of the problems has been analysed, it is usually possible to take actions to improve the situation, e.g. meetings and training sessions can be arranged for off-peak days, rest periods can be planned outside peak load in the mornings, non-urgent work can be delayed.

I would like to leave you with the thought that all information should be used for constructively approaching issues without relying entirely on these systems for running the service operation.

Inventory Control

Substantial sums of money are involved in keeping spare part stocks and, with the high cost of money, companies have put a great deal of effort into keeping their inventories low. (In the context of this book we are discussing only spare part stocks and not equipment stocks).

Inventory Goals

Inventory Controllers have often found that top management is very precise in establishing financial goals for spare part stock levels (either in money terms, as a percentage of spare parts sales values, months of stock, or other more or less meaningful parameters) but nowhere near as definite about the physical targets that need to be met. Pressure from the users (e.g. Service Engineers), on the other hand, is on the availability of parts when required.

In a well run company, therefore, it is essential to agree both the financial and the physical targets to which the Inventory Controller should manage his spare parts stocks. We know how to set financial targets, but how do we set physical goals?

Physical goals are the ability of the Store to satisfy a demand from the store's "customer" (e.g. Service Engineer or end user) at the time the demand is made. It would be unreasonable (and uneconomical) to expect this demand to be met in 100% of instances at the time of demand, as that would mean keeping relatively large quantities of every part in every store to satisfy fluctuating usage, fluctuating lead times and possibly other variables (e.g. issuing new Service Engineers with their imprest stocks, pipeline changes, etc.).

In consequence, targets on the Logistic Level of Service (LOLOS) are normally set as a percentage of instances at which a demand on any particular store echelon can be satisfied at the time of asking. A 98% LOLOS therefore means that in 98% of instances, when a Service Engineer goes to the store to ask for a component, it will be issued to him. At a higher echelon, it would mean that the demands from the field echelon could be met in 98 instances out of 100.

The next refinement that can be added to this target setting is to identify the criticality of certain components and set a higher LOLOS on these and perhaps relax the requirement on less essential parts, where a Service Engineer could help himself in some way or other if the part is not available (e.g. substitute a higher assembly, or repair the faulty component).

The difficulties for an Inventory Controller arises when the two goals are not compatible, i.e. the level of service stipulated cannot be achieved with the financial resources made available to him. His approach in this instance must be to alert management to various alternatives open to the company (e.g. increase resources, reduce LOLOS, or selectively reduce LOLOS on some parts only) and then a considered decision is made by all concerned.

Management is aware that there is not only a cost of inventory but also a cost of stock-out. That usually means dissatisfied customers, inoperative equipment, a waste of Service Engineer time and a demotivating effect on the service force. All these lead to a loss of business efficiency and a reduced profit. The skill of management, therefore, is to agree on tough, achievable and balanced targets.

Tools for Inventory Management

Once we have agreed on the financial and physical targets, the Inventory Manager must be able to ensure that these goals are achieved and measured.

The two most essential factors he will have to establich for each component or group of components are "How much to order" and "when to buy".

Reorder Quantity

The decision on how much to order is known as Reorder Quantity (RQ or ROQ) or as Economic Order Quantity (EOQ). There are a number of factors which will influence the ROQ which we can break down into a number of related groups:

(i) Usage – Lead Time – Standard Package Size – Minimum order size.

(ii) Price – Discounts available

(iii) Cost of Ownership (cost of money, alternative use of money, space required)

(iv) Cost of Ordering (in purchasing, accounting, receiving, auditing, inspecting, administering)

(v) Criticality (penalty for not having component)

(vi) Obsolescence – Deterioration

It is difficult for an Inventory Manager to develop a formula to take all the above into consideration and one of a range of simple scientific guidelines frequently used takes the most important of these factors into account in a quantitative form and the others in a judgemental form. The calculation most often used is

$$EOQ=\sqrt{\frac{2AB}{I}}$$

where A is the annual usage in £'s (i.e. number of units × unit cost)
where B is the cost of each order
and I is the inventory ownership cost in %

For instance, if the number of units used in a year is 1000 and the cost of each unit is £15, A=£15,000. If B=£12.15 and the inventory ownership cost is 20%, the theoretically most economic order quantity will be

$$EOQ=\sqrt{\frac{2AB}{I}}=\sqrt{\frac{2\times£15000\times£12.15}{.20}}=\sqrt{£1822500}=£1350$$

That means the EOQ is £1350.– worth of units or 90 units. However, if the Inventory Control Manager knows that a discount is available for orders of 100 or more, he may decide that the cost of the inventory ownership of the extra 10 units he would have to order to qualify for a discount may be worth – while, particularly as he would also save the cost of one order a year (10 orders per annum instead of 11.11 orders).

The same type of judgemental decision may be made on the other factors mentioned earlier.

This is not difficult if we deal with a very limited number of parts. What happens when an Inventory Controller has to deal with thousands of components?

The usual approach taken by inventory specialists is to use the "ABC" approach. This is an extension of the usual 20:80 rule, i.e. that perhaps 20% of parts represent 80% of the total cost, the percentages will vary somewhat from industry in industry. The "ABC" analysis breaks down into 3 groups of parts where the percentages may be, for example:

"A" items represent 5% of components and 65% of cost
"B" items represent 30% of components and 30% of cost
"C" items represent 65% of components and 5% of cost (see Figure 30).

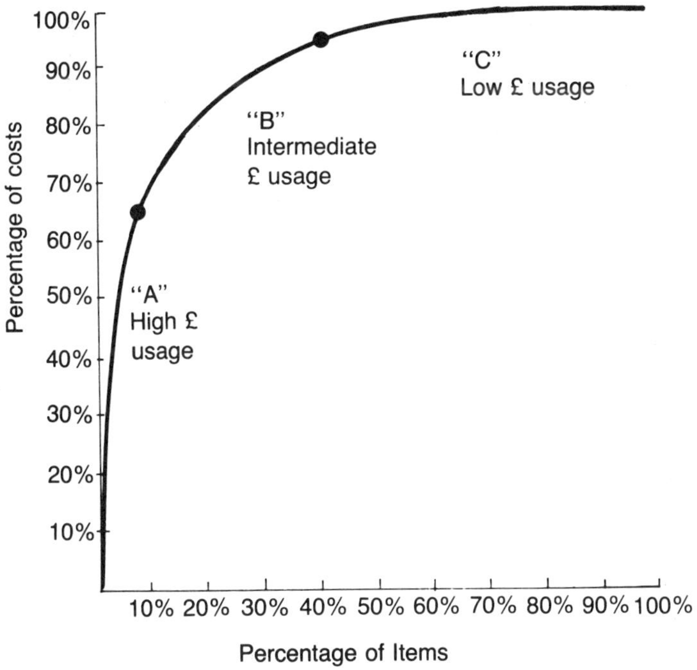

Figure 30. A, B, C Analysis

"A" items are very tightly controlled by the Inventory Manager, "B" items fairly tightly and "C" items only loosely. In this way, for example, a printed circuit board (PCB) which impacts the inventory costs to a greater extent than, say, nuts and bolts, is reviewed and controlled more often and more tightly than the nuts and bolts, which may be available in bulk to the service force. The high cost impact could be either generated by relatively few components of high cost (such as the PCB) or by large numbers of relatively inexpensive components (e.g. belts).

Reorder Level

In addition to deciding how much to order, the Inventory Controller must lay down rules of when to order; that is known as the Reorder Level (ROL) or Reorder Point (RP).

Under ideal conditions one would wish the new supply of parts to arrive at the same point in time at which the old stock is exhausted. In practice this is not feasible because there are too many variables in the provisioning of spare parts for the field. The major variables include fluctuating usage and fluctuating lead times. Both of these in turn contain a number of factors which cause uncertainties, such as accuracy of forecasting, effect of ageing equipment, transportation pipeline delays, administrative delays etc.

In consequence the Inventory Controller will want to have a safety stock at the time the new parts are due to arrive, rather than work to the ideal condition mentioned above, where he would plan for the new supply to arrive when his old stock is exhausted.

The RP, therefore, can be defined as "Safety Stock + Usage during Lead Time".

Let us look at these factors:

(a) *Usage* pattern can usually be determined from past records and superimposing the changes in the field (e.g. number of additional installations to be serviced). On a new product the usage is forecast by the technical experts. The degree of variation of usage per unit of installations will affect the size of safety stock required and the absolute value will also affect the safety stock consideration.

For example, if the demands for component "A" is, say, 1 per 100 machine months and for component "B" 10 per 100 machine months, then a variation of 1 demand will represent a large error in forecasting (100%) on component "A" whereas on "B" it will be an error of only 10%.

On the other hand if the usage of components is low, we would obviously require a smaller safety stock than for high usage items.

(b) *Lead Time*. Where lead time fluctuates widely, large safety stocks will be needed, whereas this will not be needed for small variations in lead times. Also, where the lead time is long, the safety stock will need to be high, as a great deal of usage variation can take place during this period.

(c) *Safety Stock*. Does that mean that we cannot calculate a reasonable safety stock level? Not at all. Safety stock levels are characterised, as we have just seen, by the following factors:

Large Safety Stocks	Small Safety Stocks
□ Low number of demands	□ High number of demands
□ High usage	□ Low usage
□ Long lead time	□ Short lead time

From this a formula has been developed which enables an Inventory Controller to calculate the level of his safety stock, i.e.

$$\sqrt{\text{Monthly Usage} \times \sqrt{\text{Average Demand}}}$$

There is one factor which we have not yet considered, and that is the frequency (numbers of times) with which a component is ordered on a yearly basis. By a probability study a constant (K factor) has been calculated, which refines the above formula to

$$K \times \sqrt{\text{Monthly Usage} \times \sqrt{\text{Average Demand}}}$$

Obviously it would not be practicable for an Inventory Controller (or his staff) to calculate these formulas for every component to obtain ROQ and ROL values. In the past this work was done by the use of nomographs, where it was possible to join by a straight line points on columns representing, in the case of safety stock, the monthly usage with another representing the average demand, and where this line intersects the safety stock column, the figure indicates the level of safety stock.

In more recent years all these calculations are performed automatically by a computer which recalculates ROQ and ROL values at regular intervals direct from the most recent data available as conditions change.

Link to other Company Systems

As we mentioned in sub-section 1 of Section V in connection with reporting, the expensive part of an information system is the input area. In consequence it is important for the Inventory and Warehousing systems to be linked with the input from other departments, so that data capture takes place only once.

This means that pricing data is obtained from accounting systems, lead time data from Purchasing systems and usage data from Service systems.

The reported usage of a part by a Service Engineer from the Work Control system to the Inventory system generates a number of activities:

1. Replenishing the Engineer's imprest stock
2. Debiting Service with the cost of the part used
3. Invoicing the customer for the part used (and for service carried out) if not on a Contract
4. Updating distribution records and storing data for updating ROQs and ROLs and for ordering parts at the appropriate time.

By linking Service and Distribution systems it is possible to have up-to-date information on the parts any Service Engineer carries at any moment in time, so that unproductive visits to the customer can be avoided if the part required is known. The Engineer may be able to pick up the part from a store or from another Service Engineer who is known to carry that particular part on his way to the customer.

Echelon Stocking

The number of echelons between the factory, where the component is produced, and the customer, where the component is finally used, may vary with the sophistication of the company, the size of inventory, locations of Engineers, and many other factors. Often legal and fiscal consideration will also need to be taken into account.

It used to be the practice that all components were held at every echelon level and replenishment was made from the higher echelon to the next lower one, etc.

This meant multiple handling, paper work, and stocking at many levels.

The need of this high cost approach can be frequently reduced by designating certain echelon levels for specific types of components. Let us take a large company who used to ship all their components from their international warehouse to national warehouses and from there to branch stores and local depots before issuing the part to the Service Engineer. First of all, are all these levels really necessary? And even if they are necessary, should each echelon carry the same range of parts?

With the excellent communication and data systems now available it is possible to eliminate echelons and dispatch parts carried in local depots direct from the national or international warehouse (depending on legal requirements) and there is no need for branch stores to hold these parts. Branch stores may still be required for slow moving, expensive items which could not economically be carried in many local depots. It may be possible to eliminate the branch store and hold these slow moving parts in a limited number of designated local depots. In many cases it is possible to eliminate national warehouses and supply a whole region (e.g. the European Common Market area) from one warehouse.

This type of decision must be made on the basis of individual situations and the optimal, location for any central warehouse needs to be determined. Standard Operational Research (OR) programs are available for this type of calculation where it is only necessary to change input parameters to individual company needs.

Other Applications for Computers in Service

The ease of accessibility and simplicity of some programs has made it possible for computers to be used on a very wide range of applications in Service Departments. Where a program is going to be used purely by the originator to aid his work, there is no need to comply with any restrictions and the range of applications is limited only by the ingenuity of the user. Where programs are, or may in the future, be linked to other company systems, it is highly desirable (if not essential) to ensure that it conforms to the systems architecture laid down by the company.

Let us look at the most widely used and more general applications of computers in Service Departments.

Planning Models

These models can save a Service Manager a great deal of time as for many planning activities the change of one or two planning parameters may mean the recalculation of the whole plan. In many applications, the variation of an input factor does not require the review of the whole plan but merely the calculation of the new figures. This can be done effectively by planning programs linked with other functional planning models. In this case many alternative approaches can be run on the computer before the decision is taken to proceed with one specific plan.

Territory Planning

In many companies simple models have been developed for use by the Field Service Manager or Supervisor in assigning Engineers to territories or arranging mini-team workloads of appropriate size. This allows managers to simulate a multitude of alternatives ("what if" situations) at their terminal in the office prior to discussing the preferred approach with the team in question. These models are particularly useful in service organisations handling a wide range of different models where all Engineers may not be trained on all equipments.

Response Time Models

We have seen earlier that response time may be of great importance to customers in some industries and before a Service Manager can commit his company to a specific response time, he must know what it will mean to his manpower and cost structure. We have mentioned in these earlier discussions the possible advantages a Service Manager may gain by working mini-teams and devising clear Work Control priorities. To be able to calculate the optimum approach and its costs he needs a model with parameters input from real experience in his company. That does not necessarily mean that the optimum approach calculated by the model is the one he is going to pursue – management judgement needs to be included in the decision.

For example, in one large company who had a high concentration of equipments and Engineers in the Central London area, the model showed that theoretically the best response times at lowest cost could be obtained by working all Central London Engineers as one, very large team – the additional transportation time and cost would have been more than compensated for by the smoothing of workload and the consequent more "normal" distribution curve. The approach was not acceptable for various human aspects – customers would not welcome each call to be made by a different Engineer and the Service Engineers would have felt little responsibility for satisfying customers. By a series of simulations it was then established that a reasonable compromise approach was for specialised mini-teams of four Engineers to cover a few blocks of Central London each. Although response time distribution was more dispersed, the workload in a 4-men territory could be kept reasonably well controlled and other qualitative requirements where satisfied.

Diagnostic Support

With modern equipments, micro-processors are often built into the product which will give the operator an indication of the likely problem on his machine and he is frequently in a position to help himself out of the problem situation. If he cannot do so or if the code indicates to him that he should ask for the help of Service, the call goes to the Work Control Centre. In many companies it is now standard practice for the Work Controller to try and resolve the problem over the telephone, either from the fault code read to him over the telephone by the operator or by the verbally transmitted fault reported to him by the operator. On some products acoustically coupled interrogation can be performed by the Work Controller direct with the equipment.

Until the last few years, these fault finding techniques relied heavily on the knowledge and experience of the Work Controller, both to ask the right questions and to recommend the correct solutions.

More recently diagnostic programs have been developed which aid the Work Controller on hand of a decision tree matrix to resolve customer problems. The sort of indication he would get from feeding the reported problem (or its code) into his terminal would be the likely causes for this problem in order of probability, and the type of questions which may identify the cause more specifically. This does not only avoid certain calls entirely by enabling the customer to resolve the problem himself, but even when an Engineer needs to make a call to the customer, the Work Controller can give him reasonable guidance and advice on the spare parts the Engineer may require to fix the problem. This avoids unnecessary visits for fetching parts or consumable items.

Like all other automated approaches, the human aspect needs to be considered. For instance, it may be unacceptable to try and fault-find on the telephone for long periods of time, as this may be annoying to the customer and block the Work Control telephone line for excessive periods.

The equipment often has diagnostic programs built in to aid the Service Engineer with his fault-finding.

Computer Assisted Training

When we discussed the training of Service Engineers at the end of Section III, we mentioned the potential advantage of including computer assisted training (CAT) methods together with other training techniques. The great advantage of CAT is the uniform method of instruction (not relying on individual lecturers), the possibility of each student to progress at his own rate, and to go over the same material more than once if necessary. It is also very helpful in training Engineers of varying background experience, as those who are familiar with a particular aspect of the training programme can "skip" over the sections they are familiar with, whereas others may need to cover that subject in detail. This applies not only to new trainees from other companies but also to the company's own existing service force, where the Engineers being trained on the new product may have been servicing products with some relevance to the new product, whereas others may come from unrelated products.

Another advantage of CAT is the fact that the same Trainer can now train students on different products simultaneously. His role has changed from that of a lecturer to one of a tutor. This does not necessarily mean that we need fewer Trainers, but that the company has much more flexibility to train a limited number of Engineers on a particular product rather than having to wait for a reasonable size group to make a training session worthwhile. Naturally, this also affects the lay-out of the Training Centre.

Production of Service Manuals

Computers are increasingly being utilised in text editing and graphics development work in the production of Service and Training Manuals and Bulletins. In the more sophisticated applications the Service Manual systems are linked to the Engineering and Manufacturing systems (CAD/CAM systems) to reduce duplication and to ensure that Technical Publications work on the latest information.

For international transmission of service data, the translation of service manuals into foreign languages has always been a major issue – translation is expensive and time consuming but, on the other hand, by not translating the contents, the Service Engineers in foreign countries work under a severe handicap. Computer assisted translation has been difficult for a number of reasons, the two most important ones being the multiple meanings of the same words and the problem of syntax. These problems have been largely eliminated by writing service manuals in a minimum vocabulary convention, where each word is assigned a single meaning and in telegraphic style to reduce the impact of syntax. The greater use of graphics (which used to be expensive to produce but are more easily affordable with computer graphics) has also reduced the need for excessive text. Some manual editing may still be required.

Service Administration

As in the administration of other departments, computers can substantially reduce the manual workload and enable a greater amount of data to be manipulated. Retrieval of information also becomes much easier.

In Service this is particularly useful where a service force on multiple products may not be cross-trained on all equipments or where decisions have been made to divide the work according to skill requirements. This has made it possible to utilise a multi-tier service force where this is beneficial.

The computer would therefore be used not only for standard administration purposes but also as a live skill inventory, a training status bank and for recording other essential information.

In the administration of Service Training the computer is also a very useful tool for ensuring the appropriate training programme and training schedule for each Engineer. In a large training Centre it is also used to balance space requirements and other facilities.

The computer is also an effective tool for ensuring that promotions or other appointments give candidates from various locations a more even opportunity. Without its help many decisions for desirable appointments are made from the limited localised knowledge of a small group of managers.

Involvement in Developing Systems

This paragraph is just another reminder that the user of any system should be involved in its development to ensure that it will really help him to perform his task. The very precise decisions he will have to make to ensure that the Systems Analyst and Programmer know exactly what he means, will help him clarify his own thoughts – it is a useful discipline.

The Information Systems Department should lay down clear guidelines on the systems which should be developed within the company's system architecture and only allow those with no possible link to other systems to be designed outside this architecture. It is a tedious task to try and reconcile data obtained from different and incompatible systems.

Summary of Section

☐ In this section we dealt with management tools available to Service management. I tried to point out the benefits that many of these tools or the results obtained from them can provide for a Service Manager, but also the dangers in believing that these tools or the results obtained from them can do the management job for the Service Manager. They can not! Judiciously used, they are a great help to him.

☐ We went in some detail into Service Reporting and the need to be selective in both data collection and in issuing reports. Without reports it would be difficult, if not impossible, to plan and manage service activities effectively. Reports must, however, be only used for the purpose for which they are intended as they may become counterproductive if used indiscriminately.

☐ We then spent some time in identifying the need for Service Control and established that in most service organisations, large and small, a Work Control operation is necessary to act as a nerve centre for all service activities. This work control can vary from a simple, manual activity of a part-time operator to a sophisticated Work Control Centre employing a number of highly qualified and trained Work Controllers in a fully computerised environment.

☐ We examined the importance of spare parts on a service operation and the need to have an effective Inventory Control activity. Goals for Inventory

Controllers should be physical as well as financial and we defined some of the possible physical targets and some of the calculations to ensure these targets are achieved.

- ☐ At the end of this Section we had a quick overview of some other applications to which computers can be put in a Service Department, varying from simulation models for planning, to diagnostic support, aiding service training, developing service support materials and helping with the administration of the department.

SECTION VI

Interfunctional Relationships

The great majority of people now accept that Service is a business in its own right with its own revenue (direct or notional) and cost structure. There are some companies where Service is the sole product they are selling (Third-Party Service Organisations) but in the great majority of cases Service is an integral part of the total business of a company. It is therefore necessary to examine the relationship of the Service Division or the Service Department with other functions to ensure the most efficient approach to achieving the company's objectives.

It is not easy for a Service Manager or Director to safeguard the position of the service function in the apparently diverging pressures from various functions and he must therefore understand how these pressure are generated to enable him to influence the situation. Some of the most important reasons Service is often not assigned a higher priority in top management's considerations include:

□ The impact of service efficiency is likely to be discernible in the medium or longer term only, whereas many other company activities have a more immediate visibility (e.g. number of units sold, unit manufacturing cost, debtor control).

□ Many Service Managers do not present their case in a language understood by other functions; the quantification of various options in money terms is essential. This is due partly to inadequate tools being available to the Service Manager (See Section V) and partly to his reluctance to commit himself to financial figures with his limited understanding of finance.

□ The traditional approach of top management to Service viewed it as a necessary expenditure to achieve the company's major aims. The increasing revenue and profit opportunities from service activities is rapidly changing this outlook but the relative unfamiliarity of service thinking of top management is still necessitating a continuous effort by Service Managers.

In this Section we will examine the interfunctional issues arising between Service and its main contacts within the company and how management can balance the varying needs to the total company's benefit.

Relationship with Sales and Marketing

There are three major areas of joint involvement

- ☐ Planning Activities
- ☐ Direct Sales Support
- ☐ Joint Field Programmes

Planning Activities

Service is the technical arm of Marketing in the product planning and development phase; we will discuss this aspect of the involvement of Service at a later stage. Here we will concentrate our attention at the customer oriented planning activites.

The most difficult way of managing any function is "Managing by Surprise". This is even more true in Service than in Sales or Marketing, due to the more conservative nature of service staff and to the longer lead time for many activities. Nevertheless, until relatively recently, Service was given a marketing plan after it was agreed, without fully contributing to its development. This is bound to cause inefficiencies in Service and frictions among managers as well as being demotivational to service staff at all levels.

The prime need, therefore, is for involvement of Service in the planning stages of the Marketing Plan, the Market Plan and the Sales Plan.

As Sales and Marketing Managers have not been used to involving Service Managers in this activity, it has been necessary for Service Managers to "Sell" this need to their colleagues. The only way that this can be done effectively is by demonstrating the effect "Managing by Surprise" has on the support that Service can provide to the customer and to the sales force, the additional costs involved and the likely impact on morale.

Service Managers should realise that it is much easier to influence a Marketing Plan during its development rather than change it after a number of iterations with senior management. The concept Service Managers must put over (and, of course, be fully convinced of themselves) is that Service is an integral part of the marketing mix of a company which needs as careful consideration as sales support, pricing and field coverage but where changes may take longer to implement than in some other areas of Marketing.

So what can Service contribute to the Marketing Plan? The range of subjects is almost inexhaustable but let me mention just a few:

- ☐ Offering choice of service support alternatives to satisfy varying customer needs.
- ☐ Optimising total company's costs (and thus profits).
- ☐ Identifying feasibility, time schedule and related Service costs for product launches and branch-outs and for entering new markets.
- ☐ Highlighting Service revenue and profit opportunities.
- ☐ Feed-back of customer reactions to company's Service tactics.
- ☐ Influencing advertising strategy where Service support is featured.
- ☐ Providing tools to measure distribution of Service support parameters by customer, account and product.
- ☐ Representing technical aspect in Marketing considerations (limitations and strengths of product) and explaining field implications of technical alternatives.

One of the most important effects of meaningful Service participation in the Marketing Planning process is the whole-hearted support likely to result from this involvement.

Participation of Service also has the reverse benefit of fully involving and informing Marketing of Service actions. The choice of response time for a group of customers, products or a geographical area is an example. How much additional business would we get by reducing response time by "X" minutes at a cost of "Y" pounds? Or, would we lose any business if we extended response time and saved money?

Direct Sales Support

The same considerations apply in the direct support of the sales function as we have just discussed in the Marketing Plan. The need in this case is not only for joint planning and mutual interchange of information but also the frequent review of performance against plan and the outlook of trends for the forthcoming few months. In the light of the most recent information the outlook by Sales may necessitate changes in Service plans.

Service is also required to support various Sales activities which may not be planned a long time ahead, such as local exhibitions, customer demonstrations and special sales drives. Service needs to be involved prior to any firm commitment by Sales to ensure availability of the necessary support. To enable the close co-operation needed to achieve best results, it is strongly recommended for Sales and Service to be co-located to facilitate good communications.

The technique of re-charging from the Service Profit Centre to Sales for any unplanned activity by Sales requiring Service support is becoming more usual. It not only releases the Service Profit Centre of costs over which Service has no control but is also makes it clearer to sales management what are the real total costs of any sales action; this in turn will enable future decisions, that the Sales Manager may have to take, to be made on a more informed basis.

Methods of reducing possible conflict between the sales and service force were discussed in Section IV.

Joint Field Programmes

As I have pointed out before, the customer usually does not distinguish between the "Sales Department" and the "Service Department" – he sees both as "The Company". We need to re-enforce this impression by demonstrating, "Total Company Support".

There are a number of joint activities which are worth considering:

Customer Audits

One good way of finding out what a customer thinks of our total support is to ask him! A well planned audit enables the company to discuss with its customers (or at least with some of them) any issues they may have and also cover any future requirement that may arise. It demonstrates the company's genuine interest in the customer and his problems – the only prerequisite is for the Sales and Service representatives to listen attentively to the customer's issues rather than being over-concerned to work to their own agenda.

These audits also help the company to strengthen their "One Face to the Customer" image and it is an instructive experience for both Sales and Service.

Sales/Service Contact

Every member of the sales and service forces must be made aware of the fact that their first loyalty is to the company and not to one or other of the departments. Management can underline this concept by ensuring individual departmental goals are congruent and compatible.

Joint seminars and discussion groups will also provide a suitable platform for management to put over this point. This type of joint meeting enables the company to explain the image it wants to create and the role of each of the departments in fostering this image. Previous successes or failures in promoting the desired company image can be reviewed at the same time.

Informal contact between individual Salesmen and Service Engineers should also be encouraged during which specific customer issues are very likely to be reviewed.

Representation at each other's team meetings will also ensure better understanding of the other department's problems and the smooth communication of issues.

Relationship with Engineering and Manufacturing

Service has an important role as the field link of Engineering and Manufacturing to the customer, to Sales and to Marketing. It is a two-way link, as it is also the technical arm of Sales, Marketing and the customer, back to Engineering and Manufacturing.

Product Performance

Both Engineering and Manufacturing are vitally interested in the performance of the product and any changes in the forecast performance trends. In the sub-section on "Reporting Techniques" (Section V) we discussed various ways of collecting the data (100% reporting, sampling). Engineering and Manufacturing are not interested in the raw data on individual machines (except during the early launch phase of a product or for major capital equipments such as a power station or a steel mill) but in a segmented group of machines. Service must therefore ensure that the technical data collected from field reporting is analysed in a number of different ways – for Service Management at various levels in the field and for the Product Service Department, Engineering and Manufacturing at the centre. Product Service is the technical section of Service employing highly qualified professional engineers who are in a position to actively participate in discussions with their colleagues in Engineering and Manufacturing to arrive at an optimal technical solution for the company which will satisfy Field Service requirements.

Product Service Engineers must therefore stipulate how the data should be analysed to enable them to identify specific technical issues, be they product oriented or the result of inadequate technical skills or insufficient training of the Service Engineer.

Problems which are due to the design of the product or due to errors in manufacturing must be highlighted and drawn to the attention of Engineering and Manufacturing to enable an investigation in greater depth to be undertaken.

This is usually achieved by regular meetings of the relevant Product Group, which meets under the leadership of the Product Manager and includes representatives from Engineering, Manufacturing and Product Service. Product Service reviews the latest data available and any trends that have been identified. Actions are assigned to individual functions and progress is targeted and monitored. The function concerned takes the lead in resolving the issues assigned to them with the co-operation of any other department.

When a resolution to a problem has been identified the Product Group agrees an action programme which may involve retrofitting or modifying machines in the field, cutting in changes on the manufacturing line, or deciding to defer any change until the next model is designed. Each of these alternatives can have a number of different ways of implementation. For instance, if the path of modifying machines in the field is chosen, the decision to take crash action and perform it as a top priority by making a special call on the machine – this would be done, for example, with a safety modification. If a special visit is not warranted, the modification might be carried out during the next corrective or preventive maintenance call on the machine. If the modification is necessary merely to accommodate an improved component, the old part is usually left to complete its life and the modification is performed on failure of the old component (repair by replacement).

One of the crucial aspects of implementing any of these alternative resolutions is the monitoring of results. Service Managers must implement an efficient modification status control system and this is frequently applied through the Work Control Centre. Cut-in on the production line usually is the most easy change to implement. Decisions to incorporate changes on future models are often inadequately monitored and the new model exhibits similar problems which have been demonstrated on the current equipment – this is frequently due to different management and staff being involved on the new model.

Warranties

Another area of close contact between Service and, in this instance, Manufacturing is the resolution of warranty issues. Most products of a technical nature carry some sort of warranty for defective components and faulty workmanship. Service is not only involved in performing work under the warranty but also for identifying problems found during installation of the product and for monitoring and feeding back trends in warranty work. Some companies use the recharging system to clearly place financial responsibility on the function which has technical responsibility for the problem and which has the ability and authority to improve the situation.

This is an area where field visits by Engineering, Manufacturing or Quality Control staff to the field are very useful (see later in this sub-section). I recall meeting the Manger of Quality Control in one of the branches after he had been present during the installation of an equipment on customer's premises. He was amazed at what he had seen and said: "If I had read in an Installation Report that the machine arrived in this state, I would have said that it was impossible." Having seen that it was possible, remedial action was quickly taken.

There is, however, a danger in the other direction as well. Service Engineers will tend to blame Manufacturing for problems arising during the warranty period which may not be due to manufacturing problems but due to operational errors by the customer or to bad servicing practices by the Engineer himself. It is essential for Service Engineers to know how to deal with warranty claims and not to blame other functions – customers are interested in the resolution of the problem and not whether it is the fault of Manufacturing, Service or someone else. Effective Customer Handling Skills training (See Section IV-3) is indicated.

Suggestion Schemes

Although there is some controversy about the efficacy of Service Suggestion Schemes, I personally have no doubt about the benefits of such schemes. There are the direct benefits of proposals for improved design, components, procedures and practices and the indirect benefits of motivating the service force (See Section IV–1).

In the context of relationships with Engineering and Manufacturing, we are talking primarily of technical suggestions. The objections to Suggestions Schemes for technical improvements usually come from Design Engineers, who feel that their deeper knowledge of how the machine works and its implication on other parts of the machine makes them, and them alone, qualified to make suggestions for improvements. This ignores the capabilities of the many Service Engineers who are in daily contact with the machine and the customer and who, in many instances, have very original approaches to resolving problems. It is, frankly, an arrogant position which is unwilling to accept that good ideas can originate in many places – it typifies the "Not Invented Here" (NIH) thinking.

The other group of people who may object to Suggestion Schemes are Service Managers themselves. Their reluctance is due to two main reasons: the difficulty of administering the scheme and the possibility that Service Engineers will be diverted away from their main tasks of servicing machines and maintaining customer relations, to efforts to redesign the product. Both objections are real but can be minimised by effective service management. The difficulty is that the costs of administering such a scheme are immediately apparent but the substantial benefits to the company can be quantified in the longer term only.

Administering a Suggestion Scheme raises a number of problems. We need a good communication and recording system which quickly passes the information from the Service Engineer to the first "filter", where a rapid review is made to establish whether this suggestion has been made previously and whether it has technical substance. The Service Engineer must then be informed whether his suggestion is being further progressed or not – in the latter case the reason must be clearly given. The suggestion is then passed to the Product Service Group involved, where a more thorough feasibility study is undertaken and the Service Engineer again informed of the outcome.

Having passed these two review stages, the suggestion is formally tabled at a Product Group Meeting and it is the responsibility of the Product Service representative to progress the suggestion and keep the Service Engineer informed.

The reason why the recording system needs to be good is the possibility of similar suggestions coming forward from different Engineers and one of them needs to be informed that this suggestion has already been made.

The company must also identify a time in the product life cycle, when it will no longer want suggestions, as the product is on the declining part of the life-curve.

The Product Service representative will also need to make sure that the actions agreed by the Product Group are implemented in a reasonable time frame – an excessive delay may make a suggestion less useful.

The other objection, concerning the Service Engineer devoting an excessive amount of time to suggestions, is usually based on a wrong assumption.

Many suggestions are worked out by Engineers in their own time – on customers' premises there is usually too much pressure on them. The fact that a Service Engineer uses his own time to think about resolving technical problems demonstrates his interest in his work.

Field Visits by Personnel from Engineering and Manufacturing

It is often argued that the time of Engineering and Manufacturing staff is too valuable to be spent on field visits. Considering that the product these engineers are to design and manufacture will be used by customers in the field and maintained by Field Service Engineers, this argument is difficult to support. The visits should, however, be carefully planned and the objectives identified to ensure maximum benefits from them.

It is useful experience for a Design Engineer to spend a few days in the field with a Service Engineer, to carry the latter's tool kit, to understand his spare parts issues and to work on machines on customers' premises. It may demonstrate to him the need for limiting the number of special tools, increased standardisation of parts across a product range and accessibility of components which may need relatively frequent change.

During these visits by Design and Production Engineers to the field, it is also beneficial for them to attend a meeting of Service Engineers where issues of mutual interest can be raised and discussed. The comments by the Quality Control Manager mentioned in the previous sub-section is indicative of the fact that personal experience of a situation is much more impressive than reading about it in a report.

The results from these visits should be captured by Engineering and Manufacturing management, an action programme agreed and the various points progressed and implemented. Product Service can often help in ensuring that agreed action is implemented.

In some companies, particularly in Japan, there is a regular rotation of jobs between the field and Engineering and Manufacturing. This certainly ensures thorough knowledge of each other's problems but it is also costly in training time and does not necessarily ensure the best utilisation of the individual skills and abilities of each engineer. As with many other examples put forward in this book, one cannot generalise about the most effective approach and individual circumstances will determine the feasibility of a specific solution.

The fact remains, however, that senior management must themselves believe in a particular approach to make it effective.

Relationship with Product Planning and Development

This is likely to be the area of highest pay-off for the company in utilising the experience of their Service staff and yet it is too often the area of least involvement of Service in the company's planning activities. In many companies the first involvement of service staff in a new product is at the proto-type testing stage. At this time major design changes are either going to be very costly or very time consuming or both. Senior Management is unlikely to be willing to put a great deal of additional money into the project nor be willing to delay the schedule for introducing the product and the result will be higher service costs during the whole life-cycle of the product.

Generic Goals

Service Managers should arrange for generic maintainability and operability goals to be drafted, discussed with all other functions concerned and an agreed document published for the use of all Product Planners, Designers and Production Engineers. These generic goals should be as specific as possible to be of any practical use to the engineers who will be using them. A vague statement such as the need to minimise installation time is meaningless and specific aspects need to be covered.

Aspects which would be covered in detail in the generic service design requirements would include:

☐ Product environment

☐ Transportation and delivery limitations

☐ Operator tasks and maintenance

☐ Installation condition

☐ Equipment maintenance criteria

☐ Equipment servicing criteria

☐ Diagnostic aids

☐ Tools and test equipment

☐ Machine reconditioning environment

☐ Standardisation of spare parts

Each of these aspects must then be covered in as much detail as possible.

Specific Product Development

The generic goals should go a long way towards facilitating the design of an operator and service friendly product in the early phases of a product design. As the various main groups of the design become defined in the development of the product, it will be beneficial for Service to be involved in the review meetings and to have access to the development and test areas, in order to input specific service needs to the Design Team.

This time is utilised for two purposes – as just mentioned, it is used for ensuring serviceability of the product and it enables Product Service Engineers to develop their initial thoughts on maintenance techniques and consequent training requirements of the Field Service Engineers.

At these review meetings the need for certain trade-offs between the requirements of individual functions is bound to arise; the presence of the Product Service Engineer should ensure that decisions are taken with the full knowledge of product-life-cycle costs rather than merely on short-term criteria. It should be possible, for example, to demonstrate that it is less expensive to utilise an over-specified component on one machine if it is identical to one used on another equipment instead of purchasing and stocking two components in the field. This may not be true in Manufacturing but if the total costs to the company are considered, this may well be the best solution.

Diagnostic Alternatives

A decision will have to be made early in the definition of the Product Specification concerning the level of diagnostics to be incorporated in the product. This is likely to differ by type of product, its application, the technical skills of the customer's staff using it and of the Service Engineers servicing it, the volume involved, the frequency of breakdown and by many other factors.

In the design of many products, micro-processors are included for operational reasons and their capabilities can then be utilised by Service for diagnostic purposes without increasing costs excessively. These diagnostic aids can be in coded form or in plain language, which the customer's operator can understand more easily. The operator codes may enable the operator to resolve certain problems himself or to be instructed by a Work Controller over the telephone how to clear the problem. Even in cases where the machine problem necessitates a visit by a Service Engineer, the knowledge of the problem code may avoid an unnecessary visit, if the Engineer can obtain the needed part on the way to the customer.

Machines not only include operator diagnostic codes but also diagnostic programs which can be actuated by the Service Engineer during his work on the equipment. This can considerably reduce repair time (MTTR) and avoid re-calls to the machine due to the wrong diagnosis during the initial visit.

The most sophisticated diagnostic aids are automatically monitored from a central location to determine any gradual deterioration of performance and forewarn Service of any action required.

Preventive Maintenance Alternatives

A number of alternative approaches can be applied, some of which have to be known when the equipment is originally designed, whereas others can be chosen at a later stage. As the reliability of the equipment, which is invariably indicated in the Product Specification, is likely to have the biggest impact on service calls, service hours, spare parts cost and therefore total service costs, the impact of PM's must be closely studied.

Starting at one extreme, a decision may be taken not to perform preventive maintenance at all, as it offers no technical benefit to the equipment, and has no marketing advantage for the company (e.g. cheap electronic calculators or cameras).

At the other extreme, we may have equipment where the lives of people are at risk if an important component fails or a failure has a substantial operational and financial effect (e.g. in aircraft, spacecraft or in power stations and drilling rigs). In these cases it is usual to build in redundant systems which take over when the initial system fails.

In between there are numerous alternatives. PM can be carried out at predetermined intervals of time, a certain footage produced, mileage travelled, operations performed or other meaningful factors. A combination of factors can also be used (e.g. a car service after, say 6000 miles or 6 months, whichever is the earlier). Another alternative is to divide the preventive maintenance activities into a number of separate tasks carried out during corrective maintenance visits to reduce travel time. If that is an important part of a company's strategy, then it must be known early on in the design process, so that access to specific parts of the machine does not necessitate excessive dismantling.

Another alternative is for customers to carry out their own routine preventive maintenance. This is frequntly employed where customers have technical skills in their own work environment or are likely to have their own maintenance departments (e.g. machine tools).

One of the most rapidly growing alternatives for performing preventive maintenance is the condition monitored approach to preventive maintenance tasks. In this case the machine itself indicates that the time for preventive maintenance work is approaching. In some companies this is known as "Telltales", i.e. signs that performance is beginning to fall off, or is likely to do so shortly. These conditions must be determined by each industry and each product individually. In a power station it may be a slight increase in temperature or vibration, in a machine tool a deterioration of surface finish, in a copier a reduction of light intensity – the important criteria is that the parameter should be, as far as possible, measurable rather than depend on a subjective judgement. It may seem difficult in some industries to determine a measurable factor the condition of which will indicate the need for preventive maintenance but in most cases one can be found. Let me give you an example from the reprographic industry. The need for performing a PM will be the fall off in copy quality and increased background. These are subjective criteria. The cause for the fall off in copy quality is most likely a reduction of light intensity reaching the photo-receptor. Now we have a quantifiable criteria, as we can measure the amount of light reaching the area. With the great variation of environments in which machines tend to operate, a fixed PM interval is tending to become less meaningful.

Developing Test Procedures and Criteria for Trials

Trial criteria need to realistically simulate field conditions. Service is able to help Engineering, Manufacturing and Quality Assurance in developing suitable criteria for in-house (or field) trials of prototypes, pre-production equipments and early launch machines.

Service should be involved in developing the test procedures for these trials and be involved in servicing the equipment during these trials as they will gain valuable experience.

Service should also co-operate in evaluation of the results of these trials and identify the impact any deviation from specified performance will have on service costs, customer perception and, through this perception, marketability. Recommendations to proceed or delay planned introductions should always include a reasoned comment from the Service represenative on the Programme Team. He should be part of any trade-off decisions that may have to be made.

Trade-off Practices

As mentioned earlier, the short-term impact of any decision is likely to carry greater weight with a Programme Manager than the longer term implications. Service is likely to be impacted in the medium and longer term. To ensure service issues receive the necessary consideration, it is necessary for the Product Service Representative to put his case not only in technical terms, but to also present a well considered financial impact analysis. The Service Manager must support his Product Service Engineer by arranging the help of a knowledgeable Financial Analyst to assist in evaluating the longer term implications.

The trade-off procedures in the past have often been hampered by the inadequate quantification of the financial impact. Once this impact analysis is properly performed, top management is in a position to take an informed decision.

Relationships with other Functions

The contact of Service with other functions does not differ greatly from that of other departments.

Personnel and Human Resources

In many companies Service employs a relatively large number of people and in consequence, a close relationship between service and personnel management is important. The Service Manager should take full advantage of the specialised skills of the Human Resources specialists and ensure that his functional needs are clearly understood by his colleagues in Personnel.

The skills of the Personnel Department should be used not only in the recruitment, promotion and career development area but also in developing service staff policies and procedures conducive to good personnel relations and increasing motivation. Professional advice is required to design methods of establishing service personnel's trends of attitude to their job, their management, their opportunities and the company in general.

Close contact is also indicated in the training field. The training of service staff in their professional servicing skills is usually the responsibility of the Service Department but the more general training programmes (e.g. Induction Programme to the Company) are similar or identical for all company employees.

Particularly in the area of management training, the Personnel Department can play a major role. For Service Managers, the training can be divided into general management training needs and applied service management training requirements. The former can advantageously be implemented in cross-functional training courses where the general principles of leadership, motivation and other management practices and techniques are taught. Specialised Service Management courses are then needed to teach how these general techniques of management can be applied to the management of the Service function. These can be either in-house courses concentrating on the company's specific Service issues or public service management courses where Service Managers learn, in a multi-industry environment, how to apply general management techniques to managing Service.

Finance and Accounting

I have mentioned a number of times in these pages that Service Managers should take the opportunity to utilise the services of the Finance Department in helping them to understand the financial implications of Service actions. The Accountants will gladly assist in analysing various alternatives from a financial point of view and help in the preparation of a proposal to top management.

The most important field of co-operation for the two functions is likely to be the developing of a meaningful Service Management Accounting system. To be effective, this system must give service management data in a format which enables it to analyse the results and take remedial action. It is only the Service Manager who can say in what form Management Accounts are meaningful to him and he must endeavour to ensure that he receives the information in that way. For other procedures it may be necessary to present the same data in a different way (e.g. for book-keeping purposes) but Management Accounts should be aimed at facilitating the management of the function concerned.

The advice I would give Service Managers in this respect is to give this matter considerable thought, discuss it with their opposites in the Finance Department, explain clearly what the information will be used for and then sit down with the Analyst or Accountant assigned to the project to work out details. That means, having a clear idea of what is needed but not to have the items set in concrete – rather discuss them with the Accountant and jointly come to a reasonable solution.

Information Systems

The relationship with this function was covered to a large extent in Section V. As in the case of developing a Management Accounting system described in the preceding paragraph, a close co-operation between the Service and Information Systems departments is necessary. Service needs to specify in great detail the input and output parameters and Information Systems must ensure that any developments in Service are compatible with the company's systems architecture.

Summary of Section VI

- ☐ In this Section we examined the relationships of Service with other functions with whom a close working partnership is necessary to achieve the company's aims.

- ☐ We first looked, in some detail, at the joint planning activities of Service with Sales and Marketing and the role that Service can play in the market-place in actively supporting the Marketing Plan. We also mentioned some of the support activities necessary for Service to assist in special Sales actions and finally examined various joint field programmes between Sales and Service. The conclusion we came to is that Service is no longer merely a machine repair activity but an integral part of a company's marketing approach.

- ☐ We then discussed the benefits that can be achieved by a close co-operation between Service, Engineering and Manufacturing in monitoring product performance and deciding any actions that need to be taken. We covered some other activities affecting these functions including warranties, suggestion schemes and field visits by staff from Engineering, Manufacturing and Quality Assurance.

- ☐ We then discussed the involvement of Service in Product Planning and Development. Although this area probably has the greatest impact on the longer term profitability of the company, Service often has only a peripheral role to play and gets involved too late in the development process to have a serious impact on the design of the product. We discussed ways Service Managers can help in identifying the role Service can play and how Service can specify its requirements and those of the customer. We reviewed alternative approaches to diagnostic aids and preventive maintenance practices and Service's role in the trials of early product models.

- ☐ Finally we showed that the involvement of Service with other functions, such as Personnel, Finance or Information Systems, does not differ greatly from the contact of other departments with these functions.

SECTION VII

Strategic Positioning and Tactical Alternatives

During our dicussions of various planning processes we mentioned a number of times the need to develop the strategic position of Service in conjunction with the total company's strategy. Let us now examine a number of alternative Service Strategies which are dependent on other company strategies. Some of these strategies will either influence the basic design of the product or, alternatively, the design of the product will determine the Service strategy or, at least, limit the number of choices.

Strategic Aims of Service

Before any Service strategy, policy or goal can be developed, the basic strategic role of Service within the specific company or for that particular product needs to be clearly identified. In other words, what do we expect of Service? Do we want it only to maintain and repair machines? Do we expect a major profit contribution? Does Service need to play a part in maintaining the company's customer relationship? What part do we want Service to play in software support? Can we identify a benefit in Marketing by highlighting our Service strength? Are we going to upgrade our installations and if so, can Service help us in feeding back useful data? How can Service help in projecting the desired company image? What support should our Service provide to the Sales Department? Should Service get involved in customer training and education? The scope of the questions are almost limitless.

Even after we provided answers to these questions, there are a number of alternative ways to achieve these aims. Let us examine some of these alternatives.

Who should Service our Products

This will be dependant on the answers to a number of the questions we have posed ourselves. If we have identified a role for Service in Marketing, in maintaining customer relations, in software support, upgrading of product, etc, and also contribute to the company's profits, we will opt for our own Service force. This decision may be taken irrespective of whether we sell through Dealers or through our own Sales force, or through non-exclusive Distributors. Provided a clearly defined strategy exists, we can be innovative in our industry and decide to use channels considered unusual. We can do this only if our product is, in some way, unique so that we can influence existing practices or if our company is sufficiently strong in the market-place to allow us to introduce changes.

A decision to use our own Service force has implications on the operation of the whole company. It will almost certainly entail substantial front-end investment in staff, stores, premises, training costs and, initially, limited utilisation of assets. It may necessitate a geographical concentration of our sales efforts and a need for customers to gain confidence in our newly-established Service force. All these are very real risks.

The benefits of this type of decision can also be substantial. The quality of service is in our own hands, the medium term and long term profit opportunity is substantial, we maintain customer contact through our own staff, we have the flexibility of utilising our Service reputation in promoting the company and the product, of supporting our Sales activities and gaining the strategic initiative in the market place. We have control over the level and quality of staff we use, the support that is provided and we do not have to place artificial barriers in the way of an efficiently operating Service Department. The amount and quality of technical and commercial feed-back is more easily controlled.

Some companies find the start-up cost for providing their own service prohibitive either from the financial aspect, the investment in managerial time, or the delay in establishing their own organisation is too long and they decide to use Dealers. This decision may also be indicated by the current practice in the industry or country concerned and the associated lack of uniqueness of product or strength in the market to affect a change of current practices.

There are a number of advantages in using Dealer Service organisations. In many cases the Dealer is known in his locality and thus has a reputation to maintain, which will ensure reasonable support for our product. Our cost will be much lower and the geographical coverage of his area is likely to be quite good. The Dealer may well buy his own stock of spare parts or at least hold and administer it on our behalf. If service support by the Dealer who sells the product is usual in the industry and if he is a successful Dealer who is making good profits from his present service activity, he may not be willing to take on the sale of a product which he is not going to support with his own service staff.

The obvious disadvantage of using a Dealer to service our product is the loss of part of the profit opportunity (we may still make some profit by selling the Dealer spare parts and training programmes), the loss of direct contact with the customer and the consequent loss of control of the quality of support given to customers and the chance to influence his perception of our company by service actions.

An even more dangerous approach is to leave the customer to his own devices which will make it necessary for him to utilise Third Party Service Companies to maintain his equipment. In these instances we lose all control over quality of service, feedback of valuable data and, often, any chance of continuing profits, as many non-proprietory spare parts are likely to be purchased direct from the vendor and not through us.

In some industries, almost all the maintenance is carried out by customers' own maintenance staff. In these cases we can still keep some of the benefits by providing spare parts to customers, offering to sell them training programmes, manuals and special tools, and endeavouring to support the customers' efforts and thus maintain contact and good relations for present and future business.

In many instances the approach may involve a combination of a number of the above alternatives. We may decide to support our own products in areas of reasonable product concentrations, use Dealers in more dispersed areas or in some foreign markets, and encourage customers to look after their own equipment where they have the technical ability to do so, and ask them to keep a stock of necessary spare parts to support the machine.

For products where service has become particularly lucrative to the manufacturer or dealer, third party organisations have set up in competition to the former and some attractive proposals have been made to customers. These can be either of a lower cost contract for the customer (third party service companies may have lower overheads, may service selected locations only, may be less concerned to maintain a product's image) or offer a "package deal" for all equipments of a particular type, irrespective of make, located in a particular plant or office block.

In general, the more complex the servicing of a particular product becomes, the greater is the need of the manufacturer to try and keep control of the quality of the Service Engineer, the level of management and technical support that is provided to the customer.

Where the products are sold through Dealers, the manufacturer can maintain some control over the Dealer's service standards by laying down clearly defined ground rules for the service the manufacturer expects the Dealer to provide. The more desired the manufacturer's product or name, the more insistent he can be on the service conditions he expects to be complied with. Some of the better manufacturers keep a constant, close watch on the service performance of their dealers.

Depth of Product Knowledge Required

The depth of knowledge required to service a product is only partially intrinsic to the product itself and servicing techniques may enable staff of lesser skills to perform many of the tasks.

These techniques may include the pre-installation of equipments, enabling installation to be performed by semi-skilled or unskilled delivery crews or customers themselves, the modular structure of a product enabling lower skilled staff or customers to identify faulty modules, remove these from the machine, exchange the faulty module for a good one and arrange for the repair of the faulty module by higher grade staff or under controlled conditions with more sophisticated diagnostic tools, or even have cheap, throw-away modules which do not warrant repair.

In these cases a different approach to the structure of Service manuals may be indicated. A functionally integrated maintenance system (FIMS) does not necessitate a Service Engineer to understand the operation of each part within a module and his limited training and the manual will enable him to identify faulty modules which are easy to exchange.

Another technique is to design the product in such a way that a very high percentage of problems can be resolved by staff with relatively low skills and highly qualified staff needs to be involved in only a small number of instances.

Here again, the various approaches may not be exclusive of one another. It may be a reasonable Service strategy to recruit high level staff in countries where the differential in pay between semi-skilled and highly qualified staff is low and expect them to effect repair on customer's premises. In another country, where these differentials are substantial or the availability of highly qualified staff is limited, one of the other alternatives may be chosen for the same product.

Utilising Service to Differentiate Products

With modern technology, competitive products intended for the same market segment are very similar to one another, at least as seen from the customer's point of view. There is often also a great similarity in the price of the product and companies are therefore using other areas of their package to differentiate themselves from their competitors. Service is one of the important areas where variable offers are made to customers to make "our" product more desirable than that of the competition. A number of different schemes have been developed by various companies.

The use of Warranty

As reliability of many products has increased, some manufacturers have found it possible to use extended warranty periods as a sales tool. It is intended to influence the customer by assuring him that no maintenance costs (beyond consumable items) will be charged for a longer time and by trying to indicate to him the confidence of the manufacturer in the reliability of the product, as he is willing to support it for a longer period without requiring additional payment for maintenance. With the increased use of electronic components in many equipments this may not be as expensive to manufacturers as it used to be with electro-mechanical components – the failure pattern of electronic components tends to be on the "bath-tub" distribution curve with a very long, low failure rate after the initial "infant mortality", whereas the electro-mechanical components will most likely conform to "normal" distribution curve.

The use of extended warranty periods as a marketing strategy lends itself to products which are widely advertised in newspapers, magazines and on television and radio, such as TV sets, white consumer durable goods, motorcars, etc.

The use of Coverage

Service coverage of the whole country is another strategy involving Service in the total marketing of a product. This will stress the ability of the manufacturer or dealer to support the product throughout a geographical entity. This approach is often used for interlinked products such as telephone systems, computers, word-processing and facsimile products where the final user may want each of his establishments to use the same equipment and program. For instance, a bank may require support not only in major cities but also in smaller branches in villages and small towns. The ubiquity of Service support may be an important factor which may be difficult for smaller competitors to provide.

The use of Response Time

Some manufacturers guarantee an agreed machine up-time or response time on their equipment. This pre-supposes a good geographical coverage, good monitoring systems, good decision tools and a thorough knowledge of the reliability of the product. At the time of writing, one of the computer manufacturers is using a high guaranteed up-time of his equipment at no extra cost as his main advertising pitch.

Other manufacturers use variable response times as one of the choices the customer has when signing a Service Contract with the manufacturer or dealer. In this case it is the range of response time choices which is used as a sales tool.

The use of Working outside Prime Shift

In the same way as mentioned under response time in the preceding paragraph, Service support outside the company's prime shift is offered to customers to allow them to satisfy their specific requirements. This may vary from a full 24 hours, 7 days a week coverage, to a much less extensive offer of carrying out preventive maintenance outside normal working hours.

The use of Service Contracts

A wide variety of choices is offered to customers, from a full service maintenance agreement (FSMA) which covers all preventive and corrective maintenance, including spare parts, to a much more limited contract where the customer carries out his own maintenance work and the manufacturer merely undertakes to sell him the necessary tools, spare parts or exchange modules. In many industries Service Centres have sprung up, where customers can bring their faulty machines or modules for repair or exchange. For some products (e.g. heavy goods vehicles) the manufacturer offers Service Contracts throughout a Continent (see also page 187) to enable a customer to budget accurately his total operating costs. All these alternatives are designed to give customers the type of support they require and are willing to pay for.

Establishing Customers' Strategic Needs

In Section I we discussed the parameters customers are likely to consider as important from a Service Department and how to establish the quantitative factors. When we look at customers' needs in a strategic way, we can use this earlier information only as a base on which to build future strategies.

The first step is likely to involve extrapolating present trends in the servicing approach and thus anticipating future requirements. This is obviously not enough, as we must also super-impose new technologies, innovative marketing methods and the changing industrial environment. The further ahead we are projecting, the greater the number of alternative service strategies we need to consider.

Each of these strategies will need to be tested for its feasibility from a technical, human resource and financial point of view.

To do this we will have to evaluate our present strengths and weaknesses and those of our competitors. We will need to consider not only what our company is likely to do but also develop a "shadow" strategy of the possible developments in the service strategies of our competitors.

This will result in a decision to proceed along the path of a strategy which we will review at regular intervals to check whether our logic is still valid.

We will also have developed a number of contingency plans to be implemented in case certain anticipated actions do not occur as predicted or do not happen at the time planned. These contingency plans may affect any part of our service strategy, from the level of staff to be recruited, the training to be given to existing personnel, the method of servicing or any other aspect of our plan. The need to utilise any of these contingencies may be for internal changes in our own company, the actions of competitors, differing market conditions, alterations in laws, rules or regulations or any other related factor.

If our company can be innovative in its servicing approach, it will help us to keep the initiative and force out competitors to follow our path rather than us having to catch up with developments introduced by them.

Summary of Section

□ In this Section we reviewed some of the strategic and tactical alternatives open to a company for utilising Service more fully in the overall company strategy.

□ We identified the drive from the market place towards Service involvement in the total offering made to the customer due to the increasing dependence of customers on their equipment and the lack of differentiation of product features or price, thus directing customers more strongly towards Service in their purchasing decisions.

□ Finally we covered the need for reviewing our strategies regularly and having contingency plans prepared for rapid implementation if certain assumptions in the original plan do not materialise.

SECTION VIII

The International Service Operation

In the past it was possible to develop a product, decide its marketing and servicing strategy for the home market and then, at a later date, decide to extend its scope into a world-wide operation. From the Service point of view, this would be an expensive and inefficient approach. A great deal of work will need to be done to ensure that products and strategies are suitable for an international market.

Understanding National Differences

The first requirement for developing a Service Strategy and a Product Specification for international implementation, is to understand the basic differences and then work at resolving any issues arising in a realistically cost-effective way. Let us examine these differences under three major headings:

☐ Technical

☐ Human Resources

☐ Economic

Technical

An obvious requirement is to know local conditions. This will involve understanding the environmental envelope in which the equipment will be operating (average and extremes of temperature, humidity, windforce, rainfall etc.), the existing electrical standards (not only the nominal values but also the fluctuation from these nominal values) and any other relevant, local condition (e.g. quality of roads, communication systems etc.). If these requirements become known only at a later stage, it may mean that our marketing opportunities will be limited (e.g. if our equipment can be used only in air-conditioned homes or offices), the sales price will increase (e.g. if we have to add a voltage or frequency regulator, or a transformer or converter), the service costs will be higher (e.g. need to recruit highly qualified staff or more frequent failures) or the support service that we can provide to our customers will be reduced (e.g. variable conditions).

Many countries also have their own safety and operational standards which manufacturers will have to conform to if they wish to market their products in other countries. Some of these regulations may be mandatory and others only advisory but our marketing efforts will be aided by adhering also to the advisory regulations. To do so may be difficult for manufacturers as well as the local company (be it a subsidiary of the manufacturer, a dealer or other type of distribution outlet). The decision then has to be made, whether to manufacture all products to the highest specification required with the consequent increase in unit cost but the commensurate advantage of making the same model for world-wide distribution (simpler production planning, stocking flexibility, single spare parts manual, service manual and training programme, customer benefit if moving product between countries, etc.). There is no simple answer and the best solution may, in some cases, lie somewhere in between a single model for all markets and a great variety of models. Even if the decision is for a small number of different configurations, it is still essential to plan ahead for this eventuality, so as to make any necessary adaptation as easy as possible (e.g. some motor vehicles are manufactured in such a way as to make it possible to build right hand drive and left hand drive vehicles on the same chassis and body). In some cases, the standards vary even in the same country (e.g. emission standards in California versus the remainder of the United States) and care must be taken to investigate all variations within a market.

The Regulatory bodies in the various countries are only slowly identifying their differences and highlighting these to the manufacturer. The fact that a product conforms to the UL specification in the United States has little relevance to its acceptability to BS specification in the United Kingdom or the VDE standards in Germany.

Human Resources

The situation is no simpler in the human aspect of international servicing – in some respects it is even more complex. We still need to be concerned about regulations (e.g. the weight permitted to be carried by a person is restricted in some countries) and in addition we have less predictable and more rapidly changing human behaviour differences to consider.

One aspect that will have to be examined country by country is the situation regarding industrial relations. These vary considerably from a mandatory membership of a Union (be it a Trade Union or a Company Union) to a situation where unionisation is very unusual for the service force. This is unlikely to affect the product or its specification but it may affect the service strategy and the ease of implementing any changes to it.

The cultural and attitudinal differences will have to be considered in the development of any strategy. It may not necessarily determine what that strategy should be but it may influence management's approach to implementing it. The relative status of Salesmen and Service Engineers in specific countries may influence the organisational structure or the general educational level of Service Engineer intake may have to be considered to ensure satisfactory customer relations and an adequate pool of Service Engineers for subsequent promotion to management positions.

In some countries, the technical skills required may be in limited supply and an alternative approach to the standard service policy may have to be considered (see page 194). It may be possible to break down the tasks which need to be performed in such a way that some of the work can be done by Technicians of lower skills thus limiting the number of qualified Service Engineers required, or defective sub-assemblies can be changed for good ones by the Technician and the repair carried out at the base under controlled conditions, or training periods for lower grade staff can be extended, the level of supervison increased, and the breadth of training decreased (tighter specialisation). The alternative chosen will depend on the individual situation and the manpower growth rate expected.

Expatriate management tend to underestimate the abilities of local employees to learn the skills required to perform the tasks required by the job which, at times, stems from the difficulty of communicating adequately between the manager and his staff. Due to the language barrier it must be accepted that the training period will have to be extended and the learning curve (see section III) will be less steep.

Whilst we are on the subject of language, it is desirable for training courses and manuals to be prepared in the native language if at all possible. Few companies would produce their sales literature or operator training manuals only in their own language (e.g. English) and they would make an effort to print them in the local language (e.g. French). Yet, these same companies will claim that it is no handicap to their Service Engineers to receive their training in English and be provided with English manuals only. In fact, even people who speak a foreign language fairly fluently will absorb much less of the course or from the printed page than if it were in their mother tongue.

When it comes to instructions on the machine itself, there has been a trend towards the use of internationally acceptable symbols on, say, the push buttons of an equipment and, in addition, the controls which require words to explain their functions are designed in such a way that they can easily be changed to a local language. These notices are often supplied as a supplementary kit to be fitted to the machine during installation or pre-installation.

There are also differences in the attitude of Service Engineers in various countries to the way the job needs to be performed. International Service management must be sensitive to these differences and adapt their procedures to local conditions, or, at least, be aware of the differences so as to approach the issue in the knowledge that a change from practices prevalent in that country may need to be made.

It is also my experience, that expatriate managers do not spend sufficient time, money and effort in educating local staff to take on the job of the expatriate manager in due course. It should be a clearly specified requirement in the objectives of the Service Manager to recruit and educate his successor and gradually delegate increasing responsibilities to him. In a number of instances I have seen a reluctance to delegate authority with the excuse that the local manager was not yet ready. However, when this delegation was forced on the company by the national regulations of the country concerned or the promotion opportunity of the expatriate manager, as often as not the replacement was ready.

Where it is necessary to employ an expatriate Service Manager, it is even more important for him to involve his staff in the planning and decision making process than it is for a manager who is a national of the country concerned. If we have an international or multinational company working in a national environment, there should be no suspicion whatsoever that nationals are being excluded from the management process. I mentioned a number of approaches in this book where we could do well to follow the Japanese example – in this instance I would use it as an example not to follow. The strongest criticism of Japanese managers by their national colleagues working for Japanese companies in Europe, is the so-called two-tier management structure, where the decisions made at a joint meeting of Japanese and national managers are later reviewed and sometimes altered by the Japanese managers in a separate session.

Economic

The different economic conditions prevailing in various countries may affect the maintenance strategy of a company. Let us consider, for example, two European countries, say Sweden and Portugal. The relative cost of labour and (imported) spare parts is completely different in these two countries and it may be the right approach in Sweden to use more spare parts and save on labour hours whereas the opposite decision may be best for Portugal. International Service management must be flexible enough to accept the fact that an option which may be right in their home country and, perhaps in a number of others, may not be the best solution elsewhere. This problem is aggravated by conflicting targets for the national company and the total international entity (we will discuss this more fully on pages 204–206).

There are other economic factors which make it necessary for international service management to distinguish between policies, which the subsidiary must adhere to, and procedures, which can be changed according to local conditions. Care must be taken not to swing too far the other way by abrogating all international service responsibilities – National Service Managers will frequently try and put forward their personal preferences as the economic necessity in their operation.

The difference in the working hours per day may affect many service practices. It is not only a question of a few minutes or an hour, but the ability to complete a certain number of calls per day or to give a reasonable response time to customers. What is "reasonable" in response time will depend entirely on the national practices and the national marketing strategy. This leads us naturally into the next sub-section.

Centralisation versus Devolution

The principle should always be to delegate as many decisions and responsibilites as possible to as close to the customer as compatible with the efficient operation of the company. It is a simple principle but not as easy to decide in practice which specific actions are suitable for delegation, compatible with the best interests of the company and the customer. Some service activities suitable for centralisation will be obvious, others will be debatable, often depending on the size of the company and the maturity of the market. The criteria under which we have to examine this issue must be primarily based on operational efficiency and economic factors, but there are a number of other parameters we need to consider, such as suitably trained and experienced managers, the national differences discussed on page 191, the longer-term aims of the company and similar considerations.

Service Input to Product Development and Design

Although the information for this input needs to be gathered from as wide a field as possible, the actual analysis and input must be provided by one unit, as otherwise the needs of Service are almost certain to be ignored. The need for continuous contact between Design Engineering and Service Engineering throughout the d elopment phases of the product make centralisation almost automatic. It is up to the central Product Service group to keep in touch with Service Engineers in the various countries to ensure an internationally serviceable product.

Developing Initial Servicing Strategy

As the Product Service Engineers will have been involved with the product for some time prior to launch, it will be this centralised group which will develop the servicing methods, tools and aids, and also advise on certain other aspects of strategy which will be decided on a de-centralised basis. As a rough guide we could say that the initial technical strategy will be decided centrally while the more tactically oriented commercial decisions (such as response time standards, degree of specialisation of Engineers, manpower and support levels, branch-out rate) will be decided by local management taking full advantage of any advice the central group can provide.

Service Training and Manuals

Service training and the provision of service manuals can be divided into two separate areas:

(a) The development of a service training programme and service manuals is a highly specialised and costly activity which should be undertaken only once, and it is, therefore, usually centralised.

Specialists will have been involved with the Product Service Engineers for some time in determining the best methods of both servicing and teaching the Field Engineer to maintain the product and keeping him informed through manuals and bulletins. These specialists will also be very familiar with the latest pedagogic theories, practices and methods and they will decide on the most suitable approach for imparting the necessary knowledge and information in each specific case. For this they will need to be fully familiar with how the programmes are being implemented in the various markets of the company, as this may influence the structure of the training programme. For instance, in the home environment of the company, let us say the United States, the most cost-effective teaching technique might be considered to be the usual classroom lecture plus practical sessions on the equipment, as the USA is a homogenous market, with relatively cheap transportation, single language and each course is likely to be filled by a large number of participants. If we now look at the same training requirements in Europe, we may find that due to the fragmented market, different languages, regulations and customs, the training of only a small number of Engineers at any one time is feasible. This would make a self-paced training programme under controlled conditions more useful. The company may, therefore, decide to put more effort into developing a self-paced training programme (also known as criteria referenced instruction – CRI) which might have been considered better but not cost-effective in the USA for their home market. By looking at the international requirements, the economics of the situation have altered and a self-paced programme used throughout the world becomes feasible.

The same applies to manuals where, perhaps, the more extensive use of illustrations (expensive) is not cost-effective for a market with one mother tongue, and where additional written explanations can take the place of illustrations. For the international environment additional illustrations and the consequent possibility of limiting written decriptions has a much greater pay-off, and, in consequence, the advantage of more illustrations and less words can be utilised on the home market as well.

All these considerations also have a bearing on the production aids used by the unit developing training materials and service manuals.

(b) On the other hand the implementation of the training programmes (and, perhaps also, the printing of manuals) could well be a de-centralised responsibility. In many instances it would not be a practicable solution to send all trainees to a central training centre or to print all the manuals centrally, in a number of languages. In these cases it is usual to establish a Regional Training Centre either on a geographical basis (e.g. for Europe), on a language basis (e.g. for Germany, Austria and part of Switzerland), or on some other basis. The Training Officer who will be responsible for implementing the new product training programme is then usually sent on a course to the parent company where he will not only be one of the participants of the course but he will also spend some time understanding the pedagogic approach taken in developing the training programme. On his return he will prepare himself for conducting a course in his regional centre.

A similar approach is taken on the publishing of local service manuals, where the film or the graphics for producing the printing masters is sent from the parent company to the national operation, and the translated and edited text is dropped in locally.

Reporting Systems

This is another area where there is a need to ensure a compatible, centralised approach. This does not mean that the local company cannot add certain requirements of their own to the system, but the information needed by the parent company on product performance and other operational data must be followed precisely if it is to be useful for making decisions for the future. This identical approach is not always easy to achieve and the centralised requirement must be very clearly and uniquely specified to ensure that decisions are taken from valid data. Here again it will be necessary for the centralised function to understand the national differences and make allowances for them.

As mentioned earlier (Section V) each level of management needs the data evaluated to a different depth of detail, and, for international requirements, it may be adequate to communicate national summaries only, while providing in depth information of individual machine and engineer performance to first line field managers.

In some instances it may be necessary to provide the data against two or more different input parameters. For instance, when we consider parts costs, the International Service Manager may be interested in the cost on a manufacturing cost basis to enable him to compare the product performance in various environments. The local Service Manager is much more interested to have this information on a landed cost and sales price basis to establish the profitability of his operation.

Inventory Systems

The same considerations as for reporting systems apply to inventory systems. In fact, in a number of companies the control of inventory is becoming a highly centralised activity and the Operating Companies have full responsibility only for the utilisation and administration of these assets in their own country. Inventory levels are calculated by, and supplied automatically from, a central point.

Other Data Systems

Large and expensive systems can only be justified if they are used by a substantial group of service staff. In consequence, if a company develops a computerised work control system, it will expect it to be implemented in the majority of its larger operations. This is not always easy and I have seen long delays in implementing such improvements due partially to management's reluctance in accepting ideas not developed by themselves and partially due to resistance from Trade Unions, Works Councils or other organised bodies.

This centralised development of major systems does not mean that the local company needs to use the same standards or parameters as other companies – it merely utilises the same tool to do the job but decides itself what the details of the job should be.

Commercial Approaches

There is usually a great deal more variation in the commercial approach of service operations in different countries. The headquarter organisation often merely acts as a switchboard to ensure that ideas generated in one country are transmitted for consideration to others. There is, for instance, seldom uniformity of approach to Service Maintenance Contracts or their terms and pricing. This type of decision is almost invariably a local decision with some central guidance.

Technical Flexibility

The amount of freedom allowed to individual countries to modify their equipments will depend to a large extent on the type of product and the stage of its development. When a product is relatively new in the market, most companies will wish to maintain a tight control of the configuration to ensure that any local modification may not interfere with possible future upgrades or retrofits. On the other hand, once a product comes towards the end of its life-cycle, there is usually a great deal of freedom for individual countries to modify their equipments without excessive involvement from the parent company.

Support Activities

These should be as close to the customer as economically feasible. In some small markets it is not possible to afford adequate support close to the customer, in which case it is preferable to utilise shared support to none at all. This support might be in a number of fields, but usually concerns specialists of some sort or other. The narrow national restrictions should be bypassed wherever necessary – obstacles are often more artificial and created by local managers with limited vision than that they are real "show-stoppers".

International Policy and Local Flexibility

Having decided which of our activities we should centralise and which should be delegated, we need to clearly identify our international service policy and what flexibility each operating unit has within this policy for making changes which will help their local requirements without adversely affecting the rest of the company. We will see on pages 204–206 that there are financial conflicts which need to be resolved. In this sub-section we will examine ways of making the most of matrix management in operating a functional speciality within an international environment.

Functional Service Support to Line Management

Once an operation within a country (or group of countries) becomes sufficiently large, the company is likely to wish to create a national or local image. They may be proud of their international or multinational pedigree, but they will nevertheless wish to stress their national strength and prowess. This is achieved by creating a national branch or subsidiary company, or by appointing a local or national distributor. In most cases this national representation will have line responsibility for all activities in the area concerned, i.e. sales, service, finance, distribution, administration, etc.

In some countries this will be a prerequisite for doing business in that country and there may even be a legal requirement on local participation in the ownership of any company to be established in that country.

It is, however, necessary for the international service function to offer the local General Manager all possible assistance in building up an efficient and cost-effective service operation in his country. To do this, the International Service Manager will not only have to be very knowledgeable in his field of activity, but he will also have to be highly diplomatic and sensitive to the needs of different markets and individuals. This will often be more difficult for an International Service Manager than for his colleagues in Sales and Finance. The General Manager will, usually, be more familiar with sales and financial implications, both of which will, in any case, reflect in the short-term results of his operation. The fact that, in most cases, he is less familiar with the longer-term impact any short-term service commitment may have on his operation, will make him consider Service as being of lesser importance. This has frequently polarised the approach taken by General Managers to any support offered or provided by international service management:

a) The General Manager has abrogated all his responsibilities and leaves all service plans to be developed between his appointee (e.g. the National Service Manager) and the international service executive.

b) The General Manager wants to keep all functional activities national and does not welcome any involvement by international service management.

The International Service Manager must, therefore, convince the General Manager that he and his international service staff are genuinely and sincerely concerned with helping the General Manager to develop a highly efficient service operation. The International Service Manger must be able to demonstrate that both their interests are identical and he must be sensitive to the cultural differences and tactical requirements of the General Manager. He must be able to show that he has something useful to offer the General Manager.

At the same time, the International Service Manager must endeavour to build up a relationship of mutual trust and respect with the National Service Manager. In many companies it is accepted practice for the International Service Manager to be consulted prior to the appointment of a National

Service Manager in a subsidiary operation, although this is not usually true for distributors or dealers. In multinational groups it is not unusual for candidates for the post of National Service Manager to be suggested by the international personnel and service functions to the General Manager, and often these candidates may be of a different nationality to the country in which they will operate. Dealers and distributors usually do not get the benefit of the manufacturers' personnel, although in a number of cases manufacturers' Service Mangers are assigned for a number of years to run a dealer's service operation.

This type of matrix organisation is difficult enough in a purely national environment, but it is even more complex in the international context. In addition to the cultural differences mentioned above, we have a certain language barrier, as even fluency in a language makes it sometimes difficult to detect nuances or idiomatic finesses. There is also a certain local chauvinism which, although it will be forcefully denied, will tend to make General Managers try to be completely independent. This is not necessarily a bad trend, provided the subsidiary is ready for it and the policy requirements of the parent company are safeguarded.

In this context the International Service Manager must be able to distinguish genuine reasons for a particular approach from a mere excuse. If the reason is good, he may even wish to consider the alternative approach for other countries which are in a similar situation.

Equally, a good General Manager will utilise the international service group to give him a second opinion on the service approach suggested to him by his own Service Manager. It is not unknown for National Service Managers proposing national service support expenditure which can be provided more efficiently and cost effectively from an international or regional support centre. There is, for example, a great benefit of cross-fertilisation by providing centralised or semi-centralised training centres. In addition to this cross-fertilisation, it is often possible to train in more economical groups, use more sophisticated training aids and more suitably qualified trainers in a centralised environment, the benefit of which may far outweigh travel expenditure.

The National Service Manager will want to use the international service function for a great variety of reasons:

☐ Provide international comparisons

☐ Support in specialised areas (training, publications, product specialist, inventory control)

☐ Opportunity to discuss ideas

- ☐ Share development resources (e.g. systems, tools)
- ☐ Information and assistance for product launches
- ☐ Advice on experience in other countries
- ☐ Support for proposals to his General Manager.

In developing an international servicing policy, the International Service Manager will consider the experience in the various countries and he will clearly separate the policy statements (which should be few and succinct) which cannot be altered without specific agreement, and the much broader advisory statements, which can be adapted to local requirements. It is usual, for the International Service Department to be informed of any deviation even in the latter case.

Implications of Multinational Users

For many products, it is not only the manufacturer who provides Service on an international basis, but the users themselves are multinational companies. If they wish to purchase certain equipment, they may insist that the same product must be made available and be able to be serviced in numerous markets. If the service practices or terms differ widely, they are likely to question variations which they consider to be unreasonable. Many multinational suppliers, therefore, try to ensure a certain consistency in their marketing and servicing approach, if there is a likelihood of their customers being themselves international companies. It causes a great deal of friction and wasted time to try and explain to an international customer why his product can be maintained on a Full Service Maintenance Agreement (FSMA) in one country, whereas in another service is available on a Time and Material basis only.

Where the product is portable or transportable, the manufacturer's warranty document should state to which countries the warranty is applicable. Complications often arise when one subsidiary disclaims responsibility for servicing a product sold by another subsidiary of the same manufacturer. The International Service Manager needs to agree an acceptable procedure for the sake of customer relations.

Another issue that frequently arises is the international customer who qualifies for a major accounts quantity discount in one country and then assumes that he qualifies for the same discount in another country. Management in the second country, however, claims that he does not qualify, as he does not justify a quantity discount in the second country, the first country's subsidiary being a different legal and administrative entity.

All these issues are soluble, but it helps if they are resolved prior to customer problems arising, so that each operating company and customer knows exactly where he stands.

Conflicts between National Profit Targets and International Company Benefits

At first sight it does not seem possible for a conflict of interests to occur between the national subsidiary and the international company. In practice it happens frequently. As the national subsidiary will have very specific profit targets to achieve, its General Manager can be forgiven if he concentrates on his specific target to the detriment of the company as a whole.

Let us look at a few Service orientated areas where conflict may occur.

Spare parts

An international price-list for spare parts exists. A national subsidiary finds that it can purchase components claimed to be equivalent to the original spare part locally at a price lower than the landed cost of the spare part.

If the subsidiary decides to buy locally it will increase its profit at the risk of a lower quality component. The international company, however, will be left with excess stocks of the spare part, will perhaps have to purchase in smaller lots and loose quantity discounts from an outside supplier or have idle capacity in its own plant, and it will loose the uplift it charges to its subsidiary on its cost price.

What is the solution? The subsidiary should put the parent company in touch with the manufacturer to establich whether the component is genuinely equivalent, in which case this component may be purchased either by the subsidiary or the international company on a controlled basis to ensure that no excess stocks accumulate anywhere in the company.

Refurbishing

A detailed study has shown that the most efficient way of refurbishing a machine which has been traded-in by a customer is at a Regional Centre operating under central control. This is a controlled process giving a high quality refurbished product, but it is also fairly costly to the subsidiary. By short-cutting the refurbishing process the subsidiary can refurbish the machine more cheaply in its own country.

If the subsidiary decides to carry out its own refurbishing process it will increase its profit, save tranportation costs and possibly have the machine available more quickly. The risk is in the lower quality. From the international point of view excess capacity will be available at the Regional Refurbishing Centre and the reputation of the company name is at risk if the subsidiary operation does not produce an acceptable quality when refurbishing the product.

What is the solution? Again the decision should be made jointly. It may be that the traded-in machines should be classified into machines requiring only minimal refurbishing which can be satisfactorily performed locally, and the rest, which require more thorough refurbishing, at the Regional Centre. Clear criteria for this classification need to be laid down and strictly adhered to. Sufficient notice to all units needs to be given for any planned change to enable resources to be balanced and suitable spare parts for the refurbishing process to be re-allocated.

Training of Service Engineers

Say, a Regional Training Centre has been established for the training of Service Engineers speaking the same language – e.g. in Germany for German, Austrian and Swiss Engineers. The Austrian and Swiss subsidiaries pay the German subsidiary a "per capita" charge for every Service Engineer they send for training to Germany. Although the Austrian and Swiss operations agree that the training in the German Centre is much better than they could provide locally, the pressure on profits is such that they are willing to lower the quality of the training, perform it themselves and save the "per capita" charge and the travel and subsistence costs.

The Austrian and Swiss subsidiaries would improve their short-term profit situation at the likely risk of a longer learning curve for their Engineers. The German subsidiary would under-recover planned expenses and therefore their profit would be unfavourably affected. The International Service Manager would be concerned about the quality of Service Engineers in Austria and Switzerland and at the under-utilisation of the German facility and trainers.

What is the solution? As always, there is not just one solution but it must be achieved by all parties agreeing on a specific approach. The two approaches which suggest themselves are:

(a) Make the German Training Centre into an international facility operated as a non-profit unit with costs shared pro rata by the three companies utilising the Centre. The method of pro-rating would need to be clearly agreed beforehand (e.g. relative revenue of subsidiaries, numbers of staff on board, numbers of staff utilising the facility, or similar criteria).

This would form a commitment for all the subsidiaries to contribute a specific proportion to the Centre's costs and not to the profit and loss account of one of the subsidiaries.

(b) Whether "a" is implemented or not, consider whether the simpler and shorter training sessions could, efficiently, be carried out by Trainers from the Centre in various cities of the area – i.e. bringing the Trainers to the Engineers, rather than the other way around. This is likely to be cost-effective only if the machine is relatively simple (short training period), small and not requiring sophisticated training aids and provided a reasonably sized group of Service Engineers could be freed at the same time in each city. The latter is likely to be difficult to achieve without reducing the level of service to existing customers – it is easier to absorb the workload of one or two Engineers sent, say, from Vienna, on a training course to Germany than to arrange the training of 8 to 10 Service Engineers at the same time in Vienna.

I believe these three examples illustrate the type of conflict that may arise between national profit pressures and longer term benefit to the whole company. In some instances it may be necessary for more senior line managers (e.g. Regional General Manager or International Operations Manager) to take a firm decision for the benefit of the whole company without removing the profit target goal of the subsidiary's General Manager. After all, there are likely to be many more aspects affecting profits on which a corporate view must be taken.

Summary of Section

□ It is always beneficial to know beforehand that a particular product is intended for an international market. This will make it easier to sell and service the machine in the different environments.

□ We need to understand all the national differences, be they technical, economic or affecting the human relationship between the company's staff and the customers. Some of these differences are unlikely to be overlooked, whereas others are often ignored or added as an after-thought to the company's planning process.

□ One of the aspects of management that will have to be resolved is the extent of centralisation. The principle that needs to be adhered to is to decentralise as many responsibilities as close to the customer as is compatible with an efficient and cost-effective operation. This is unlikely to be a static situation and will need continuous review, as it may be possible to delegate an increasing amount of activities. Certain parts of the Service operation are likely to be permanently centralised (development of major programmes).

□ When we consider the development of an international service policy we need to identify policies which must be adhered to and practices which can be modified locally to provide management flexibility. The proper utilisation of international or regional functional support by national line management needs to be implemented in a sensitive way to ensure the synergism of the matrix organisation.

□ We also identified that it is not unlikely for conflicts to arise between national profit targets and benefits for the whole company internationally. Most of these conflicts can be resolved, or at least modified, by an open discussion between the parties involved and the subsequent adherence to the agreed approach.

SECTION IX

Future Trends in Service

In what direction is Service developing at the present time? Various considerations exert conflicting pressures, so let us analyse some of these trends from the technical, economical and human points of view.

Technical Developments

The relatively lower cost of micro-processors and other electronic developments will have a strong impact on the servicing of a great many products of the future. They are initially incorporated into products for purely operational reasons, but once they are built into equipments, they will be increasingly used for servicing purposes as well.

This may lead to better protection of equipments against the mis-use or mal-use of operators. We are already finding cameras which will not work in inadequate light conditions, cars which will not start if the engine is in gear, machine tools which will cut out if a tool is becoming blunt, office equipment which will indicate to the operator where he or she has gone wrong in setting it up and household equipment which safeguards against overloads or injury, etc. The next step, into which we are currently moving is that the equipment will tell the operator what he has done wrong and advise him how to ensure proper operation.

The impact on Service is likely to be the elimination of unnecessary calls, which in some Service Departments still comprise a substantial part of their work – they are often known as "Mickey Mouse" calls.

Telling the operator how to use the equipment correctly, leads us into telling him also how to repair simple machine faults by himself. The technical skill needed to effect repair or change a component as well as its accessibility will determine whether the operator will be advised to call for help from Service or to help himself (see page 211 where we discuss customers' choices).

The same micro-chip can also be programmed to help the Service Engineer with his diagnosis, which will reduce the time necessary to get the equipment operational again and thus increase machine up-time.

Where major capital equipment is concerned it may not be necessary for the customer to monitor the equipment as it will be possible for the Service Organisation to monitor the performance from its Work Control by acoustically coupled probes which will indicate a machine condition which may cause a breakdown in the near future. A timely preventive call may limit any damage to the machine and reduce down-time.

At the other extreme of technical development there is likely to be an increase of throw-away modules, where intervention by a Service Engineer becomes unnecessary. The typical example, today, is the cheap calculator or torch, where the customer may exchange the battery, but beyond this, the product or module is so reliable and inexpensive that repair is not being undertaken.

Mechanical and electro-mechanical components are being increasingly replaced by more reliable electronic components. On the other hand equipments are becoming more and more sophisticated so that there is a certain balancing effect on Service requirements.

The implication on Service are wide-ranging. A study recently undertaken indicates, that the Service industry is one of those, where the total manpower needs are likely to grow, at least in the foreseeable future. The skill levels required will be discussed on pages 210 and 211.

Economic Trends

In the Introduction we mentioned the changing role of Service in the present decade and the reasons for this change. These changes are likely to continue into the next decade and will be accentuated for economic reasons.

With the increasing integration of various equipments in the factory, office and the home, customers will be dependent to an ever greater extent on the operation of each unit within the chain. The quality, reputation and response of the supplier's Service Department will be of great importance in the purchasing decision.

The cost of supplying this high quality service is likely to continue to rise – the manufacturer will have to endeavour to compensate increasing costs of service labour by more service-friendly design and the company supplying Service will have to utilise improved service tools and service management techniques to increase service productivity in a climate where pressure for shorter working hours and more pleasant working conditions is likely to continue.

The customer is likely to be willing to pay a reasonable price for good quality and highly responsive Service – it will be increasingly necessary to be able to demonstrate to the customer that he is obtaining value for money from his service expenditure.

Customers who are not so dependent on first-class service support are likely to do more of their own servicing work, but they will still need to purchase spare parts, replacement modules, service manuals, special tools and test equipment.

The pressure on margins when selling equipment is likely to continue due to competition. The trend of many manufacturers to obtain an increasing percentage of their profits from their Service Departments (servicing and associated sales of parts, training programmes, etc) is likely to continue for some years to come.

The implications on Service are an increasing involvement in the total councils of the company. There will be a need for Service Managers to be genuine business managers in addition to managing Service. Their understanding of the operation of other functions will need to improve, with particular emphasis on management accounts and financial controls.

Human Aspects

We need to look at the human aspect from two points of view – one being that of the customer and the other that of our own staff.

Customers' Personnel

The public, in general, will become much more "technically" orientated and will have a better understanding of the equipments on which they are working.

Due to this greater technical knowledge, and also due to the relatively high costs of calling for help from Service, customers' staff will be able to effect simple repairs themselves, guided by the equipment's own instructions or from guidance from a manual or obtainable over the telephone from the manufacturer.

Many more customers are likely to have their own maintenance departments to carry out simple repairs and standard maintenance activities to increase the up-time of their equipments. Only the more complex repairs will be performed by the manufacturer's Service Department.

In consequence, the Service contracts which will be available to customers will be much more varied to enable each customer to buy the extent and the level of service cover he requires. The customer will make the choice according to the amount of "insurance" he believes he requires to safeguard his operation.

Manufacturer's Service Personnel

It is likely, that there will be a more distinct division between the various levels of service staff which will be employed. They are going to be utilised in small groups consisting of one or two highly skilled Service Engineers and a number of Technicians of lower skill level; all of them will be very effective in their customer handling skills. The Work Controller will be able to identify from the fault code reported by the customer what type of assistance is required and send the engineer with the requisite skills and parts.

As it will become possible for the customer to choose the type of service support he wants to buy, it is likely that the number of Service Centres to which customers will bring their machines or modules for repair will increase. At these Service Centres the simpler repairs will be carried out on the premises, whereas the more complex repairs, requiring more sophisticated tools and test equipment, will be sent to a Regional Centre. The customer will purchase a repaired module for the traded-in defective unit.

As Service will be an increasingly profitable part of a company's operation, the number of Third Party Service Companies will increase and their quality improve to compete with the manufacturers' own Service Departments. This increased competition will make it even more necessary for the Service Departments to be managed by highly professional Service Managers. Manufacturers' Service Departments will seek to service not only their own equipments but endeavour to become Service Dealers for associated equipment produced by other manufacturers, to be able to offer customers the same total service that Third Party Service Companies are using so effectively in their sales arguments to penetrate the market. This will again necessitate the Servive Manager being a total business manager to ensure that the correct business decisions are made.

This will mean that Service departments will have to make choices to ensure quality support at reasonable cost to customers and still ensure an increasing flow of profits – some of these choices we will discuss in the next sub-section.

Service Alternatives

With the pressure on reduced down-time and the consequent shorter work-times and off-premises repair of modules, the reduction of travel time becomes more important. (The proportion of travel time to total time of work plus travel becomes higher). This will give increasing benefits to large service groups who have a high concentration of equipments in relatively tight geographical territories allocated to small groups of Engineers, thus limiting travel time.

It may well be possible to sell customers modules to be held on their own premises, to enable quick repair to be effected by the customer himself or by the Engineer, who would be unable to carry a complete range of spare parts for a large variety of products. The spare parts position could also be alleviated by large Service Organisations utilising mobile radio-telephone controlled stores in areas of major concentration. These mobile stores could reduce the total value of stocks held in the field, as the parts actually carried by the Engineers could be drastically reduced due to their easy availability.

The other choices which will have to be made is the amount of diagnosis and repair to be performed in the field – the limiting factor is likely to be the MTTR.

Service Engineers in the field will have easier access to main-frame or minicomputers at a suitably located base through audio-coupled, portable terminals or personal computers. This will again speed up the repair process and streamline the total service activity.

The support to customers and Service Engineers will be on a multi-tier basis, so that the wide range of products which will be serviced by each team of Engineers can receive the necessary back-up.

There will be much more aggressive marketing of Service due to increased competition and the attractive returns which can be achieved from investment in Service. There will be a more careful segmentation of the service market by type and size of customer, his location, importance, type of industry etc. The flexible market approach will necessitate first-class support tools (mainly in Work Control) to be able to measure, provide and control the agreed LOS. Obviously, all these parameters will have a price tag attached to them. There will be a drive to sell Service Contracts and it will be as important for a Salesman to sell a Service Contract as it is to sell the equipment, its software and consumables.

The status of Service Management will be enhanced by the greater professionalism required for the job and with the company's recognition that its future orders are, to a large extent, dependent on the perception the customer has of the company's service support.

Summary of Section

☐ The future direction of Service will be governed by three major factors – the technical developments, the economic pressures and the human aspect of both customers and own staff.

☐ We looked at each of these three areas and extrapolated present trends to come to the conclusion that Service will become of increasing importance to a company, not only as a useful source of revenue and profit, but also in ensuring the customer's confidence in the after-sales support he can expect from the supplier.

☐ To be able to provide this high level of support at acceptable prices and still achieve a reasonable profit, every level of Service staff will have to become increasingly professional. Support must be given to the Department to ensure this professionalism, including the use of modern management techniques and tools.

☐ It is particularly important for the Service Manager to become a business manager with all that this entails, rather than specialise in his own field only. This does not mean any less professionalism of the service function, but additional knowledge of other aspects of general management.

Glossary of Terms

Attrition Rate	The ratio of the number of a group of employees who leave the company to the whole group. (Also known as Turnover of Staff).
Available Hours	The number of hours during which an engineer is available to take customer calls (i.e. excluding holidays, sickness, formal training).
Burn-in	The practice of more extensive testing of electronic components to pass over the infant mortality period.
Configuration	The current state of units, assemblies, modules and modifications comprising a particular system
Consumables	Materials which are being used up in the normal operation of a product (e.g. petrol in a car or ink in a pen).
Corrective Maintenance (CM)	See Customer Request Call (CR)
Criteria Referenced Instruction (CRI)	An instructional method allowing a student to establish his knowledge in a particular area, so that he can bypass the detailed learning process if his knowledge is shown to be adequate in the specific field.
Cross Fertilisation	Assist by the interchange of ideas.

Cross Training — The training of an engineer skilled in one product on additional products or product families.

Customer Request Call (CR) — A service call initiated by the request of a customer. (Also known as Corrective Maintenance (CM), Uncheduled Maintenance (UM) or Emergency Maintenance (EM) call).

Direct Costs — Those costs which can be clearly identified to a specific product or service (i.e. excluding overheads).

Direct Time — Number of hours or percentage of time that can be utilised for work and specific associated activities such as travel.

Down Time — The time an equipment is not available to perform its function (see also Mean Down Time).

Economic Order Quantity (EOQ) — See Re-order Quantity (ROQ)

Emergency Maintenance — See Customer Request (CR) call

Engineering Change Order (ECO) — See Modification

Environmental Envelope — The extremes of environmental conditions in which an equipment will be expected to operate.

Failure Rate — The number of failures per unit of measurement (cycles, miles, time, units, etc.).

First In First Out (FIFO) — A warehouse practice of issuing the oldest item in stock before newer items.

Full Service Maintenance Agreement (FSMA) — A maintenance contract which includes all service support to a customer, normally including labour costs and spare parts costs but not the cost of consumable items.

Functionally Integrated Maintenance System (FIMS)	The method of preparing documentation based on a functional grouping of components instead of the usual schematic layout.
Hardware	Physical product, equipment, or their parts.
Hot Line	A telephone contact direct to a source of knowledge or skill to enable a Service Engineer in the field to make a customer's equipment operational as quickly as possible.
Imprest Stock	Predetermined stock on loan to a store or to an engineer.
Imputed Revenue	Income which is not received specifically for a particular activity but which is nevertheless included in the calculation of a price to the customer (e.g. payment for warranty). Also known as notional revenue.
Indirect Costs	Those costs which cannot be clearly identified to a specific product or service – i.e. costs shared among a number of products or services.
Indirect Time	Number of hours or percentage of time an engineer is available in the field but cannot be utilised.
Infant Mortality	The very early failure of components (usually electronic).
Last In First Out (LIFO)	The issue of the newest item in stock on first demand.
Lead Time	The period of time estimated to be needed to accomplish a task.
Learning Curve	The rate at which additional knowledge or skill is gained.
Level of Service (LOS)	The level of support provided by a service organisation to a customer.

Logistic Level of Service (LOLOS)	The level of support provided by the logistics organisation to customers and to the service organisation.
Mean Down Time (MDT)	The average time an equipment cannot perform its task.
Mean Time Between Failure (MTBF)	The average time (or operations, distance etc.) between breakdowns.
Mean Time Between Maintenance (MTBM)	The average time (or operations, distance etc.) between maintenance calls (corrective and preventive maintenance).
Mean Time Between Service Calls (MTBSC)	The average time (or operations, distance etc.) between service calls (i.e. MTBM plus calls caused by faulty customer operation)
Mean Time To Instal (MTTI)	The mean time to instal an equipment.
Mean Time To Repair (MTTR)	The mean time to perform a repair task.
Mean Time To Travel (MTTT)	The mean time to travel from one customer to the next.
Modification	The change to a machine configuration to correct a fault, improve its performance or bring it up-to-date (Also known as a Retrofit or an Engineering Change Order (ECO).
Module	A separate physical and functional unit or sub-assembly which can be replaced as one entity.
Nomograph (or Nomogram)	Graphical presentation of relationship between three (or more) quantities, whereby the value of one is established by joining points representing the others.

Non-Available Hours	The number of hours an engineer is not available to take customer calls (due to holidays, sickness, formal training, etc).
Non-Proprietary Item	An item which is generally available, i.e. not specific to any one manufacturer's products.
Notional Revenue	A revenue not received directly by the department concerned but the value of which has been included in the total price charged to the customer. (Also known as imputed revenue).
On the Job Training (OJT)	A practical training process performed while working in the field as opposed to training in a classroom.
Operational Availability	The time or percentage of time an equipment is functionally available to a customer (Also known as Up-time).
Operations Research (OR)	A quantitative technique to simulate complex problems on a scientific model.
Overheads	General costs which cannot be uniquely identified to be incurred by one product or service.
Paid Hours	The standard number of hours per year for which an engineer is paid .
Pipeline	The support chain from the point of procurement to the point of usage.
Preventive Maintenance (PM)	Maintenance carried out to avoid the breakdown of an equipment. (Also known as Scheduled Maintenance (SM)).
Proprietary Item	An item, the design of which is specific to a manufacturer and is owned by him.
Rebuild	The process of disassembling a product and reassembling it using new or repaired parts, to a standard procedure. (Also known as Recondition).

Recall	A repeat call, usually implying that it is for the same reason as the original call.
Recondition	See Rebuild
Redundant System	A back-up module which comes into operation when the prime module fails, so that there is a continuous functioning of the complete system.
Refurbish	The process of preparing a product for re-use by carrying out necessary cleaning, repair and replacement activities on an 'as needed' basis.
Reliability	The specific period during which an item will perform its function without a failure.
Re-order Level (ROL)	The point to which a stock item should be allowed to deplete in an inventory system before additional items are ordered (Also known as Re-order Point (RP)).
Re-order Point (RP)	See Re-order Level (ROL).
Re-order Quantity (ROQ)	The amount of an item that should be ordered at one time to obtain the lowest total cost of carrying inventory and costs associated with ordering (Also known as Economic Order Quantity (EOQ)).
Repair Time	See Mean Time To Repair (MTTR).
Response Time	The number of working hours between receipt of a customer's request for a service visit and the arrival of a Service Engineer at the customer.
Retrofit	See Modification
Safety Stock	The quantity of an item held in stock in excess of normal usage to ensure a specific level of confidence that supply can be maintained even it there is a delay in some link of the supply chain.
Scheduled Maintenance (SM)	See Preventive Maintenance (PM)

Software — The activity required to operate a piece of hardware, often applied specifically to computer programs.

Third Party Service Organisation — An outside company without a formal agreement with the manufacturer or dealer acting as a service sub-contractor; often working in competition with the manufacturer.

Time and Material (T+M) — A contract where the customer pays only for the labour hours expanded and the materials used to perform work on his specific equipment.

Total Hours — The number of hours an engineer is paid for, consisting of Paid Hours (standard time) plus Overtime.

Trade-off — The balancing of alternatives to achieve an optimal compromise solution in operational and financial terms.

Turnover of Staff — See Attrition.

Unscheduled Maintenance (UM) — See Customer Request (CR) call

Upgrade — Bringing a product to a more recent state of modification or increasing its capabilities by additional modules or by supplying a more powerful model.

Up-time — See Operational Availability

Utilisation — The percentage of
Direct Time to Available Time (Operational Utilisation)
Direct Time to Total Time (Total Utilisation).

Warranty — A guarantee by the manufacturer or supplier to effect repair free of charge to the customer, if the fault is due to faulty workmanship or material.

Work Control A service operations centre to which customers direct their requests for service and which ensures that the problem is resolved either on the telephone or by a visit of a Service Engineer, and which is responsible for allocating engineers to calls to satisfy laid down priorities.

Subject index